THE
DESIGN
PROCESS

THE
DESIGN
PROCESS

KARL ASPELUND

UNIVERSITY OF RHODE ISLAND

FAIRCHILD PUBLICATIONS, INC.
NEW YORK

Executive Editor: Olga T. Kontzias
Acquisitions Editor: Joseph Miranda
Assistant Acquisitions Editor: Jaclyn Bergeron
Senior Development Editor: Jennifer Crane
Development Editor: Sylvia L. Weber
Production Editor: Elizabeth Marotta
Art Director: Adam B. Bohannon
Production Manager: Ginger Hillman
Copy Editor: Vivian Gomez
Interior Design: Emily Mitchell
Cover Design: Adam B. Bohannon
Cover Typography: Emily Mitchell
Cover Art: © Corbis

Library of Congress Catalog Card Number: 2005933567
ISBN: 1-56367-412-2
GST R 133004424
Printed in the United States of America
TP13

CONTENTS

Today's design world is remarkably different from the one I graduated into 20 years ago. The altered landscape requires more skills of today's young designers. The blurring of distinctions between high-end and mass-market design has continued to a point where a design aesthetic is to be found at practically every price level, resulting in an enormously increased demand for educated designers. At the same time, the waning of Modernist influence has resulted in a broadening of the stylistic field, allowing designers greater freedom of play. This newfound freedom is reinforced by the advent of Computer Aided Design and Manufacturing (CAD/CAM) to create any designs, no matter how unorthodox they are. Massive improvements in communications and computer technology have imploded our frames of reference and created a wired world where information moves at the speed of light and accessibility is everything. Globalized industries now require businesses to view the entire world as their competition, while design, procurement, and manufacturing can be continents away from one another, outsourced and offshore. While robotics and CAD/CAM have altered manufacturing methods to an astonishing degree, environmental concerns and a demand for sustainable practices are increasingly changing the approach to methods and materials. The greater number of choices, expanded communications, improved technology, and greater distances involved require a greater degree of clarity and a commitment to an idea well in advance of what used to be strictly necessary. In addition, today's climate of speed demands a constant flow of information and availability that requires a designer to be consistently on track, moving a project forward with certainty and knowledge to its goal.

Over the years, it has been my goal to convey to students that designing, regardless of what is being designed, has a clearly definable process. Apparel, artwork, aircraft, book covers, film sets, tea sets, and Web sites all follow a remarkably well-delineated path in their creation. The process of design can be broken down into stages, each of which contains its own set of goals. By following a path that arrives at each stage in turn, a project's development becomes clearer, easier to navigate, and more assured. Moreover, focusing on fulfilling the needs of each stage before moving onto the next allows the project to meet its goals and makes revising it much easier. A staged process is also very beneficial to teamwork and helps continue the design's progress, even when the team's energy is not at its peak.

Throughout my career, I have worked on theatrical and film costumes and sets, couture, art direction of fashion layouts and advertising campaigns, exhibition and graphic design, murals, and large-scale public artwork. I have mined my experience heavily for the ideas and methods presented in this text. Varied as these experiences have been, they have served to confirm the similarities of their processes.

In teaching design, it seems to me that guiding students through a design process throughout the course of months requires a guidebook that maps out the road to take. It requires a book that describes how to travel the path from the World of Imagination to the World of Objects and helps the students sustain themselves creatively on this journey. There are numerous books that address the artistic and technical sides of executing and presenting designs. There are other books that address creativity or brainstorming; a few speak to the actual search for ideas, define sources of inspiration, and explain how to stay inspired, which are crucial to a designer's methods. However, in 14 years I have not found a single book that walks student designers through the process of design from inspiration to production. I have found no books that deal with a designer's role as a manager, a coordinator, an artist, a performer, a dreamer, a communicator, and a problem solver. Clearly, a book is needed that answers fully, at each stage, the student designer's question, "What next?" While there is no way to quantify and systemize a creative process, there is a way to guide designers through the stages in which they will find themselves and give them the cognitive tools and examples so they can move to each subsequent stage. This book aims to fulfill this need.

ORGANIZATION AND LEARNING FEATURES

The book's main body is divided into one introductory chapter and seven chapters that specifically correspond to the seven stages of design as follows:

1. Inspiration
2. Identification
3. Conceptualization
4. Exploration/Refinement
5. Definition/Modeling
6. Communication
7. Production

The division of the book into these stages allows readers to recognize and discover answers to any design project questions. Communication, for instance, is a concern throughout the entire design process, but since it is toward the end that communication increases exponentially, it is presented here as a stage in its own right, at the point where clarity becomes completely crucial: before handing a project over to production.

Since the introductory chapter gives an overview of each of the stages, a quick mention of concerns will suffice here.

Stage 1: Inspiration allows readers to examine various sources of inspiration and avenues for becoming inspired. The exercises will allow readers to relate to inspiration personally.

Stage 2: Identification allows readers to examine a structured method of identifying concerns and constraints surrounding their projects. This stage will also explain the importance of recognizing environmental concerns and working within sustainable practices.

Stage 3: Conceptualization outlines concepts through both written and visual means.

Stage 4: Exploration/Refinement encourages readers to explore methods for exploring and experimenting with concepts quickly and efficiently so they can fully reveal the potential of their ideas.

Stage 5: Definition/Modeling teaches readers how to commit to decisions with confidence, and how to determine the level of needs their designs should fulfill. Then they will look at issues relating to modeling their designs.

Stage 6: Communication allows readers to explore various techniques for design and provides them with an approach to create samples and prepare presentations. These lessons reinforce the idea of clear communication with clients, colleagues, and production staff.

Stage 7: Production outlines the ideal manner in which to keep track of and convey information at the production stage. The text reviews various prototyping options and discusses issues of collaboration. It will also explain how students can, at the close of the design process, analyze what they have learned so they can apply their knowledge to future projects.

Each stage includes the following:
- *Objectives and Key Concepts* that indicate the chapter's content and the goals that students can reach by reviewing the text and completing the exercises.
- *Perspectives* of seven professional artists and designers who have very graciously taken the time to share their thoughts and experiences. These invaluable contributions give readers direct insight into the philosophies and experiences of these highly regarded professionals, which greatly widens the book's scope.
- *Exercises* that bolster the material presented in each stage and keep the students' design projects moving forward. The exercises aim to leave the student designers with a body of

work that eventually leads to a completed project. As students complete the exercises, they keep a visual and written journal, which creates a volume of work in students' portfolios that will be attractive to interviewers and clients alike.

- *Illustrations* act as visual aids to better explain each stage. They are therefore of a varied sort, and it is my hope that they will contribute to the enjoyment of the book as well as sparking thoughts beyond the text itself.

Five appendices provide reference material that students can use either as a basis for further research or as supplementary material to increase their awareness of the numerous sources of information and inspiration available to them.

- *Appendix 1* provides a refresher on the elements and principles of design.
- *Appendix 2* is a reference list of books that may be interesting to any student of design, in school or out.
- *Appendix 3* lists in chronological order architects and designers, beginning with William Morris in 1834.
- *Appendix 4* discusses trendspotting and postmodern culture.
- *Appendix 5* contains a timeline of Zeitgeist-altering events and significant moments in design.

WHO SHOULD USE THIS BOOK AND HOW?

This book is primarily intended for design students who are working on their own projects, either as an independent studio project or in a classroom setting. The breakdown into seven stages is fairly detailed and results in each stage being carefully explained. Students can therefore refer to specific stages as needed (i.e., each stage is a stand-alone text) or read the entire text step by step. The manner in which the book is used depends on the course structure and level of supervision students will receive.

An Instructor's Guide and accompanying CD-ROM are available to instructors. The Instructor's Guide provides suggestions on how to use the text and exercises in different circumstances, as well as points for generating classroom discussions. It also provides rubrics for evaluating the exercises either by peer review or individual critique. The rubrics provide a framework toward possible solutions, without spelling out specific answers or predetermined results. The rubrics can also be used as the basis for classroom discussion on the methodology of the project at hand. The guide also contains spreadsheet templates for grading and scheduling. The CD-ROM contains Microsoft PowerPoint slides related to each stage for lecturing purposes.

This text serves well as a handbook for professional designers. It can prove to be helpful to designers, as well as those who must manage and coordinate design teams. Because of the rigors and deadlines of professional life, sometimes designers lose touch with the discipline and joy of design work. My own experience has confirmed that revisiting the concepts discussed in this text can be beneficial. It is my hope, and my intent, that students who use this book in their classrooms will continue to find it helpful long after they graduate. The thoughts that eventually became this book were inspired, developed, and field-tested in various venues and circumstances throughout the past 20 years. Twenty years of designing and 14 years of teaching design have allowed me to meet numerous people: collaborators, coworkers, students, clients, and audiences, all of whom have, in some way, shaped the thoughts contained in this text. Some of these people, through their support and faith

ACKNOWLEDGMENTS

in my abilities, allowed these thoughts to take root and blossom and should be mentioned.

My four years of teaching at the Reykjavik Technical College were a formative adventure, during which my ideas for the book began to take shape. After teaching illustration and design for two years, I was asked to set up and head a department of design for its first year. There, I had the amazing opportunity to design courses and put my ideas of design instruction to the test. Ingvar Asmundsson, the dean; Gudrun Erna Gudmundsdottir, my initial department head; and Sigurdur Orn Kristinsson, the director of programs, deserve my sincere thanks and appreciation. Such trust placed in someone so young required quite a leap of faith—startling in hindsight—for which I am very grateful.

At the University of Rhode Island's Department of Textiles, Fashion Merchandising, and Design, the department heads, Dr. Linda Welters and Dr. Martin Bide, along with the entire faculty and staff deserve my sincere thanks as well. The past nine years at URI have flown by, and the school has been an extremely supportive and enjoyable environment, without which I would not have been able to develop the ideas and methods presented in this book. Dr. Welters, in particular, has my deepest gratitude and appreciation for *her* leap of faith in hiring me when I was newly arrived in the United States.

I owe an enormous debt to all my students for putting up with the experimentation that was required to explore the ideas presented in this text and appreciate their contribution to the formulation and focus of the exercises. I am very grateful to my students for their perseverance and for giving me the privilege of sharing the joy of their achievements.

One student requires special mention. Thanks to Jennifer Penswick for allowing me to use photos of her designs from my classroom as illustrations. Two other illustrators, my children Karl and Julia, created wonderful illustrations used in the discussion of Stage 4. They have, in their growth and development, also unknowingly contributed to the views put forward in that stage. Thanks to them for both contributions.

Three groups of people have influenced the manuscript directly. The first group is made up of the reviewers of the first draft chosen by the publisher: Nancy O. Bryant, Oregon State University; Barbara Giorgio-Booher, Ball State University; Janette K. Hopper, University of North Carolina–Pembroke; Jean M. K. Miller, Towson University; and Roberto Rengel, University of Wisconsin–Madison. I thank them for their time, careful attention, and illuminating comments that made a great difference in the creation of the book. It is far better for their efforts. Since the manuscript went through an anonymous review process, I cannot address my special thanks by name to "Reviewer #2," whose detailed questions and enthusiastic marginal notes prompted a number of beneficial additions and revisions to the manuscript.

The second group, whose contribution has also made this a better book than I could ever have written otherwise, consists of the seven interviewees, who so generously shared their thoughts and experiences. Many thanks to Leifur Breidfjörd, Ian Cunningham, Pálmi Einarsson, Brower Hatcher, Tomoko Mitsuma, Yeohlee Tang, and Mark Zeff for their time and gracious, sincere participation. Their contributions are worth the entire effort of putting the book together. Also, thanks to Shizu Yuasa, at TIS in Tokyo, for translating Tomoko's interview.

The third group is the excellent team at Fairchild, without whom there would be no book at all. Olga Kontzias, executive editor; Carolyn Purcell, former assistant acquisitions editor; Joseph Miranda, acquisitions editor; Amy Zarkos, former senior development editor; Elizabeth Marotta, production editor; and Adam Bohannon, art director, have all been wonderful. I must, however, extend my very special thanks to Sylvia Weber, my development editor, for her unfailing support and encouragement. Sylvia's rapid-response e-mail, intelligent and lighthearted—I last counted one hundred of them—will be sorely missed.

Brenda, my wife, deserves a great thanks for her support, proofreading, patience, and illuminating discussions. A wonderful teacher, her guidance continues to be invaluable.

The thoughts that did not grow out of the past 20 years took root in the 20 years before those. It is therefore with much love and gratitude that I dedicate this effort to my parents, Erling and Kolbrun. From the very beginning, they have provided me with a lifetime's worth of inspiration.

—Karl Aspelund

Introduction

OBJECTIVE

To successfully steer an idea on its journey from the world of imagination to the world of objects, a designer must keep focused on where the idea is going and make a number of important stops along the way. This book examines each stage of that process. This introduction describes the nature of a designer's journey, maps the path a designer will take, and explores the path by explaining what happens at each stop.

KEY CONCEPTS

- A designer's work is concerned primarily with solving problems by developing and explaining ideas. The "look" of a product is just one of many possible problems.
- An idea's evolution is essential to the creative process.
- The design process, regardless of discipline, has seven basic stages: inspiration, identification, conceptualization, exploration/refinement, definition/modeling, communication, and production. These stages are not necessarily linear but can be examined as such.
- Ideas that go through the seven stages will result in a tangible design.

The journey from the World of Imagination to the World of Objects ranges over a wide territory.

DESIGNING IS UP CLOSE AND PERSONAL

We are surrounded by design. As I sit here at my computer, I can consider the design of its casing and the user interface of the software. I can also consider the design of my clothes. The keyboard, my teacup, the telephone, the graphics on a CD cover, the CD case, and the window frame are all designed; even my daughter's rock collection on the windowsill has been designed. Each rock has been chosen on the beach as a candidate for the collection and then intentionally placed on the windowsill as decoration. The setup is designed, even though the rocks themselves are not.

What then is designing? For that matter, what is a design? The answer lies in the decisions a person makes. A landscape designer decides the placement of a line of trees, a celebrity lends her name to a line of clothing, an architect sketches an outline on a napkin, an engineer calculates the need for a gauge of steel and the number of bolts necessary for a structure's base, a software developer creates a diagram of actions that a program will perform. These are all examples of designing. A design is a plan of action, created in response to a situation or problem that needs solving. This plan often needs to be laid out to be clearly understood by a viewer. Designing is about forming ideas, planning and explaining the execution of those ideas, and making choices based on the evolution of those ideas that will lead to an end result. Designing is a journey that has a number of stops and detours along the way.

A designer must deal with deadlines and budgets. There are collaborators and clients who need to know what to expect and who must, very early in the process, be informed about a number of details. A designer makes decisions about technical aspects and materials. All of the decisions that go into a project can delay that project or even completely change its direction. A project evolves as a designer learns more about it and its needs.

While an idea exists only as a possibility in a designer's imagination, it can be anything at all. As soon as a designer makes a decision for the design, the idea has been isolated from an infinite number of other possible ideas. The designer must also determine whether the unexplored ideas contain something that is worth examining. For this reason designers must grant themselves time to develop their ideas despite deadlines, budgets, and schedules. It is the designer's job to keep an eye on the ideas' development and possibilities. Can we do this to it? Or that? Or both? Or not? By asking questions like this, designers can learn what an idea is capable of and figure out what they ultimately want from it. Perhaps a designer does not want the most obvious solution. Perhaps there are ways of doing something that have never been done before. Perhaps the normal approach is not the best solution.

There is a path all designs take on their journey from the world of imagination to the world of objects. By allowing the path to meander and twist without much restriction, making sure that the process makes certain well-defined stops along the way, designers can examine and explain the idea at each step of its evolution without stunting its growth. In this book, you will map and follow such a path. It is a journey that requires a high level of personal involvement.

THE DESIGN PROCESS: A RELATIONSHIP

The design process can be likened to a romantic relationship. In the first stage, *Inspiration*, an idea has taken hold of you. Everything is exciting, and everything about your idea is fun and wonderful. You are infatuated. You stay up all night with your idea, take it everywhere with you, and love being seen with it. Strange behaviors emerge. You find yourself taking risks and acting impulsively.

For a relationship to survive, the energy of the infatuation must be transferred into a more sustainable form. The relationship then enters the *Identification* stage, where the idea becomes an understandable entity with definite parameters. The abstractions of the initial inspiration begin to solidify into recognizable, defined forms. Things have happened that cannot be undone. The identity of the idea is forming and acquiring a character of its own.

In the *Conceptualization* stage, the idea's constraints and needs become clear. The idea becomes specific—a concept—with its own characteristics. It begins to have a shape and a life of its own. The initial parameters are already defined, and they are now developed into a set of loosely understandable outlines. You and the concept are now officially "an item." You must recognize that there are ways to approach the concept and ways to behave in relation to it. It can be treated certain ways, and it will not accept certain things.

When the *Exploration/Refinement* stage begins, you must establish boundaries and structures. Any implications that exist when the idea is conceptualized become fixed in this stage. If you step outside the boundaries, there may be serious consequences. If these definitions are changed or modified, the relationship changes.

Designers must therefore commit to these structures in order for the relationship with the concept to continue. However, commitment is tricky, and it is very hard to give up the freedom to make choices. It is normal to have doubts about decisions and to wonder whether your choices are excluding future possibilities. To clear this hurdle, a little reinspiration is necessary. You must remind yourself of why the idea was a good one in the beginning. It is good to revisit the heady first days and recall the impulses you felt at that time and the risks you felt capable of taking. This reinstills confidence and the sense of enjoyment from that initial moment of inspiration.

You must prepare for this and deal with it to move forward to the next stage, *Definition/Modeling*. At this stage you begin to build on what you have discovered so far. Here is where the experiences you've had and the discoveries you've made about your idea are used to create a structure that is the best possible design for the situation. At this stage you also begin to look toward a future that contains your idea as a permanent entity by creating models and examples that allow you to examine the effects of the real world and test your design's viability.

In *Communication* and *Production*, the focus turns to all the details involved. In both these stages, designers establish and work with decisions already made. The focus is outward, toward communicating the design to others and leading it through production to its ultimate end as a physical creation in the world. If anything new comes up at this point, it is usually because the requirements of previous stages have not been fulfilled.

There can be numerous details to address. Some of them are difficult, and some require compromise. If the details are approached as a source of inspiration, life gets much easier. One way to do this is to look at the idea from the inside out. Your design can be seen as a sum of its parts. Each detail, each element has something to contribute to the whole design. Designers who continually reaffirm their commitment to the whole concept will find that it isn't difficult to become excited about making all the details work together.

The mundane can kill a romance.

ALREADY, I SEE THE DETAILS PILING UP...

DESIGNING IS IN THE MIND

This book does not aim to quantify the design process. Rather, it shows how an idea can travel from the world of imagination to the world of objects in an organized, timely fashion, evolving as it goes but keeping its original purpose and energy intact.

A designer's job begins with a problem that requires a solution. Unlike a mathematical problem, a design problem is not always clearly stated at the outset. Designers must begin by identifying the problem and determining what they are being asked to do. Ideas begin to form as soon as the problem is examined; the problem's nature, once it is recognized, usually implies where its solution lies. Designing is about ideas: needing and finding ideas, examining and identifying their nature, and, most important, illustrating and explaining them so they can be realized.

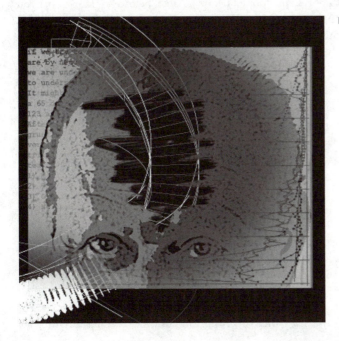

Designing is in the mind.

It is a common misconception that design deals exclusively with the surface of things and, that designers are primarily concerned with the look of their designs. There are also the notions that true design must be the work of one person, that a collaborative effort is less authentic, and that a design arising from practicality does not qualify. Nothing could be farther from the truth. No matter what is being designed—clothing, cars, or computers—the design problem exists not only in carrying out a stylistic vision but also (and often more so) in the final product's functionality. Think about all the things around you that first and foremost are functional. Look through your kitchen drawers or toolbox. Think about medical and military devices (usually some of the best functional designs around). How do they work? What are they made of? How are they constructed? How do end users interact with them? In both their training and practice, designers must always ask such questions.

In large-scale global manufacturing, it is possible that there are several designers or even teams working on each level of a product's development. Whether you are the lead designer supervising the creation of an overall vision or a member of a design team working on a specific aspect of a project, you must recognize what needs to be done and communicate and cooperate at each stage.

The movement of an idea from one stage to the next involves an evolution. An obvious truth about designing is that it must involve development. Indeed, the changing and evolution of an idea is highly necessary to the creative process. Designers examine, question, and redirect the idea at each stage, as needed. In doing so, they bring it closer to its ideal solution, even if that solution turns out to be very different from what was originally imagined. At the outset, ideas in any creative process are nebulous ghosts, slow to reveal themselves. People are quicker to know what they do not want and what something shouldn't be. As a designer's vision is directed toward what the creation *should* be, rather than what it should *not*, the designer develops a dialogue with the project to learn what it needs. An idea should be allowed to change and evolve until it is as close as possible to what it needs to be. The idea must not become formed before its time, before you know what you want it to be (or what *it* wants to become). But designers must be careful that the idea doesn't evolve beyond recognition. Designers must keep track of the nature of the idea and its details at each stage so that the idea's original purpose is fulfilled. Tracking an idea's development allows designers to be confident that it is developing in the right direction.

THE MAP: FROM THE WORLD OF IMAGINATION TO THE WORLD OF OBJECTS

To formalize the idea of a journey, let us examine a map describing the path you will take. An idea's path from the world of imagination to the world of objects passes through the seven stages described above. By stopping at each of these stages in turn and taking the appropriate actions, you will inevitably arrive at your destination with a set of designs that are ready for production.

The nature of this book requires you to visit these stages in a linear fashion, but be aware that the design process is not completely linear. The stages do not dovetail neatly into one another. Communication, for example, is a concern throughout the design project because clients and colleagues will need information from start to finish. Also, conceptualizing doesn't end after the initial outlining of a project. A concept will and must evolve. For this reason designers must revisit their thoughts from time to time, making sure they are on track.

Designing requires traversing a vast landscape.

INSPIRATION

You will begin your journey at Inspiration. Whether it is just one or a series of trips, you need to have something that drives your creativity. Even the most mundane, practical designing requires a positive, energetic attitude.

Finding and maintaining inspiration is an extremely important but often neglected part of the designer's work. It is an emotional, often almost spiritual exercise, and the need for it often arises during times of stress when there is little or no time for reflection. Stage 1 shows readers how to recognize and tap into sources of inspiration.

IDENTIFICATION

In the Identification stage, the focus is on examining and defining the project as much as possible. You will create a design thesis for your project that will serve as a guide for the remaining stages. A large part of the designer's concern lies in identifying the project's constraints, which should include environmentally sustainable practices.

CONCEPTUALIZATION

In the Conceptualization stage, it is important for designers to explore concepts fully and understand their impact before translating them into workable objects. The best approach is first to visualize an idea without being too concerned about problem-solving. Practical problems tie up designers in search for solutions. This can be detrimental to the project if it causes the designer to lose sight of the bigger picture. It is very tempting at the beginning of a project to jump right in and begin to solve everything at once, especially if the deadline is close. It is important to resist this impulse. The time for acute problem-solving arrives later.

Designers often create only an impression of the idea at this stage. They create metaphors that become the basis for illustrative models. This occurs, for example, when a fashion model wears something on a runway that would be practically impossible to wear anywhere else and when architects produce fanciful drawings of structures that defy engineering. These metaphorical creations make perfect sense later in the design process, when more usable designs have been developed.

Designers often use collages or tear sheets to illustrate their concept. They describe through these means the various aspects of a design with a visual reference that is immediately recognized and understood. In tandem with a thesis statement, this can be a compelling way to introduce a concept to a client or production team. This is also an excellent way for designers to clarify their concept in their own minds.

EXPLORATION/REFINEMENT

At the Exploration/Refinement stage, designers must begin to explore their solutions in more detail. The outlines created in the previous stages must be filled in by fully defining each element of the design. This step may require changes to the outlines. If certain elements are impractical, this may demand a reevaluation of the concept. At this stage designers can get bogged down in details, and their overall view dissolves unless they keep their vision clear. Here, designers maintain their focus by reinspiring themselves.

DEFINITION/MODELING

For designers, Definition/Modeling is often the most difficult stage of the process to get through. It is at Stage 5 that designers commit to their concepts. Unfortunately, things are not always that clear-cut. Practically speaking, design decisions may rely on other decisions that aren't always in the designers' hands. Deciding to include one thing often means excluding another, and this can be confusing and difficult. If an attachment to a certain solution has been formed, it can be difficult to decide that it is not the best one. Designers must rely on their inspiration and be confident in the foundations laid in previous stages to get through this one.

Making decisions.

COMMUNICATION

From the first meeting with the client through the final presentation of a finished design and even as a design goes into production and is marketed, communication is crucial to a project. However, communication becomes a focal point just prior to the production stage, as the challenge becomes to communicate to clients, collaborators, manufacturers, management, and others precisely what has happened so far. Making samples and technical decisions is paramount, and if a production team is involved, it begins to play a larger role. In fact, the art of presenting the design becomes as weighty as the designing itself, and artful illustration and modeling become important communication tools. In this stage, designers must be able to communicate about issues concerning a broad range of disciplines, such as engineering, construction, detailing, and texturing.

PRODUCTION

The final stage occurs when the design goes to Production. No matter how large or small the production is, designers must communicate with a number of collaborators. Prototypes are made, and the feedback from these necessitates decisions, possibly prompting final revisions if materials and construction techniques do not work out as planned. Planning, scheduling, and budgeting loom large, and these tasks begin to take over the project's pace and direction. Finally, production preparation and new knowledge gained can be recycled for future designs.

THE FIRST JOURNAL ENTRY, A REVERSE DESIGN

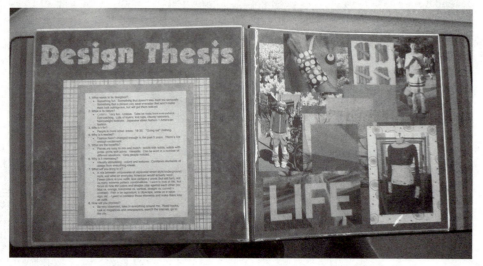

A design journal.

THE DESIGN JOURNAL

This exercise is the first installment of your design journal. Each subsequent chapter in this book will include exercises that contribute to the journal, creating an illustrated account of the design process. Journals such as these serve well not only in job interviews and presentations, but also as a way to refresh and inspire designers for future projects.

Before beginning this exercise you should decide on a format for the journal. Choose a sketchbook or folder of standard size to hold sketches and clippings. Anything larger than 11" x 17" becomes unwieldy and difficult to pass around at meetings or interviews. Anything smaller than 8.5" x 11" requires care because sketches may be too small to include significant detail. Choosing standard sizes matters because these journals can be used for years and may be added to a portfolio at a later date.

REVERSE-DESIGNING

Reverse-designing an object requires you to choose an object as close as possible to the one you intend to design and then trace its progress back through the seven stages. Reverse-designing an existing design is meant to create questions and give you points of reference for your own process. Once this exercise is completed, you will have a very good general idea of the path you will take.

Consider each of the design stages and write down any thoughts that come to mind. Use illustrations as much as possible to explain your conclusions. Use sketches and clippings; print downloaded images and anything else you need. Write about whatever you can't illustrate. Eventually, attempt to illustrate these writings. It is important at this time not to slow down but rather to let the thoughts flow. Include anything and everything you can think of at this point. You can always edit later. A designer's job is to solve problems and answer questions, so the more questions you create, the more material you have to work with.

Take it apart. See how it works.

STAGE 7: PRODUCTION

Imagine the creation of the final designed object in its construction stage. What do you think are the main issues in the construction and production? Is anything unusual or innovative? What does the designer have to communicate very clearly to the production team? If you were to construct something like it, what might be improved or different?

STAGE 6: COMMUNICATION

How would you create a model or sample to explain a design to a production team? What materials and methods would you use? What features would you highlight? Is there anything that cannot be adequately illustrated or modeled? How might a designer deal with this? What would be a good way to present the sample (i.e., two-dimensional representation, full-scale mock-up, scale model, or computer-generated model)?

STAGE 5: DEFINITION/MODELING

Consider the following for the design of your choice:

Form

Why do you suppose it has the form that it does? What requires it to take this form? Is anything superfluous? How much of its form is derived directly from its function?

Materials

What prompts the choices of materials or media? What are the practical constraints? What are the decorative decisions?

Color

What do you suppose might influence the choice of colors? How much does the choice of materials influence the color choices? Is there any sense of practicality in the choices? What is purely decorative?

Detailing and Decoration

What, if anything, serves to decorate this object? Why do you suppose it is decorated this way? Why would it be unadorned? Are the decorative elements applied, or do they arise from the functionality or nature of the design? Is the decoration relevant to the total design, or can you separate the style of decoration from the style of the object itself?

Function

Having considered form, materials, color, detailing, and decoration, how many of these features are influenced by the functionality of the design and how? Conversely, how do aesthetic decisions affect the functionality?

STAGE 4: EXPLORATION/REFINEMENT

Simplify the object so that it is in its most basic state. Strip it of details and embellishments. When does this begin to impair its functionality? When does it begin to lose its identity? Having removed as much as possible without transforming it into another class of objects, describe the design in the simplest way.

STAGE 3: CONCEPTUALIZATION

Describe the object metaphorically. Then think of ways to describe its individual parts or components. How would you describe it if you had never seen anything like it before? Illustrate your thoughts on the design so far. Create a collage of found images (from magazines, Web sites, photocopies, and so on) to describe the design. Refer to form, color, texture, detailing, functionality, environment, and emotional response.

STAGE 2: IDENTIFICATION

Use the results from your examination of Stages 7–3 to write a design thesis for the final object. The design thesis is a way of establishing a starting point for a project and creating guidelines for the process. Describe the various design elements and discuss the intent of the design. Use the following guidelines:

1. What did you design? Describe briefly the object or product.
2. What is its nature? What is the function of this design?
3. What is the target market or audience for this product?
4. Why is it necessary? What was the problem that required the design as its solution?
5. What are the benefits of the design? How does this design solve any problem that may have been identified in the previous question?
6. Why is this interesting? What challenges do you suppose this project presented?
7. What could you have brought to it had you been working on its design? What is your vision for this product? What new solution could you come up with?
8. How would you proceed? What methods would you use? Where would you begin?

STAGE 1: INSPIRATION

Considering all of the above, what would have been a good source of inspiration throughout the design process of this object? Why?

You have traced the steps backward and begun your design journal. You should now be familiar with the material covered in the remaining chapters. Take a moment to review your thoughts and make note of questions you have or gaps in your knowledge. As you go through the seven stages, revisit this exercise and see whether your questions can be answered.

The journey begins.

Inspiration

OBJECTIVE

This chapter argues for the need to have inspiration and explains its nature. It examines a few strategies before presenting twelve exercises that design students can complete to uncover their sources of and methods for attaining inspiration.

KEY CONCEPTS

- Designers must be inspired.
- Inspiration is a tool that furthers designs; it is not an end in itself.
- Designers need to seek inspiration rather than wait for it to come.
- Designers can find inspiration and should actively seek it in a variety of sources.

The journey begins with inspiration.

INSPIRATION: AN ACT OF CREATION

Our journey on the road from the World of Imagination to the World of Objects must begin at Inspiration. In any creative act, there must be a force that drives the creator and infuses the created object with energy. A designer's motivation for working on a project must be strong enough to produce the best possible end result. The creative energy going into the design should be clearly visible in the final product.

The word *inspiration* is derived from the Latin verb *inspirare—to breathe into*—as in the action of gods breathing life into their creations, a scene found in creation myths worldwide. This infusion of life is crucial to even the simplest design because the joy of creating is not there without it. Without joy, working on a design can prove to be tedious.

Inspiration can take countless guises and exist in many places. A poet's inspiration may also serve to inspire a dancer, painter, sculptor, or designer. No matter what form it takes, inspiration is an energy that drives people to be creative and infuses their creations with life.

As students begin to work on their projects, they should have some idea of where they are going. Their inspiration will take form based on the needs of the projects and the styles and energy with which they would like to infuse their projects.

FINDING INSPIRATION

It is necessary for designers to reinspire themselves throughout the creative process. Sources of inspiration exist throughout everything and should be infused in the design process so that it becomes constant in the creative process. Inspiration keeps the idea for a design moving forward.

Take a moment to consider the general nature of the design project you would like to begin. You will examine it in more detail in the next chapter, but for now just think about how and where you might get started.

BEWARE OF THE MYTH

The myths regarding inspiration are not true. Inspiration is something that cannot be waited for—designers should always actively seek it.

In the Greek myths, inspiration was bestowed by one of the nine muses.[1] Each of the nine was responsible for one of the arts. Without their visitation, creativity was a lost cause, as described in this passage from Plato's *Phaedrus*:

> And a third kind of possession and madness comes from the Muses. This takes hold upon a gentle and pure soul, arouses it and inspires it to songs and other poetry, and thus by adorning countless deeds of the ancients educates later generations. But he who without the divine madness comes to the doors of the Muses, confident that he will be a good poet by art, meets with no success, and the poetry of the sane man vanishes into nothingness before that of the inspired madmen.[2]

Muses are all around.

Since ancient times, people have widely interpreted this idea to mean that madness (or at least a wild eccentricity) and lack of control are essential in some way to a creative person, resulting in the misplaced romanticizing of depression, alcoholism, drug abuse, and numerous celebrated suicides. Often, self-destructive tendencies are the only things a person knows about many artists throughout history. It is not unusual to find people who have heightened and sensitive emotions in any artistic field, but it is inaccurate to assume that emotional imbalances are prerequisites for being an artist who is inspired.

The Greeks (or at least Plato and his followers) equated inspired creativity with the shamanistic trances of the oracles and priestesses. The *Phaedrus* highlights the beneficial nature of this belief.

> [. . .] *but there is also a madness which is a divine gift, and the source of the chiefest blessings granted to men. For prophecy is a madness, and the prophetess at Delphi and the priestesses at Dodona when out of their senses have conferred great*

benefits on Hellas, both in public and private life, but when in their senses few or none.[3]

Even though we may not have experienced prophetic trances, we can all relate to the notion of being entranced during a moment of intense creativity or excitement about someone else's creativity. We lose ourselves in dance or song or are moved to ecstasy by an orator. We forget time and place, our emotions well up, we laugh or cry, or we scream and applaud. Indeed, we take leave of our senses for a moment. The "divine madness" seems to be the ability to let go, the willingness to open up to the influence of a creative energy and to allow our emotions to surge where and how they may. Inspiration is attainable when we can follow our emotions, control them, and rein them in when necessary.

GENIES DON'T RETURN TO BOTTLES

Releasing your inspired energy into the world is like releasing a genie from a bottle. You can never be quite sure what is going to happen, nor can you make it go away once it's out. Thoughts and ideas have this power. Once they are out, they do not go away.[4] For this reason, we must watch carefully where our thoughts take us at the beginning of a project. As soon as we begin to look at a certain source or entertain a notion, we have created a momentum that is often arrested only with great effort. If we are fortunate and have chosen our first steps well, this momentum takes us to where we want to go. If not, we have to start again with a brand new idea.

Genies don't return to bottles.

When people seek inspiration, they must be careful not to let the energy they find speed them in a direction in which they don't intend to go. Designers should be wary of immersing themselves in the works of other artists or designers; doing so will result in ideas that are heavily influenced by this already existing work and rob their own ideas of originality and creativity. For this reason, designers should question whether they are opening up to the style, narrative, technique, or vision of other artists or designers. Inspiration should be the energy behind creativity—driving it—not leading it. You must therefore always be careful to choose the most ideal source of inspiration and be vigilant about where your idea is heading as a result of your inspiration's driving force.

PLAY SOMEWHERE ELSE

Beware of the tendency to get tunnel vision: If you are going to design watches, don't seek inspiration exclusively from other watches. Look to architects, painters, woodcarvers, or even filmmakers and musicians. Always remember that inspiration for any specific design project can come from anywhere—even the most unlikely source.

Good designers are continually on alert for new stimulation, new challenges, and new approaches to old problems. Follow their lead and become a collector of impulses; keep scrapbooks and journals. Always add to your knowledge of art, music, and film. Make a point of experiencing, seeing, and listening to something new every now and then. Don't shy away from trying something that didn't work out the way you expected on a previous project. Experience builds on itself, and as your horizons broaden, previously rejected ideas may become ideal avenues to explore for other projects.

You can find inspiration everywhere you go.

ALL WORK AND NO PLAY DOESN'T WORK

When discussing his vision, Pablo Picasso said the following:

> *Reality is more than the thing itself. I look always for the super-reality. Reality lies in how you see things. A green parrot is also a green salad and a green parrot. He who makes it only a parrot diminishes its reality. A painter who copies a tree blinds himself to the real tree. I see things otherwise. A palm tree can become a horse.*[5]

This notion should be very familiar to you. As children, we have all taken a simple prop and transformed it into an amazing thing. For example, a stick in the backyard can become a guitar, a sword, or a magic wand. It can be *all* of these in a single afternoon. This playful view of the world allows us not only to see the world differently, but also allows us to show others the world in a way they may have never considered before. The ability to create new worlds out of things that are all around us is indeed a valuable gift.

The way of viewing the world that Picasso refers to is one of the more powerful creative tools people are born with. Playtime is necessary for ideal human development. It teaches children about the world and how it works. It allows them to experiment with roles and situations that they may encounter later in life. Unfortunately, as children grow and reach adulthood, they tend to lose touch with this ability.

For creative endeavors, it is essential that designers tap into their imaginations, that they engage in playtime just like when they were kids. Playtime becomes the time designers use for experimenting and thinking. My former mathematics professor used to refer to *couch time*, which he advocated heavily as an important means for solving problems. He recommended that his students study a math problem, seek a solution, and sit on the couch to ponder it. After a few moments, when the students went back to work on the problem, they'd find the solution. "Eureka moments"[6] often come while scientists are taking baths, sleeping, gardening, or doing something else unrelated to their work. You'll often hear them say, "Suddenly, there it was. The solution was right before my eyes." Studies found that people who have eight hours of sleep after learning and practicing a new task remember more about it the following day than people who stay up all night learning the same thing.[7] Our brain requires processing time to make connections and explore possibilities and seems to be better at this when we are not actively engaged.

Couch time is an important tool for solving problems.

Zen masters instruct without speech or by asking questions such as, "Where is my fist when I open my hand?" These are designed to shake students out of their normal thought patterns. When this inspired strategy doesn't work, the masters hit the students upside their heads. Students are so surprised that normal thought becomes suspended. Their moments of revelation do not come as a result of concentrated thinking, but precisely when the thinking stops.

Designing always involves deadlines, and the available time for experimentation and pondering is therefore always limited; however, you must never think of playtime as time wasted. It is possible to view the entire design process as one large game. Play involves rules, and each design project requires a new set of rules or at least a modification of the last set of rules. Play is also a challenge: Can you solve the problem? Can you beat the clock? Can you make it more fun?

INSPIRATION IS JUST THE BEGINNING

It is dangerous to believe that inspiration is an end in itself. Such creativity is fine, if this is what you set out to do. Design, however, involves a need to go beyond this and use an idea and the philosophizing surrounding it to create something else: a product that is physical, useful, and more than just an expression of a concept.

It is also all too easy to get carried away with inspiration and get lost in research. Gathering information and impulses is exciting because everything is new. Be that as it may, deadlines must be respected and projects must continue to move forward. Time is limited, so research and couch time have to have an end and a purpose.

No stopping here!

All too often, designers lose themselves in their research for their projects, only to have to sacrifice something else due to time constraints caused by the detours. Admittedly, it is difficult to avoid reading one more book, trying one more experiment, calculating a curvature to a greater degree, or going back to the museum if there is a chance that a problem will be solved. Perseverance certainly pays off, and your umpteenth visit to the library may yield a spectacular find. Sometimes the initial research is a lot of fun, and you can fool yourself (and others) into thinking that you are doing something essential when you actually are avoiding to make decisions about material you already have. Call it creative procrastination, if you will.

If you are within your deadline obligations, go ahead and add to your knowledge. But, if you don't have the time, move on.

PERSPECTIVE

YEOHLEE TENG, FASHION DESIGNER

Yeohlee Teng came to New York from Malaysia to study fashion at the Parsons School of Design. She has worked primarily in New York City, where she established her own house, Yeohlee Inc.

Yeohlee believes that "clothes have magic." She dresses the "urban nomad," defining a lifestyle that requires clothing that works on a variety of practical and psychological levels. She is a master of design management and believes in the efficiency of year-round, seasonless clothes, which have been termed "intimate architecture."

I thrive on information; it inspires me. I don't think I can isolate it to one subject; it's really everything. For instance, I can give you a small snapshot of the past couple of days: I went to a restaurant last night called Freeman Alley. The place had really good Eastern European food, and it was mobbed with a crowd of very interesting people. It made me think about dining in New York because prior to that I was at a place called Beds where the prices were much higher. They had tables, but it was basically also beds, so you could lie around and have your dinner in bed. All of this is interesting to me. Maybe it translates—who knows how information translates? So I sit there and think about the possibilities of places like Freeman Alley being discovered; who are the people who are dining there? Are they really in the know? What about the cuisine? Is it really very fashionable? Because food goes in and out of fashion, just like clothes. And as a matter of fact, I also had lunch with the former food critic at the *Times*, so we discussed fashion and food. These are the kind of things I think about. And that's just from the last couple of days. As far as information is concerned, it comes from everywhere. I talk to everybody; I don't have any prejudice; I'm not elitist. It's my sense of curiosity. After the World Trade Center incident, I talked to taxi drivers to find out how the local economy was doing. I'll talk to the UPS guy to find out how the fashion industry is doing. They know because they know how much product they pick up and ship.

The problems I enjoy solving have to do with diminishing resources in a very, very general sense—and with time. So I spend a lot of time thinking about design that's very efficient as far as the use of fabric and the manufacturing process is concerned.

I don't think that within a certain realm of fashion enough time is spent on how useful clothes can be, how efficient they are, and how you can manage your life with less clothes. For example, for a collection some years ago, I took a fabric that was extremely expensive and labor-intensive to make, and instead of doing more to it, like sewing by hand, adding 60 hours of hand labor to it, I tore it. I was intrigued by that because if you are paying a lot for the fabric and you can construct it with a minimum of time and labor, you can even out the cost.

I devoted another collection to making fashion that had very few cuts and very little stitching. The clothes were very packable and didn't occupy a lot of space. They were made of very efficient fabrics that one could launder and they didn't wrinkle very much and were very low maintenance.

In a general sense, a lot of the things I make are classic and timeless, so if they withstand the test of time and laundering, that's terrific as well.

I like materials that are kind of seamless and can go from season to season and through different times of day and through different geographic regions. Not all the fabrics I use can function this way, but some of the basic fabrics that I use do. I look for fabrics that wear well, that are comfortable, that have some elasticity to them, that don't over-wrinkle, that are easy to maintain, and that you can machine wash and hang dry.

This fall season, I was on the hunt for an interesting fabric that you can make into coats, that actually had Lycra in it. For the spring season I am working with a lot of fabrics that are extremely high-maintenance because they have a chintz finish and are very stiff. So I'm collaborating with Nano-Tex because they think they can make some of those fabrics crease-resistant, and we are in the process of testing it. This kind of prototyping I might do once or twice a year, but only when the need arises; I don't necessarily seek it out. But when there's a lot of linen in the collection, there's obviously a need to seek out some kind of crease-resistant technology. . . . I explored textiles that are utilized in other industries. I saw these polyester fabrics that are being made into valves for the heart . . . .

I'll find things like this and then just think about them. I don't really go out and seek specific things. I observe, they filter in, and then I try to educate myself. But when I find that a concept isn't working, I'll just chuck it out. This can happen throughout a collection's process. I'll start off with certain ideas that I'll abandon because other ideas are more interesting and seem to be more appropriate for the collection or the timeframe. Then sometimes I'll come back to the ideas later. Ideas are like opinions—everybody has them; some pan out and some don't. Generally, if you overwork an idea, obviously something is not right about it. I don't get hung up on my ideas.

I am also inspired by architecture and travel—actual journeys or virtual ones through movies, books, and music. I come from a family of architects and engineers, but I don't think

there's a structure to my developing an interest in architecture. I think it just happened. With my family, the thing that we did was we drew together—we had drawing competitions. That's the thing I remember; we were always drawing.

One of my collections was inspired by Kansai International Airport, but it wasn't really the appearance of the airport alone that interested me. It was a combination of things. I looked at all the people in the airport, and they looked really "Industrial Revolution." Then I looked at the space and its materials and construction, and it [looked] like the 21st century. So it made me think of fashion as opposed to architecture. I think fashion has dwelt too long in reliving different eras rather than applying itself to what the future or the present really is about.

Again, I was not really looking for architectural inspiration when I stumbled onto the work of the architect Louis Barragán. It was very serendipitous. Before a trip to Mexico City, I visited the architects Tod Williams and Billie Tsien, and in their work space is what Billie called a "Barragan stairway." And I said "Oh, who's he?" Then, off I went to Mexico, and that's Barragan's world. His spectacular use of geometry and color inspired my fall 2005 collection.

I need to see my designs out in the world—to feel that the work has been successful. When I started my first collection, I only made five pieces. My criterion was if I can sell my five pieces, if there's somebody out there who would want to buy them, then maybe there's a reason for me to go into business. I was successful in selling that collection to Bendel's, which in the eighties was where I thought my customer would shop. Then I managed to sell it to Bergdorff Goodman and Nieman's.

Bendel's put it into their catalog, so from a five-piece collection, I ended up with huge orders. I actually hadn't thought through the process of how I was going to manufacture them and get them into the store; I wasn't thinking in huge numbers.

But now I knew the ideas worked, not just by the fact that the director at Bendel's recognized the collection as good, but that other people did as well. And then, when Bendel's bought it in-depth, people came and bought it from the store, and *that's* what gave the collection life. If you make something, and it's truly beautiful, and you can't market it, if what you are doing is functional design, then you are not being very successful. If it were a piece of art, then you would only need one collector to buy it for you to be a success. When you're a designer, such as I am, and you are doing ready-to-wear, you need to succeed on a certain level. I am not confused about what I do—I make clothes—and because of the price point and the marketplace I'm in, they're fashionable clothes—designer clothes. My success depends on how many people I can convince to wear my concepts and ideas. And the more people I see in my clothes,

the more successful I am. There's another school of thought in the world of fashion where it's only fashion if its not wearable and nobody wants to buy it. I think differently. I think that really good design is universal and should have universal appeal. It's like good art; if something is really successful, everybody recognizes it. You don't have to be elevated and be a person of special taste and education and refinement. It should have some kind of visceral appeal.

I don't resist my work being elevated to art. What I'm trying to explain to the people who are interested is this: Within the world of fashion and clothing design, one should be able to have a dialogue, referencing history and anthropology and different eras of fashion. You should be able to view a designer's work in that context, just as art can be viewed in a painting context or in the sculptural context. You shouldn't need to validate good design in fashion by likening it to a piece of art. You should be able to do it in its own world. How many times do you read a review where the person writing about a fashion show, in addition to having an opinion, is educated about textiles? Excuse me—if you don't know anything about textiles, how dare you write about clothes? I think that what I am really trying to do is to point the way toward having our own books and references on fashion that will make fashion as a discipline more significant against other disciplines. For instance, architecture has more respect than clothes; the museum of Modern Art will hold an exhibition on architecture and not on fashion. I think it's because we don't have people who write about it other than from the curatorial or educational world, so the critics are not necessarily as steeped in our techniques and our craft. I'm not criticizing anybody; I'm just saying that fashion reviews fall into a very narrow confine. In the world of fashion, a design is validated by who wears it. This is important—but if you can have that focus and have a broader context for what you're looking at and have some historical and social references, it becomes more potent. I'm not distancing myself from the world of art or architecture. All I'm saying is they are relevant references, but let's also have our own references.

It's not a deliberate act, but I tend to want to challenge tradition. We have these demarcations, like night, day, sportswear, activewear—all these areas were created by the industry, so that you could specialize and have more business. If you can make a pair of pants that can succeed both in the workplace and a black tie event, you've reduced the number of buys from two to one. It's driven by the marketplace. All I'm doing is saying to my clients, "You don't have to be so rigid about what you wear and don't wear. If it looks good and you feel good in it—hey, it works!

Designing requires a strong personal involvement since the designer must be able to iden-tify with the client, end user, and/or consumer of the final design product. Designers may have to assume the personalities of the people for whom they are designing. Designers must be able to find and depend on resources of inspiration to explore situations and reactions to situations that they have never before encountered.

The following exercises allow you to gather sources of inspiration and tells you where such sources may be found in the future. The 12 exercises prompt you to look into your mind from 12 different angles.

The exercises will help you to

- know how and where to find the muses when you need them;
- release the appropriate genies from their bottles at the right times;
- explore and play; and
- move on.

CREATING A DESIGN JOURNAL

Brainstorm

The quotations that introduce each set of questions are from a variety of sources. They rep-resent one of the facets of creative thinking. You should look for similar examples in authors, designers, artists, and architects you encounter on your own.

This is a meditative exercise, so don't be hasty. Read each question, and write down everything that comes to mind: Make lists, write down keywords, and jot down impulsive thoughts. Give yourself time to think about the questions and your notes before you edit them into clear answers to the questions. Not all the questions will have clear answers at first, and the questions are not designed to be easy. These answers will be the basis for your search for inspiration, not only for now, but also for future projects.

Visualize

Since designing is a visual skill, use your thoughts and answers to create visual statements in a sketchbook or folder. Collect images and photographs. Create collages and sketches to illustrate each section. Think of this as an open-ended project, a journal that you will add to as your insights evolve. Do not try to be logical. Let your impulses and instinct control your choices. A good strategy is to focus on the exercise, impulsively collect images, whether they are sketched or clipped, and once you have a good stack, start to arrange them into a collage that describes your thoughts on the topic.

1: FOCUS

"*. . . with me it's the Muse who causes poetry by focusing the world.*"—May Sarton[8]

As we may expect from a poet, Sarton's choice of words is interesting. The Muse *causes* poetry. She doesn't allow, create, or induce it; she causes it. The Muse makes the creation inevitable by sharpening the creator's (Sarton) perception.

To "focus the world" is to reveal things in a way that their meaning is clearer than before. Poets, painters, and designers find ways to expose things that have been hidden from view so a new context or an entirely new meaning can result. On the one hand, we can examine artists and writers in search of revealing insights and interpretations. On the other-hand, we may enlist a Muse to help us focus the world in a manner that lets us see things we have not seen before.

The muse focuses the world.

1. What have you seen, read, or heard that made you understand something in a way you had not or could not before?
2. What can make your perception clearer? What can help you to focus the world?
3. What, where, who could be your Muse? How?

2: ENERGY TRANSFERRED

"A poem is energy transferred from where the poet got it . . . by way of the poem itself to, all the way over to, the reader." —Charles Olson

Energy is never destroyed. The energy that goes into a creation will radiate from it forever. We can stand in front of a painting that is decades old and sense the painter's approach and the energy of his or her emotions. A concert of music that is centuries old can stir our emotions every which way, and poems written more than one thousand years ago can bring tears to our eyes.

Energy is transferred.

We sense the artist's joy, anger, or excitement—the reigning emotion of the creative moment. The energy of the artist's creativity and inspiration is transferred to you through the artwork, perhaps hundreds of years after the artist lived. On the one hand, you can be aware and open yourself to influences from all possible sources. On the other hand, you can let this knowledge spur you to animate all you create with your own energy. Either way, your objective is to use this transfer of energy to fuel your creativity.

1. Have you been completely thrilled and energized by a poem, a piece of writing, a work of art, a film, a performance? What was it?
2. Describe what happened. How did the energy manifest? How do you think it managed to do this?
3. If you haven't been so energized, don't stop until you find a work of art that transports you, now! Where will you go to look for this?

3: THE BEAUTY OF THE WORLD

. . . What a piece of work is a man! how noble in reason!
how infinite in faculty! in form and moving how
express and admirable! in action how like an angel!
in apprehension how like a god! the beauty of the
world! the paragon of animals! And yet, to me,
what is this quintessence of dust? —Hamlet, *Hamlet*, II, ii

People, especially because of their contradictory nature, are an endless source of inspiration for all the reasons William Shakespeare wrote about and more. Hamlet, a man in turmoil, was overflowing with admiration at the glory of human beings, while he contemplated killing one. We can admire people as individuals and as types, we can love them and fear them. We cannot always understand why we feel a certain way, yet, we still feel something.

Designers must understand their clients and collaborators, and often they won't have much time to relate. Work on understanding people, but also genuinely like them for what they are. Learn as much as you can about people and what makes them tick. You have to care about people to create good things for them.

People: The beauty of the world.

1. What are the best qualities of people who affect you strongly and positively?
2. What excites you about them? What do you admire?
3. Who is your favorite person? Why?

4: IRRESISTIBLE FORCE

. . . I should want to show by my work what is in the heart of such an eccentric man, of such a nobody [as I am in the eyes of most people].

This is my ambition, which is, notwithstanding everything, founded less on anger than on love, founded more on serenity than on passion. It is true that I am often in the greatest misery, but still there is within me a calm pure harmony and music. In the poorest huts, the dirtiest corner, I see drawings and pictures. And with irresistible force my mind is drawn towards these things.

More and more other things lose their interest, and the more I get rid of them, the quicker my eye grasps the picturesque things. Art demands persistent work, work in spite of everything, and a continuous observation. —Vincent Van Gogh, in a letter to his brother Theo, July 1882

Opening your heart and self for a creative drive can be difficult and debilitating. For professional designers, continually giving in to the "irresistible forces" can become a drain on their energy and cause them to burn out. We all have limits and must know what we are capable of accomplishing. However, by allowing yourself to be drawn to the edge, you find out where that edge is and how it allows you to learn to control the forces that pull at you. Therefore, the strength of the focused and directed creative impulse becomes that much greater.

Irresistible force.

1. What interests you to the point of being drawn to it with "irresistible force?" What would you like to be so interested in?
2. What can make you *need* to create?
3. What "puts you over the edge?" How do you come back?
4. What is the wildest impulse you've ever had? Did you act on it? If not, why not?

5: THE NOISE THAT KEEPS YOU AWAKE

"Musicians, painters, whatever, they have no choice but to describe where they live," said Bono, whose ordinary conversation is often true to a tradition of Irish bards. *"Sometimes it may seem hard to keep your ear on the street because there's a lot of stuff you don't want to pick up. But as Bob Dylan said, 'He not busy being born is busy dying,' and I think the death starts in your record collection. I like to feel alive. I think I'm awake, and this is the noise that keeps me awake."*[9] —Bono

Bono.

Design what you know. But what happens if what you know is limited or not recently renewed? Think about your background and environment. How does this define your vision and thoughts? What can you do to add to that?

Is it possible that you are missing something by not being aware of your surroundings? Open yourself up to new influences in all the arts and in your daily life. You may find treasures you didn't expect to find.

1. In terms of your influences, what is your environment? Where are you from? *What* are you from? What are the forces, things, people, and situations that shaped you into who you are?
2. How do you think your current environment affects your opinions and tastes?
3. What makes you feel alive and awake?
4. What do you need to listen to, look at, or experience to keep your ideas fresh?
5. Experience artistry that is unfamiliar to you. What would that be?

6: REFLECT INFLUENCES

From the time the D&G collection was launched, its design philosophy has remained constant. Domenico [Dolce] and I get a lot of our ideas from the street; we are very influenced by what

kids wear to go out at night to the clubs. We try to reflect these influences in a positive way.
—Stefano Gabbana, of Dolce & Gabbana

What is out there?

Going out and looking at the world is as necessary, if not more so, than any other research you conduct. You can choose influences and how you work with them, but you must seek them out; don't wait for them to come to you.

An influence should be just that; it should influence you. It should not be something that you recycle into your designs. Copying an influence is easy. To be truly creative means you add your energy and interpretation to create a design that is more than just the sum of its parts.

1. By whom or what would you like to be influenced?
2. Where will you go for this influence?
3. How will you reflect these influences to make the creations uniquely yours?

7: COMMUNICATE FEELINGS

Fashion is not enough! . . . I try to communicate a feeling, a sensation . . . I'm always telling stories. Stories about women. From the spy to the Madonna, via the heroine, the goddess, the "petite parisienne," the secretary. I then created clothes that men and women can wear in these imaginary adventures. I direct them. —Thierry Mugler

Thierry Mugler in his studio with
Jerry Hall.

There is a side of designing that is about dreams and fantasies. A designer creates a vision of the world, as it should be, instead of molding designs to the way the world is. Sometimes the impetus for a new design is simply that we, our clients, or even the world at large, are bored with what is available. It becomes our job not only to create the design, but also to create the context that calls for its existence. We must show the environment that this new design belongs in and ensure it looks desirable.

Western society has in the recent past become more driven by a consumer economy. The demand for "new" is greater than ever and continues to grow. The influence of popular culture on design increases and design trends, even in long-term applications such as architecture, are increasingly affected. With this has come a demand for the increased expressiveness of design. Modernism, and the cool structured functionality that went with it, has given way to the (sometimes) playful anarchy and retro-referential style of the postmodernist and Deconstructivist movements.

It is extremely important to be aware of the trends and movements that shape designs. Our reason for observing them may be so that we can run counter to them or ignore them. If we are astute at spotting trends, we can use them to predict what the next trend will be and so be ahead of the curve. A trend can be recognized only in the context of where we are and where we have been. What is the Zeitgeist, the spirit of our time? What is changing? What is old? What is bubbling under the surface? A spirit creates an emotion, and we can either tap into it or create an alternative view. Designers can put a unique stamp on this world and in doing so bring dreams to life.

1. Where does your imagination like to go?
2. What bores you?
3. How would you change the world if you could?
4. What are your favorite adventures or fantasies? Why?
5. What is the spirit of our time? (See Appendix 4 for a brief discussion of this topic.)

8: BE COMPLETELY QUIET

There is no need for you to leave the house. Stay at your table and listen. Don't even listen, just wait. Don't even wait, be completely quiet and alone. The world will offer itself to you to be unmasked; it can't do otherwise; in raptures it will writhe before you. —Franz Kafka[10]

"Don't even listen, just wait."

This seems at first glance to contradict the idea of the need to look at unlikely sources for inspiration to create specific designs. However, the idea presented here is grounded in the perception that your consciousness is your own. No one can think your thoughts. No one can see through your eyes. Everything you experience in the world and all your ideas, thoughts, and impulses are within you and nowhere else. But, trying to access your thoughts is not always easy in the middle of the noise and activity of daily life. All our increasingly convenient gadgetry seems to be making this not better but worse. It becomes very difficult to take the time to be still and think, digest, and meditate.

Outward noise is not the only problem. Have you ever tried listening to the chatter that's going on in your brain all day? We tend to either be thinking of something that has already happened or about something in the future and not what is going on right now. The present is fleeting enough as is, without us ignoring it. If you cannot be still, you will not see clearly. By quieting all this mental fidgeting, you can focus on the present and tap into thoughts and impulses.

This idea is closely related to Zen practice in that the impulse itself, the act of waiting and listening, is even too much action. The anticipation of discovery clouds the view. You probably know how difficult it is to get a good idea if you are forcing it to happen.

Find a place where you can be quiet and still. Become accustomed to your silence. Eventually you won't have to withdraw yourself; you will be able to quiet yourself in the middle of a stressful situation. This will help you access your own thoughts, experiences, and beliefs and harness them to your work.

1. Do you have an opportunity to be alone and quiet? How? Where? When?
2. If not, why? How can you make this happen?

9: THE BEGINNER'S MIND I

If your mind is empty, it is always ready for anything; it is open to everything. In the beginner's mind there are many possibilities; in the expert's mind there are few.
—Shunryu Suzuki, *Zen Mind, Beginner's Mind*

Clear your mind.

Being able to see the world with a fresh, unformed view is of great importance. This enables designers to have a new vision in designs, find new approaches, and see new solutions to old problems. If you find yourself coasting along on preconceived ideas, stop, go back, and question all of them.

1. When have you best been able to accept new knowledge and ideas?
2. Why do you think that was?
3. How would you prepare yourself to do that again?
4. When are you best able to generate new ideas?

10: THE BEGINNER'S MIND II

You can't do this kind of work with total jerks, but you can't do it with total professionals either. They are far too knowledgeable about the normal way, and that gets them completely blocked. —Ole Sheeren, OMA Project Manager, on working with the architect Rem Koolhaas.[11]

Rem Koolhaus showing a model of the Seattle Public Library.

Too much knowledge can be as much of a stumbling block as lack of it. You cannot undo knowledge or unthink a thought, but you can open your mind to be receptive to the different, strange, or seemingly impossible. Once we become accustomed to a certain method through study or training, it can be very difficult to break those habits. Always question your previous methods, opinions, and knowledge. Keep in mind that *normal* is a very relative term.

1. Define *normal.*
2. Have you ever gone against the normal mode of thinking? How? Why? Why not?
3. How would your design go beyond notions of normalcy?

11: PAIN

The birth of a new idea comes best when everything is going well and will be painful. Don't attempt to tamper with the process and don't deny the pain. —Andy Law, Founder, St. Luke's Advertising Agency, UK

The birth of a child is an often crazy and messy situation, involving a lot of pain and stress. In the midst of it, it can be difficult to imagine it ending well. However, when labor is over, all seems well once a small, warm bundle is in your arms.

Resisting the pain just delays the inevitable and can cause complications. In the creative process, trying to stay away from the agony of choices and decisions does just the same. Trust the process and go with it.

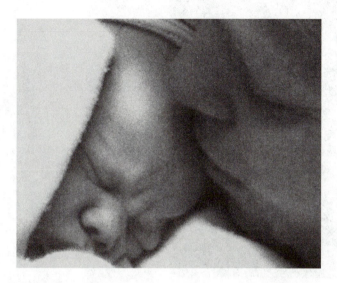

The birth of a new idea is painful, but the pain is quickly forgotten.

A new idea needs to be carefully attended to at the time of its birth. A healthy atmosphere and environment will facilitate things, but the process will still require a degree of tension and pain. A good design requires the expenditure of a lot of energy, the keeping of strange hours, and the agonizing over details and solutions.

By preparing for the process, you can make sure all goes well. There are no shortcuts, so make sure you are ready for each step of the way by having resources of inspiration and keeping your eyes on the ultimate goal.

In addition to this, knowing your limits prepares you for times of stress. You know when you can go on and when you need to hunker down. Being able to look back and say, "I could handle that!" will allow you to be less apprehensive the next time a high-stress situation occurs.

1. When are you at your strongest?
2. What needs to happen for you to be content with the world and feel that all is well?
3 When have you had to endure mental or physical pain to achieve a worthwhile goal? If you have, could you do that again?

12: GET UP AND LOOK

People are always blaming their circumstances for what they are. I don't believe in circumstances. The people who get on in this world are the people who get up and look for the circumstances they want, and if they can't find them, make them. —George Bernard Shaw, *Mrs. Warren's Profession*

"The people who get on in this world are the people who get up and look for the circumstances they want, and if they can't find them, make them." –George Bernard Shaw, *Mrs. Warren's Profession*

A professional needs to be proactive about opportunities, processes, and solutions. If something doesn't work, fix it or do it again. If an idea isn't developing, don't wait for it to resolve itself. The creative drive must also drive one *to* creativity, not just through it. Get up. Go.

1. What needs to happen for you to be a more creative person?
2. What steps can you take to make this happen?
3. What could you do routinely at the beginning of a design project to energize your creativity?
4. What can you do today?

Identification

OBJECTIVE

This chapter covers the process of a designer identifying his or her idea and dealing with several steps that occur in this second stage, including reviewing constraints and coming up with solutions to the design problem within these constraints. Also covered is a designer's responsibility toward the community and society as a whole when faced with choices that can affect people's safety, health, and well-being.

KEY CONCEPTS

- A designer's main concerns are solving problems and making decisions.
- Design depends on recognizing and working within constraints.
- Every design has both inherent and imposed constraints.
- Designers must be aware of the larger, and often unintentional, consequences of their work.
- Sustainable practices and the protection of the environment are concerns that today's designers cannot ignore.

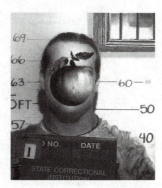

Identifying the problem is the first step in capturing an idea.

IDENTIFICATION

There are many ways to go about identifying a project. The project brief may arrive as a request from a client, it may be a self-directed new design, or it may be an improvement on an older design. Whatever the project's origin, designers need to identify what the design needs in a coherent way and what its limits are. A project's needs and limits are its constraints, and by identifying them, we understand what we need to engage with to create an effective design. We can then tap into our sources of inspiration and apply them to our projects.

CONSTRAINTS

Q. *Does the creation of design admit constraints?*
A. Design depends largely on constraints.
Q. *What constraints?*
A. The sum of all constraints. Here is one of the few effective keys to the design problem: the ability of the designer to recognize as many of the constraints as possible, his [or her] willingness and enthusiasm for working within these constraints—constraints of price, of size, of strength, of balance, of surface, of time, and so forth—each problem has its own peculiar list.
Q. *Does design obey laws?*
A. Aren't constraints enough?
(Excerpt from *Design Q & A* by Charles and Ray Eames, 1967; appears in Volume 4 of the *Films of Charles and Ray Eames*)

A design, like a river, needs constraints to have form and direction.

A design project is a problem that needs to be solved and explained by a designer. The problem can be simple or complex, or it can be practical or whimsical.

Each problem has its own list of constraints, some more fixed than others. The constraints come up at different stages, and sometimes they are not apparent until after the final design is already in the hands of the end user. These constraints will, more than any other aspect, define the project as the idea or the solution, which begins to grow and evolve. It may seem at first that the design process will be more difficult if there are many constraints. However, the opposite is true, as long as the designer is willing to work within the constraints. Designers must not approach these constraints in a negative manner. "To constrain" seems like a negative action, but we must be aware of them as a frame and a guide that keep us from going into undesirable places. Think of a river, constrained within its banks. If designers ignore constraints, then the project may develop in an unwanted direction, which may require that a designer redesign or even cancel the project. Clients expect results as agreed, so if designers step outside the boundaries, they must do so with care.

Igor Stravinsky at work. "The more constraints one imposes, the more one frees oneself of the chains that shackle the spirit. The arbitrariness of the constraint only serves to obtain precision of execution." –Igor Stravinsky

Constraints can be either inherent or imposed. *Inherent constraints* are those directly connected to the essential character of the object being designed. For example, a clock should have some way of measuring and displaying time, and a spoon should have a handle and a bowl. The best way to recognize a design's inherent constraint is by questioning whether the object would lose its essential nature if a certain aspect were to be removed. A clock that tells the wrong time is still a clock, but a clock that measures no time at all isn't really a clock. Therefore, an inherent constraint defines an object's functionality. A raincoat should repel water, and a chair should hold its occupant in a sitting position. Conceptual artists and surrealists in the past century had a lot of fun ignoring or contradicting the inherent characteristics of objects and causing their audiences to question their perceptions and understandings of the world.

Man Ray: "The Gift." By contradicting the object's inherent functionality, the artist makes us question the object's nature. This can prompt a wider questioning of reality in general and of our understanding of the world.

Imposed constraints are characteristics of an object's desired design but are not essential to its existence. The imposing of constraints usually (and ideally) involves choices that designers make at the beginning of a project, when the desired result is defined. If designers move outside imposed constraints, they will still find that their designs are still identifiable as objects of their class, but they aren't exactly the planned end result. For example, instead of designing a steel-encased clock, you design one with a ceramic shell. It is still a clock, but the qualities brought to it by virtue of its casing have changed.

Constraints can be imposed unexpectedly at any point during the design process, all the way into the manufacturing stage. For example, if you learn that a component needs to be a required size, it may affect and change the intended manufacturing technique, which constrains the choice of materials, requires specific coloring processes, increases the budget, and so on.

Ideally, all constraints are evident at a project's start, but the specifics and budget may have been prepackaged from a client who was not aware of the constraints. In this case, a designer must realign the project, usually at a cost of time, money, or both. For this reason, it is very important to try to define all constraints at the beginning, keeping in mind that there is no shortage of possible constraints.

Concept map of constraints. Design depends on the sum of all constraints.

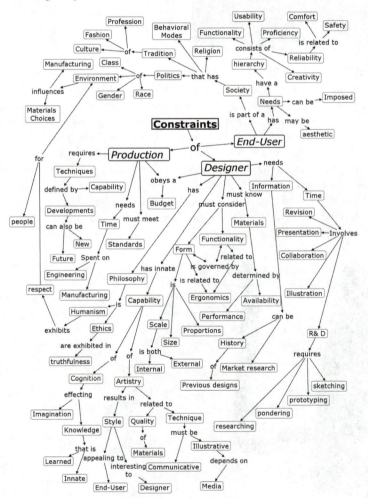

When looking for the constraints of a design problem, there are three main, largely overlapping areas in which designers should seek. Constraints are determined by the needs or desires of the *end user, designer*, or *fabricator*. In addition, an ever-present constraint is *responsibility*, which applies to the other constraints in one way or another.

END USER CONSTRAINTS

The constraints that relate to the end user are perhaps the most obvious at the outset. Whatever the client needs (inherent) or wishes for (imposed) is added to the list of characteristics the design must have. Whatever the design, you have to deal with people. They will inhabit, view, wear, use, build, or at least be affected by your work. Keeping the human factor in mind is absolutely necessary, whether it is directly, by working toward ergonomic solutions, or indirectly, by anticipating human interaction with your design. Ergonomic design is the art and science of working with human scale. It is a way of considering design options to ensure people's capabilities and physical limitations are taken into account.

Functionality and Form

What an object does or how it should behave is determined by constraints, as previously mentioned. "Form follows function" is probably one of the most quoted maxims of modern design. It is generally taken to mean that an object's form should result from its function. The statements of any creed tend to lose their power when they are quoted excessively, usually out of context, and this particular maxim is no different. In its worst case, when it is treated as an article of faith, it has been responsible for many bad decisions. It has relieved designers of the responsibility for aesthetics. It was the architect Louis Henri Sullivan, in reference to the problem of designing tall buildings in the late 1890s, who said the following:

> *Whether it be the sweeping eagle in his flight or the open apple-blossom, the toiling work-horse, the blithe swan, the branching oak, the winding stream at its base, the drifting clouds, over all the coursing sun, form ever follows function, and this is the law.*[1]

In the late 19th-century, people believed they had mastered all the laws of the universe and were excited about the industrialized future. It is understandable that such a period would generate the idea that process, or function, should determine the shape of things. This is, however, a misreading of nature. Nature does not "decide" or make choices about its form *or* its function. A natural system functions *within* the capabilities of its form. A bird does not grow wings from a desire to fly; it flies because it has wings. Things in nature do what they can simply because they can.

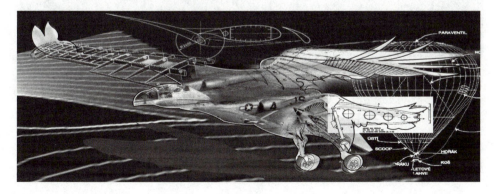

A natural system functions within the capabilities of its form. A bird does not grow wings from a desire to fly; it flies because it has wings. Humans fly by design.

Strict functionalism also tends to ignore the possibility that aesthetic appeal or decoration may in itself be a design function to consider. Essentially, the Modernist/functionalist aesthetic was a response (and a refreshing one at the time) to the top-heaviness of Victorian design and an answer to the demands of industrialization. Think of form and function as joined. Let one inform and acknowledge the other in any order you like. Your main challenge is to make sure they do not conflict with each other and that both fulfill the end user's needs and desires.

Societal Constraints

Our world is increasingly globalized, especially as far as business and communications go. Our world is also becoming increasingly fragmented culturally and politically. This highlights problems of marketing and manufacturing in other cultures. A huge portion of the world gets its imagery and ideas from the same entertainment media, while cultures that used to be under a multistate umbrella rally around their common heritage and language. To be aware of emergent trends, we must focus on the local and particular, as well as the global and general, and be careful not to assume anything about one or the other. Just because the whole world can watch the same television program does not mean that we have the same preferences. Religion, gender roles, and racial and class consciousness are all as intensely relevant as they are difficult to discuss. Don't presume to understand the needs and references of a culture unless you are of it, have studied it, or have a guide.

Human behavior is predictable only on a large scale and even then only very generally. Even more difficult than prediction is regulation. People will not behave in a certain way just because a designer wishes them to do so. Expecting common sense should never be a basic assumption in any design that involves public interaction.

> Human behavior is predictable only on a large scale and even then only very generally.

A staggering example of a collision between design and "humanity" is the memorial fountain to the late Princess Diana Spencer, unveiled in London in 2004. Designed at a cost of $6.6 million dollars, the memorial is a large oval stone channel set in a sloping, landscaped site. Water runs through the oval, and the project was introduced with the idea that the waters were to be waded in. The whole thing was to "reflect the turbulence, excitement, and energy in Diana's life."

But water, children, dogs, and park pigeons make for a mean mix, and soon it was determined that the water was heavily contaminated with bacteria. To make things worse, waders who played on the wet granite began slipping on the stone and getting badly injured. There were even more problems involving drains clogged by leaves falling off nearby trees and other debris. Three weeks after the memorial's grand opening, it was closed.

Fences have been erected around the memorial and fitted with gates so that staff can manage the number of visitors. The texture of the granite stone has been roughened to prevent slip-and-fall accidents, and new guidelines instruct visitors to paddle their feet and dip their hands only if they are sitting on the edge of the fountain.

As part of a new safety plan, six "staff trained in crowd management and first aid" supervise the site during the summer. The heightened security raised the expected running costs of the memorial by more than $170,000 a year.

Safety

If safety is not a central concern right at the beginning of a design project, then it is usually the last thing on anybody's mind. There are indeed entire fields of design where safety concerns are minimal.

However, if there is even a hint of danger in a situation, it must be examined very carefully. The example of the memorial fountain for Princess Diana shows how common sense cannot always be expected. Designers can go too far with their safety concerns, and a lawsuit-happy culture does not help matters any. This leads to warnings that bath sponges should not be flotation devices or that hot coffee is actually really, really hot. This is really an exercise in futility that only aims to prevent lawsuits.

Designers must be aware of the standards and laws governing materials, chemicals, and electricity. Building in redundant safety measures is always a good idea. If in doubt about the safety of your designs, research similar situations extensively and increase whatever safety factors you have already built in.

CONSTRAINTS OF PRODUCTION

The most immediate set of constraints are determined by matters related to production. The questions of materials, techniques, and capabilities are there from the start, and very few designers have the luxury of shooting out ideas first and asking production questions later.

With computer aided design (CAD) increasingly taking over as the tool of choice in design studios, the line between designers, model makers, and engineers is becoming blurred. In architecture and industrial design, the line may never have been as clear as we are led to believe. The constraints of production are especially important to consider, now that CAD plays such a large role in every aspect, from rough sketching and modeling to printing construction diagrams. The software allows for the creation of any shape, texture, and configuration, and a regular reality check is necessary. Can what is being represented actually be constructed? Can the printer deal with the color nuances? Will the structure actually stand using this gauge of steel for support?

Reality checks are also necessary when working with nondigital media. It is just as easy (if not easier) to design an "impossible" design with a pencil and paper as with a computer and mouse. The danger involved in CAD is that the speed of execution, constant precision, and cleanliness of the output, printed or on-screen, lend "believability" to the image that a hand-drawn sketch will generally not be able to achieve.

Will you be ready when production begins?

Computers aside, we must be aware of the processes involved in the manufacturing of our designs. However, we must not be so consumed with manufacturing issues that we are unable to experiment with our ideas and designs. Working within constraints and using them to create something new is immensely satisfying. The constraints of materials, engineering, and fabrication have in the past century been great sources of inspiration in all fields of design. For centuries, architects and builders have used the quirks of materials and construction to create rhythms and textures; the 20th century took this to new extremes. The functionalist tendency took hold everywhere, allowing apparel designers to use seams and fasteners as visual elements and architects to highlight structural components and raw textures.

The true art of design lies in the collaboration between builders and makers and designers. Design is more than worrying about how the final product looks; how a product works is just as, if not more, important. Talk to the fabricators of your designs often and early in the process. Learn from them as much as you can and be respectful of their expertise. Strive to be well-informed and aware of the limitations of their methods, and keep track of new developments that can do away with the constraints of old technology.

The Pompidou Museum, Paris; a striking example of late-Modernist architecture.

Vivienne Westwood ready-to-wear, autumn 1997: The zipper, a functional element as a design statement.

CONSTRAINTS OF THE DESIGNER

Information

In designing, information is crucial. A designer must communicate well. In order for the end of the project to be accurate, we must be sure that the information going in is clear. The lack of information about any aspect of the project may become a constraint. In designing, what you don't know usually does hurt you. You may opt to design for a "best case" or "worst case" scenario.

My tutor at art school used to annoy me by saying that "designer" should read "decider." I later found that she was absolutely right, and the key to making a good decision is to have good information.

One of the problems with decision-making in design is that designers need to make decisions well before they have all the information. The only way to deal with this is to create flexible plans that you can revise as you go. Make yourself and your clients aware of any uncertainties, and update them whenever there is a revision. What may seem obvious to you may not be so clear to someone who encounters the project only intermittently.

Time

Designers have deadlines. Constraints of time are perhaps the most acute constraints of all. Time is distressingly difficult to make up once it's lost. We are often surprised and frustrated by the fact that every time we need to meet a deadline we work up until the last minute. This becomes easier to bear if you understand that last-minuteness is, in a way, part of the process. If a project has not come to a satisfactory conclusion or is still offering possibilities, we always take all the time given to us. The flip side is C. Northcote Parkinson's Law, which states, "All work expands to fill available time." Parkinson (who was being sarcastic about the British Civil Service) maintained that every job takes all the available time allotted to it because nobody works longer or harder than they need to. This principle is unfortunately often used by managers to justify tight schedules and is really not all that helpful in planning.

The Tailor's Rule: First, Do the Math

Take the time available and divide it by the number of tasks that need to be done. Say you have a presentation due next week that includes 12 ideas mounted on boards. You have an entire week of ten-hour days. If you don't intend on working on the presentation day itself (never a good idea!), you have six days. So, you have half a day, say five hours, for each drawing in the presentation. However, there may also be other things that need to get done in this timeframe. You may have to get supplies and samples or do some research. Once you create the drawings, you also have to account for assembly of the presentation; you'll need time to do the following:

- Mount them
- Write captions
- Assemble and mount any supporting material (color swatches, detail views, diagrams, samples, and so on)

Finally, let's say you need to have daily meetings to show your client or colleagues preliminary sketches. Suddenly, instead of just 12 drawings you needed to do, you now have three additional tasks for each. Your task list is suddenly up to 55. It would seem you have, on average, a little more than an hour for each of the tasks you have to perform in the next six days. This also doesn't account for the fact that you may want to factor time for the following:

- redoing something
- dealing with unexpected problems
- leaving time for personal errands

Applying the Tailor's Rule, or doing the math, is often a sobering exercise but allows people to see why we are so often scrambling at the last minute to finish projects and presentations.

The Tailor's Principle: Everything Takes at Least 15 Minutes.

When you plan your time, you need to take into account that every significant action will probably take at least 15 minutes. In other words, you can't realistically fit more than four tasks, on average, into an hour. Regardless of whether it actually is 15 minutes or 10 or 20, the point is a good one because it keeps planning "real," if not entirely reasonable.

Let's say you had 60 hours to complete the 12 drawings. You decide you can finish the research and supply gathering in one day (ten hours), leaving you 50 hours in the five remaining days for the presentation boards. Put aside one hour a day for lunch and breaks. Now you have 45 left. You decide to allow two hours for each illustration—one hour for sketching and drawing and one hour for finish and color—which takes 24 and leaves you with 21. Your daily meetings and other activities with clients, associates, and others will take about 90 minutes a day. You now have about 14 hours left to assemble support material, mount the drawings, and write captions for all 12 drawings. This leaves you with $14 \div 12$ hours = 70 minutes to create each drawing's presentation, and as each of these involved three tasks, you have just a little more than 20 minutes to complete the three tasks for each. Therefore, to create a presentation of 12 drawings you must finish something every 20 minutes for the next five (ten-hour) working days. Note that this doesn't allow time for any mistakes or downtime over the course of one week, which is neither normal nor healthy. This is where the greatest mistakes in planning creative time happen. We tend to assume that we can work flat out, at a constant rate, with no interruptions for days on end. However, most of us need to amend the Tailor's Principle.

A day in the life of a designer: The multi-faceted nature of the job makes rigorous time-management essential.

Amendment to the Tailor's Principle: Plan for Lag Time

One week of ten-hour days does not sound too bad. No matter how focused you are, unless you have a place to hide with your work, there will be interruptions. Life and its attending chaos intrude into the most carefully laid-out plans. You must therefore plan for the interruptions, such as the phone ringing, meetings not beginning or ending promptly on schedule, and so on. Planning time only to work is fine, but you have to realize that you need to be creative, not just busy, and as you saw in the Inspiration chapter, you must have time to refuel.

The solution is to factor couch time into your planning. This will help keep you sane in the long run. We decide to give ourselves 12-hour days instead of ten-hour days. The two extra hours a day are divided between extra assembly time and life's chaos. By adding two hours to each day, we have made sure that we won't have to add 12 hours to the last day. Without factoring the math, we may very well be in danger of showing up at our presentation without having slept and with unfinished or hurried-looking work.

Time constraints are frustrating. We never feel there is enough time, and we usually feel that having a little more time will make things so much better. The best you can do in a given timeframe is always the best you can do, whether it's the best you can do in three days or three years.

Plan for every step of your process. What if each step takes a little more time? Might you need to stop along the way?

Materials

Materials must conform to both inherent and imposed constraints. You need to learn about materials, what they are, and how they behave. The capabilities of the materials you choose will direct your project throughout. From the time you begin sketching through preparing for production to the eventual cost of shipping, the material you choose will be a constant factor in your work and decision-making. If it is not immediately clear what materials are going to be involved in your project, research by considering both form and function and how each will be influenced by material choices. Strength, comfort, weight, and aesthetics should be considered, as well as production issues of standards, price, and availability. There may be color choices involved and often materials can carry an emotional, psychological, or political message, such as in the field of "green" or environmentally friendly design.

Many designs allow designers to use materials in a new or unconventional way, so be very careful that you understand the materials' capabilities. The constraints placed on you by your material choices should be evident as soon as you begin to sketch.

You may not know what materials you intend to use until you see the forms you are designing, and the same is true for functionality. The materials may need to provide a function, such as strength, conductivity, or warmth. Production affects the choices as well. We must consider techniques and capabilities and whether our choices are suited to them. If they aren't, we must search for a solution, often through modeling and experimentation.

Sometimes material choices are at odds with one another. The best-looking material may also be the least tolerant, and the lightest material may also be the most expensive. You must be ready to compromise and revise your plans, but this is one of the more compelling reasons to be fully aware of the purpose of your designs and its constraints.

Budgets

The most difficult set of constraints has to do with money. Like other constraints, budget constraints can make the project less cumbersome, if not easier. It is a rare design project that has an open-ended budget, and that is a good thing. During my first years designing for theater, I was resident at a theater that had not implemented line item budgeting for its productions. Every time I asked the question "How much can this cost?" I received the answer "As little as possible." This drove me to distraction, as the definition of "little" and "possible" was left entirely up to the designers. Needless to say, production costs tend to be high when there are no budget constraints. A good budget in design (just like anywhere else) must be clear and realistic.

If, for example, we know that we have only one dollar for fabric, we can begin to plan for scavenging and soliciting donations. We eliminate a legion of problems and solutions right off the bat. This is much easier, not to say efficient, than having to scramble to find fabric for one dollar. Time, in this case, is being wasted by questions of money.

In the same way as when we plan for time, budgeting should include contingency plans. It is not uncommon to routinely add 25 percent to budgets for "unknowns," and designers who do generally base this on experience. This can also work in reverse. If you are handed a fixed budget to work with, estimate your numbers to 75 percent of its total.

Look at your project, and try to spot which elements will be the most expensive and which carry an unknown price tag. Give the unknowns extra-careful consideration because odds are they will become larger figures than anyone expects.

Apply cost-benefit analysis to your decisions. Is a small detail worth a disproportionate amount of the budget? Yes, if the detail is what gives the design its character. It is good to keep in mind Pareto's Principle—also known as the 80/20 rule—which states that 80 percent of the resources will go toward 20 percent of a project's needs.

Pareto's Principle, also known as the 80/20 rule, states that 80 percent of resources will go toward 20 percent of a project's needs. This appears in many guises; for example, when 80 percent of your time goes into planning 20 percent will go into your activities or when the top 20 percent of the wealthiest people use 80 percent of Earth's resources.

It is good to remember that the budget is there for a reason and that it is very often high on your client's list of priorities. You may have the opportunity to reason with your clients about the wisdom of their budget decisions, but more often than not you go with what has been decided and work within these established budgetary constraints.

CONSTRAINTS OF RESPONSIBILITY: UNINTENDED CONSEQUENCES AND SUSTAINABILITY

Planning: Expecting the Unexpected

In a process as multifaceted as even the most basic design will be, things are bound to go wrong. Inevitably someone will invoke Murphy's Law: "Anything that can go wrong will." To most, Murphy's Law is just a wry comment, and its fatalistic overtones are not given much thought beyond the moment of their use. We allow this to affirm our belief that the universe's odds are stacked against us, and we move on.

The law was named after Captain Edward A. Murphy, an engineer working at Edwards Air Force Base in 1949. One day, after finding that an experiment didn't work due to a mind-bogglingly wrong setup of equipment, he declared, "If there are two or more ways of doing something, and one of them can lead to catastrophe, then someone will do it."[2] Shortly afterward, Dr. John Paul Stapp, an air force doctor who took part in the experiment, said at a press conference that their good safety record on the project was due to a firm belief in Murphy's Law and in the necessity to try to circumvent it. In other words, Murphy's Law is not a fatalistic, defeatist principle, but rather a call for alertness and adaptation.[3] By vigilantly exploring the possibilities arising from our design's interaction with the world and adapting to the implied problems, we can reduce the "things that go wrong," if not eliminate them entirely.

Consider again Princess Diana's memorial fountain. It seems that everything that could go wrong did. People slipped on wet granite, leaves clogged the drains, and the water became contaminated. But the inevitability of the mishaps seems very clear. Foresight could not really have been that difficult. An alert walk through the park would have alerted the designers to the fact that water in a green area collects leaves and debris. Creating a model made from the materials would have shown the designers that granite gets slippery when wet. To be fair, perhaps they did all this and thought, as the chairman of the memorial committee did, that "people would [show] a little bit more respect given that it is a memorial."[4] This is what the sociologist Robert K. Merton called the "imperious immediacy of interest," referring to instances in which an individual wants the intended consequence of an action so much so that he or she is compelled to ignore other unintended effects.[5] It is precisely this kind of thinking that designers must avoid.

Dr. Stapp coming out of the experiment in which Murphy's Law was born.

Sometimes the more stressed you are, the likelier you are to make mistakes. However, the universe is out to get you.[6] The natural world is one large system of order that fights entropy and loses continuously. The natural order of things is toward dissolution, and nature, through being overwhelming and relentless, always finds the chink in the armor. Besting that requires being alert and planning continually for entropy and chaos in any and every system. Murphy's Law is *not* a defeatist principle, but rather a call for vigilance.

A series of events required for making something happen (such as the creation of designs) can be viewed as a system, and systems have interdependent probabilities. Phase A must precede phase B, which must precede C and D, and so on. Let's say you have 16 steps to take to complete a project. Let's also say that you have a 98 percent chance of succeeding in the first attempt at each step. Are these good odds? No. Your total chance of overall success is 0.98 to the 16th power or 71 percent. Your odds are slightly less than three out of four for success.

A 98 percent likelihood of success diminishes to 71 percent in 16 steps. Do the math! The odds are always stacked against you. Stop being surprised about it. Work with it. Murphy's law is not a defeatist principle.

More often than not complex systems are driven by probabilities, and the way to win is to create a system where the odds are heavily stacked in favor of success. You do this by being determined not to insert any actions or processes into your designs that may have an unacceptable outcome. If you must include undesirable possibilities, you have to alleviate the "bad" outcome by designing acceptable safeguards. Better to design out the unintended consequences altogether.

Unintended consequences is a term originally coined in sociology but that is now widely used in medicine, economics, civic planning, and politics. It can also be applied very effectively to the theory and planning of design. When testing a new design, it is important to keep in mind that not everything can be tested and planned for. No matter what the situation or design, the more complicated the world's interaction with it is, the likelier that there will be unanticipated, and sometimes unintended, consequences, which may not come to light until long after the design is finished. Oddly enough, people will put things to uses that the inventors never intended. The Internet, for example, has its origins in the 1960s system designed to keep the lines of command open during a nuclear attack. No one intended it to be used as it is today.

Sometimes, new designs are developed in response to the problems inadvertently caused by other, older designs. We've seen the invention of answering machines, resulting from the need to deal with untimely or unwanted telephone calls. Then there was voice mail to deal with large numbers of calls and mobile phones to deal with being away from the home or office.

The first and most complete analysis of the concept of unintended consequences was done in 1936 by the sociologist Robert K. Merton. In his article "The Unanticipated Consequences of Purposive Social Action," Merton identified five sources of unanticipated consequences. The first two—and the most pervasive—were inadequate knowledge and error. The third was "imperious immediate interest." The last two belong more clearly to the sociological sphere but are nonetheless interesting to us. The fourth concerns when a person's fundamental values do not allow for the consideration of further consequences, and the fifth is when a prediction of the consequences of a system becomes part of the system, and as such, influences the outcome.

Merton's five sources of unintended consequences are a remarkably helpful set of guidelines for design because designing is in the end a social exercise. Merton provides us with a guide to expose where problems may inadvertently arise. Seeing that we cannot anticipate everything, we can at least try to identify the areas from which the trouble may arise, like old maps where unexplored areas were left blank and labeled "Here are monsters." If we know the areas from whence the monsters could arise, we can either avoid them or go in armed to the teeth. As we begin to plan for the production of our designs, we must be very aware of what we don't know, where we are in danger of error, and what could be our "blind spots." This awareness becomes our ammunition for the monster hunt.

We must know where the dangers of our journey lie, even if we don't know exactly what they are.

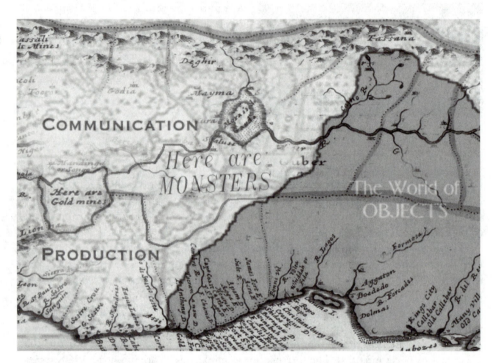

Identify the gaps in your knowledge. Go through your designs, and find the areas where you need information or expertise beyond your own. Be very honest with yourself about your knowledge or lack thereof. Make shopping lists of missing information, and find what you need. It is very likely at this stage that you already have people around you who can help. Recognize other people's experience and expertise and get them involved. If you do not have experts at hand, make time for research or find experts. Get a brainstorming session going and *create* an expert. As long as you are not dealing with proprietary or classified information, people are always willing to help.

Next you need to look for possible sources of error or mistakes. One of the most common mistakes to make is to work under the assumption that because something worked in the past it will work again. This may be safe to assume most of the time, but you may find that you are doing things out of habit and neglect to notice that the circumstances are not *exactly* the same.[7] Another error is to assume that you have all the information (or that anyone else does, for that matter). The more links there are in your chain of information, the greater the danger that your information has been misinterpreted along the way. The information you disseminate about your designs needs to be extremely well-organized and accessible to its intended recipients—do not assume people will understand. Murphy's Law is in full effect here: What they can misunderstand, misconstrue, misinterpret, mangle, fold, and mutilate, they will. Never rely on second-hand information, and never assume anything. Remember, you are not paranoid if the universe *really is* out to get you.

Some serious introspection is in order. How large are your blinders? Are you so focused on the intended effect that you don't see the side effects? There is not necessarily anything wrong with desiring an outcome and being focused on it. Such focus may in fact be highly motivating to you and others. However, question the outcome of your designs. If you feel there is any doubt about the veracity of the picture as you see it, plan for a reality check. Look at similar designs and how they behave, and examine the environment your design will live in. Create a prototype and test it in as real an environment as you can. Make sure your testing is also properly designed so it does not just give you the results you desire.

Merton's fourth factor's relation to design problems is less immediate, but it is found everywhere and therefore worth a look. It involves the fundamental values you live by and with which you approach the world. You have a set of beliefs and priorities according to which things are done, and these are not questioned on a day-to-day basis. The inherent danger is "the fact that when a system of basic values enjoins certain specific actions, adherents are not concerned with the objective consequences of these actions but only with the subjective satisfaction of duty well performed."[8] In other words, the practice becomes more important than the outcome. It becomes important to build something a certain way or communicate along certain channels, never questioning whether there might be a better way to do it. In my experience I have encountered this most often when trying to get someone to go against the grain of their training. I have asked scene-painters to paint sloppily, seamstresses to tack something clumsily together, and graphic designers to make their techniques and fixes clearly visible. They understood what I wanted, and usually why, but they still had to concentrate much harder on doing the job poorly. "Badly," however, was the desired and, therefore, "better" effect.

Question your methods. Do you know how or why they work? Do they in fact *really* work? Are you stubbornly holding on to techniques and approaches that are outdated and obsolete just because it's the way it's always been done? How do your personality and views play into your choices and decisions?

The concept of unintended consequences implies that "Public predictions of future social developments are frequently not sustained precisely because the prediction has become a new element in the concrete situation, thus tending to change the initial course."[9] This is the factor most tied to human behavior and points to the use of design as a force of social change.

The designer is a member and often a leader of a team; a designer has responsibilities to the team as well as to society at large. The design goes out into the world and has an effect. Social interaction is a complex model of events and movements, and designers must be aware of the ripple effects they set in motion. Merton uses the example of how socialist proselytizing in the 19th century actually delayed or even hindered the revolution they prophesied and wished for. They called such attention to the plight of the working man and got labor so organized that the lot of workers actually improved. In this way they lessened or even negated the need for revolution.[10]

In a similar vein, designers can use their abilities and positions to avert disaster and perhaps bring about a revolution of their own. Designers can educate their colleagues and clients about the dangers our environment faces and advocate for the practice of sustainable design.

SUSTAINABILITY

The largest issue facing designers today is sustainable or "green" design. This type of design is more than a choice or constraint for a project. Sustainability is a philosophy that encourages people to respect the planet and its resources.

In the scheme of unintended consequences, the largest of all is the treatment that human development has on the environment since the industrialization of Europe began in the 18th century. The human race has increasingly taken resources from the planet at a rate way beyond its capacity to replace and renew. To design for sustainability means to reject the notion that we can take what we think we need from Earth and its ecosystems without regard for future inhabitants. Its goal is "to meet the needs of the present without compromising the ability of future generations to meet their own needs."[11]

Earth is a closed system that has a finite amount of resources. The use and distribution of these resources at the beginning of the 21st century has been highly wasteful and skewed and has inflicted irreversible damage on the environment.

Sustainability is a philosophy that encourages respect for our planet and its resources.

Twenty percent of the world's people from countries with the highest incomes account for 86 percent of global consumption.[12] For example, if ten people represent the world's population, then two of them represent the wealthiest. If you give everyone three cookies—one to eat, one to share, and one to save for later—then have them divide the 30 cookies so the wealthiest have 86 percent of the cookies, the two high-income people will each get 13 cookies. Each of the remaining eight people gets half of one. Adding insult to this injury, note that the inhabitants of North America and the European Union generate, on average, 3 to 11 times the amount of solid domestic waste as the inhabitants of developing countries.[13] The largest part of this waste is not being put to any use, and as a matter of fact, 93 percent of the manufacturing resources in the United States are turned to waste before the product even reaches the consumer.[14]

Global consumption expenditure has more than doubled since 1980 and is driving development the world over. While this has many positive effects, the inequalities remain and are in fact increasing as the wealth generated from this increase does not get distributed evenly. Wastefulness is also on the rise. The increase in consumption generally leads to economic growth, which is directly linked to an increased use of resources. Even though the developed nations have in many cases managed to uncouple economic growth from an increase in resource consumption, this kind of efficiency is still relatively unknown in the developing world, and it is there that the growth is now greatest.[15]

The challenge is to take a step beyond just limiting resource use. The more affluent countries need to adopt lifestyles that are within the planet's ecological means. In this way, they limit the damage caused by their economic growth and become a model for developing nations on how to sustain growth without causing further harm to the ecosystem. The idea that perpetual growth is the defining characteristic of a healthy society is no longer tenable.[16] It is also necessary to move away from the mindset of "fixing" and toward a philosophy of betterment.

At the Earth Summit in Rio de Janeiro in 1992, more than 178 governments (including the United States) adopted Agenda 21—a program of action for sustainable development worldwide. Its first principle reads as follows:

> *Human beings are at the center of concerns for sustainable development. They are entitled to a healthy and productive life in harmony with nature.*[17]

Tackling these concerns, however, cannot be the responsibility of governments alone. As the tenth principle states, "Environmental issues are best handled with the participation of all concerned citizens." [18] Designers, whatever their discipline, are in a key position to participate in this effort and contribute toward its goals. As we have seen, a designer is the hub of communication for a project. The designer communicates with everyone involved, from colleagues to end users, and can inform, educate, and motivate them at every stage. Manufacturers and retailers have begun to and will continue to go along with sustainable practices when it makes economic sense. The ability of a product to claim some measure of environmental sensitivity has begun to be seen as a selling point, especially in Europe, but increasingly so in the United States. Consider how much the products we design are in fact alike. Cell phones all look like one another, and jeans all look like one another, even if the brands are different. To be able to add the incentive of environmental friendliness is "just good PR" in the words of one executive.[19] There is a subset of customers who is willing to pay more for "green" products, and that group is growing.

"Follow the money" is always a good maxim and, in this case, completely valid. In the past 300 years (if not longer), the market has led to greater and swifter progress than has altruism. Designers who are interested in promoting sustainability will be far more successful by working inside the consumer culture than by protesting against it. By designing products that are less taxing on the environment, we can begin to raise consumer awareness and change deeply embedded patterns of consumption.

"Human beings are at the center of concerns for sustainable development. They are entitled to a healthy and productive life in harmony with nature."

By educating ourselves and others about the benefits of sustainable practices and making choices based on these, we can become a force for global change. This is not a difficult task; all it requires is keeping some points in mind when making choices for your designs.

Using Resources Efficiently

We need to use less to make more. This involves taking a look at the entire life cycle of a product: being aware of the product's development from the gathering, harvesting, or mining of resources to the manufacturing, packing, shipping, and distribution. We also need to look at retailing, usage, and eventual disposal or recycling. Where is the waste? How can the waste be minimized or put to use? Clearly, designers do not have ultimate control over how their designs are used; however, by designing the product in such a way that it has minimal environmental impact at each stage, you will assert whatever influence you can. We are the only lifeform on the planet that creates waste that is not subsequently used in some other natural process. A sustainable society would eliminate the concept of waste. Waste is not simply an unwanted and sometimes harmful byproduct of life; it is a raw material that is out of place. Waste and pollution demonstrate a gross inefficiency in an economic system, since they represent resources that are no longer available for use, and/or create harm in humans and other species.20 We must look to nature to inspire us to design products that cycle their materials through the economy. The ultimate goal is that all waste will become fodder for another product, therefore, minimizing the impact on the planet. The impact we have on the planet is quantified in the ecological footprint. It is a measure of how much bioproductive land and water we utilize to produce all the resources we consume and to handle all the waste we make, much of which is made up of forests for absorption of carbon dioxide.

The average world citizen has an ecological footprint of 5.6 acres, the average German's is 12 acres, and the average U.S. citizen's is 24 acres. The drain on Earth's resources will only increase as the developing regions increase their consumption (as they have every right to do) and thereby expand their footprints.

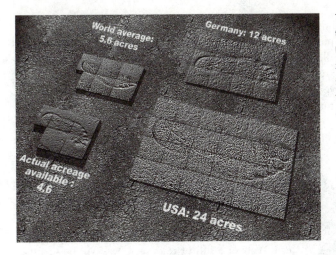

There are 4.6 acres of bioproductive land per person on the planet. However, the average world citizen has an ecological footprint of 5.6 acres; the average German's is 12 acres; and the average USA's citizen is 24 acres.

As there are only 4.6 acres of bioproductive land per person on the planet, we are currently running a deficit of 20 percent, with the capacity decreasing every year, through the increase of the world's population.[21] This deficit may be what accounts for the fact that in the years between 1970 and 2000 populations of terrestrial and marine species dropped by 30 percent, while freshwater populations plummeted by a stunning 50 percent. Equally alarming is our energy footprint, dominated by our use of fossil fuels such as coal, gas, and oil. This is the fastest growing component of the ecological footprint, increasing by 180 percent in the last 30 years of the 20th century. Fossil fuel dependence is unsustainable for more than a few decades. It took 10,000 days for nature to create the fossil fuels that humans of the early 21st century consume in one day.[22] Designers would do well to focus on the energy requirements of their designs by making sure they are designed, manufactured, transported, marketed, and finally operated within the following three constraints:

1. A product's life cycle involves the greatest possible *conservation* of existing energies.
2. A product is designed so that its life cycle requires a greater *efficient* use of energy.
3. A product's manufacturing and use reflect an increased drive to switch over to cleaner, more *renewable sources* of energy.

Principle 3 of the UN's Agenda 21 states, "The right to development must be fulfilled so as to equitably meet developmental and environmental needs of present and future generations."[23] Unless we begin to seriously redesign our products and methods, there will be less available for future generations. There is room for a lot of top-of-the-hierarchy creative thinking. A looming target is the 93 percent wastage that happens before products get to U.S. consumers. Study that for your product. Where does it happen? How can you design to eliminate it? How much can be solved by reducing transportation needs? Can you influence this with fewer components, less materials, and more localized production? Aim to design not only a product but also a life cycle that uses materials sensibly and highlights recycling and thrift.

Eliminating Toxic, Persistent, and Biocumulative Substances

Our environment is clogged with pollutants. Our industries are throwing toxic substances into the biosphere faster than the natural systems can neutralize them. Compounds are accumulating in the food chain (biocumulation) of which we are the top link. The list of chemicals to avoid in manufacturing is getting longer each year. Our life expectancies are increasing and so is the buildup of these substances in the environment and food chain. Longer life means the biocumulation in our bodies reaches damaging levels more often and more effects come to light. Allergies, cancers, retardation of fetal growth, and delays in children's mental development are just a few examples of these effects.

First of all, make sure your designs' life cycles are free of the most toxic compounds. Your designs should be manufactured, marketed, used, and eventually recycled with the greatest possible avoidance of environmental contamination. This should include emissions produced in manufacturing and transportation, as well as secondary implications, such as the usage of batteries.

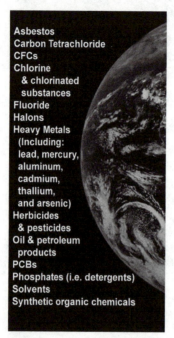

The Earth is a closed system. The substances released into the ecosphere during manufacturing have nowhere else to go.

Asbestos
Carbon Tetrachloride
CFCs
Chlorine
    & chlorinated
    substances
Fluoride
Halons
Heavy Metals
    (Including:
    lead, mercury,
    aluminum,
    cadmium,
    thallium,
    and arsenic)
Herbicides
    & pesticides
Oil & petroleum
    products
PCBs
Phosphates (i.e. detergents)
Solvents
Synthetic organic chemicals

Educate yourself on these substances and their uses in production. There are a number of governmental agencies as well as private foundations such as the National Center for Environmental Health[24] and the Children's Health Environmental Coalition[25] that have Web sites full of resources. You will be surprised how widespread toxic substances are in the manufacturing of literally *everything* around you.

Increasing Durability, Reuse, and Reparability

Increasingly, as the 20th century drew to a close, consumers in the United States were habituated to the disposability of goods. Once something stops working or even if we just stop using something, we don't get it repaired or give it to someone else. We throw it out. Most electronic goods are now so cheap to produce that they would cost more to repair than to replace—if you could even find someone who could repair them. All this contributes to an ever-growing mound of materials that have become waste long before their lifetime is over. The economics of obsolescence have a stronghold on consumer economy, and new paradigms will not see the light without resistance. But again, economic politics will win if consumers as well as manufacturers can see the larger benefit of durable, repairable goods.

Recycling of materials and components is gaining popularity. There are several large-scale initiatives taking place and more in the works. A Dell "recycling tour" in 2004 took place in 17 U.S. cities, collecting nearly 1,000 tons of unwanted computer equipment. In its first two years, Operation Fonebak, a nationwide mobile phone recycling scheme in the United Kingdom, processed more than 3.5 million mobile phones for reuse and recycling. Wherever possible, phones are fully refurbished and sent to developing countries. Irreparable or older phones are recycled for their materials and parts. In the U.K. there are an estimated 45 million cell phones in use, with users replacing them every 18 months. The lifetime of the product, however, is about eight years, so essentially the refurbished product has a longer lifetime in its new home than the original user gave it.

European automakers are redesigning their cars to be very efficient in terms of reuse, in anticipation of new European Union legislation that dictates that every vehicle scrapped after 2006 must be taken back at no charge from the last owner. Volvo, for example, is aiming to be able to recycle 95 percent of the materials in its cars by 2015.

The common incentive for manufacturers is that there are recoverable valuable metals, such as gold, silver, copper, and platinum, that are put back into use. Materials that cannot be reused find their ways into other products. Mixed plastics (those that contain metals and plastics) from cell phones are sent to a specialist recycler in Sweden who incinerates the plastic and uses the energy to heat the local village. Other plastics are sent for granulation and end up as traffic cones, among other things.[26]

In designing products for recycling, reusing, and reparability, you must think in terms of components and commonality of materials. What can be reused where and how? How much energy is involved? When dealing with plastics, consider how they would be recycled or whether they can be recycled at all.

What appears to be a technological question—how much of anything do we really need—is actually a social one.[27] Do we really need everything to be new, colorful, and shiny? Can we be satisfied with something else? When is "enough" enough? Is there something missing in a user's interaction with an object? (How, for instance, would you redesign a cell phone so that its user keeps it for its entire lifetime?)

It is a big misconception that green design has to be somehow "lesser" in quality. This is not the case at all. If everything becomes raw material for something else, then the stigma of "recycled equals old" will disappear through sheer redundancy.

Devising New Models of Consumer-Producer Relationships

Related to the issue of reparability is the possibility that if products become components and materials for replacing and reusing, then ownership of the product may become a fluid concept.

In the United States, Interface, the leading manufacturer of commercial carpeting, has recently inaugurated an innovative Evergreen Carpet Lease. Customers lease the carpet and accompanying maintenance services. Interface retains ownership of the carpet and takes it back after use for additional uses or recycling, thus retaining the value of the carpet as an asset and controlling all liabilities of the carpet in landfills. They sell only the *services* of the carpet: color, design, texture, warmth, acoustics, comfort under foot, and cleanliness but *not* the carpet itself.

Here you are designing a situation as well as a product. Ask whether the consumers really need to *own* the product or whether leasing is an alternative. Can a product's function be equally or better met by a service instead? If so, how does this change the nature of the product? Think about what would happen to it at the end of the lease term. It would obviously need to survive intact and be reparable or reuseable. What does that mean for its components? How will you design it to meet the needs of care and maintenance *during* the lease term? One thing to consider is where the maintenance will be most needed and design that part, area, or component so that it is easily swapped out.

Changing the Relationship Between Developed and Developing Countries

The exploitation of poorer nations' resources and populations for the enrichment and comfort of wealthy and more powerful nations is a paradigm that must change if we are to live in a truly global community. Our products cannot continue to require cheap labor and resources to the degree that they have so far. All ideas of justice and equality aside, it is simply inevitable that developing nations will reach a level of affluence where they will no longer be content to be the producers of other people's wealth. Where will we then go for our inexpensive labor? We have also learned in the past 30 years that environmental damage is not a local issue. Toxins tend to spread throughout the globe's ecosystem and the depletion of resources influences generations to come. The sad possibility is that nations that are now struggling to achieve the level of prosperity enjoyed by those of us who live where the first wave of industrialization took place, may never achieve it, as the resources will simply not be there. The same may apply to our immediate descendants.

All gone.

The only way out for us is to do more with less. There is no excuse for up-and-coming designers not to participate in an attempt to make the world a better place for everyone, now and in the future.

The Brundtland Report spells this out directly and dramatically as follows:

> *Many present efforts to guard and maintain human progress to meet human needs, and to realize human ambitions are simply unsustainable—in both rich and poor nations. They draw too heavily, too quickly, on already overdrawn environmental resource accounts to be affordable far into the future without bankrupting those accounts. They may show a profit on the balance sheets of our generation, but our children will inherit the losses. We borrow environmental capital from future generations with no intention of repaying. They may damn us for our spendthrift ways, but they can never collect on our debt to them. We act as we do because we can get away with it: Future generations do not vote; they have no political or financial power; they cannot challenge our decisions.*
>
> *But the results of the present profligacy are rapidly closing the options for future generations. Most of today's decision-makers will be dead before the planet feels the heavier effects of acid precipitation, global warming, ozone depletion, or widespread desertification and species lost. Most of the young voters of today will still be alive. In the Commission's hearings it was the young, those who have the most to lose, who were the harshest critics of the planet's present management.*[28]

Which side of this discussion do you choose to be on?

BROWER HATCHER, ARTIST

Brower Hatcher's work ranges from gallery-scale artwork to large architectural designs. In a career of more than 30 years, he has consistently explored the notion of a "visual field," through the use of space-defining wire frame structures. Brower lives and works in Rhode Island, but his work can be found all over the United States. His recent work incorporates biomimetic principles: allowing sculptural forms to develop using principles of biological growth.

Conceptualizing is a distillation process, which I think I do indirectly. In the first step I sort of fill myself up—I become a sponge. I like to wander in books; it's a mental wandering where I fill myself up with reading and looking around. It doesn't really matter where I am. It's great if you can partake of the world, you know, go to great cities, but I don't think that's requisite. You just keep filling yourself up, and then when you have this problem in the back of your head and listen for solutions, the ideas just sort of come to you. But I think it's sometimes more like a hunt. You're looking for something; you come around the corner, and suddenly you see your quarry. Then you get your bow and arrow: "This is the big one."

I work at it all the time. I'm always ready. I like going back to nature. My wife is a ferocious gardener, and I like to watch all that unfold; I like watching things grow. I might be digging in the garden, and there's a worm, and I think "Wow, look at that great looking worm! Look how that worm's put together!" In my early days, I was hanging around with all these heavy Modernists; they were all so deadly serious, which was fine—I learned an awful lot. But my first works were very rooted in nature. Somehow that made me feel really good. I guess I like things that have one foot in a pretty sophisticated cultural aspect, but have the other foot in nature. I find that very intriguing.

If you've got a job scenario where you have to deliver, then you have to reach closure, some kind of summing up. There are always other things going on, so I can't keep the wandering up for long. In some ways that makes me more frantic; I don't want to lose half an hour. . . I need to be sure I'm using all the time I can. I'm reading; I'm thinking; I'm working. I'm working in an opening up expanding way, before I have to close down. I know the time will come when I have to make decisions. I have to define things, draw the forms, model them, and make a spatial plot. Whatever it is I'm thinking about has to get done. . . . It has to come out of this dream state.

It's at work even on my downtime, when I can't absorb any more. I completely relax, and

often in these times I can visualize, sometimes very effectively. There's that time just before you sleep when you can kind of see things. When you just wake up, something will click; things will come together. I think it's important after you've been actively filling yourself up that you take time to relax and let things process.

But also then it depends on what you're doing. Somehow, in the different stages, the manifestation is different, the medium changes. First you are absorbing; you're a sponge soaking up what you can. This becomes a dreamy manifestation, which then goes to a second level of manifestation where you're making models, and the piece keeps changing. There's a clarification, and there's also a creativity pumping in. There's something you thought up; maybe you had this vision. You thought it was the thing, but then it's really not the thing. Say you decide you want to put a rhinoceros over there. You now have to deal with the specifics of that decision. Then maybe this allows you to see that the rhinoceros wasn't such a good idea anyway.

Finally, you get around to the stage of making the thing physically and that's another kind of thought process, where I think you have to be very open to materials, let the stuff talk to you. You put it together; it creates certain situations and certain forms. Ideas come out of that. You're going along one way, but then you see that it would be better to go the other way.

Every time you do anything, it opens the door to something else. This is why I like to have work progressing on many different things, and a number of people at the studio. Often there's work that I more or less know how to do. But I really like the edge, when you're out there doing stuff you didn't know how to do before.

I used to do very solitary work, doing my own little thing. I found that kind of lonely and a little bit extreme. You want to do bigger and bigger things, but it's not just that. It's kind of being in the world; the art is interactive, taking place in the world. It's a very complicated process. You're involved with a lot of people. I guess I enjoy the society of the crowd and working with everybody's talent. I guess I'm also a major collaborator. I like having a team. I recognize that all these people have all these talents and abilities, and if you can bring them in on the larger picture, the potential is enormous—it goes way beyond me. I'm beginning to feel that I'm more just the muse or something. Well, I guess I'm the leader, the conductor—but you're not going to get much music if you don't have an orchestra.

I think it's all very fun, but there is also a fair amount of hardship. It's different from having a job where you are just providing a service and being compensated for it. You're often out there flapping in the breeze. By sheer willpower and some maniacal dream, you make it possible. Basically I imagine these things, and somehow I get myself into the position where people seem to become interested and find that I can provide them with something no one else can. And then I have this entire team pulling along with me, which makes it all possible. I suppose there's a symbiosis.

All the time you have to be aware that there's an audience out there. They are your clients, and they are also the ones with the expectations. They hired you because they believe that you can deliver on their expectations. They think you are going to create something absolutely amazing. I love the challenge that somebody is expecting me to come up with something amazing. In many ways that gives me a lot of license to do what I want to do or be the way I want to be. It's extremely liberating when people have those kinds of expectations. You do want to rise to the occasion, and it's very exciting to actually do that and then have somebody stand back and go "Wow, that's amazing." But by that time I've usually had enough of the piece in question. The creativity is over and what remains is to take it somewhere and install it. I mean, I've had my fun. . . . The installing of the work and then standing around while people say nice things, that's all very nice, but I don't find that particularly important. It's a courtesy, like going to an opening. It's part of the give and take of operating in this arena. I do like to stand back, to be a fly on the wall, and to listen to what people say. I find that very interesting because ultimately the work is not complete until it enters the world. I may be personally done with it, but the work gets to a point where it has a life of its own. That life is bigger than I am, and beyond me, and in order for the creation to really be the thing we want it to be, I have to go away. I have to let go; it's not me anymore; it's out there in the world doing its work, which it does by itself, but I've infused it with all these little triggers. Then when it's done, I like to go home and putter around, dig in my garden, and become a sponge again.

It's become so now that there are so many gigs, and they sort of run right into one another. And they feed on one another. For everything you do, there are things you couldn't do. It's a garden of forking paths and you decide to go down this path and that path. But as you're going down your chosen path, you look to the side, and there's another path, and you look down that and think, "Oh, that's kind of neat," but you don't have time to explore it, so there's always the possibility to come back to one of those.

Unwinding is actually getting centered again, coming back to a core in your life, back to something that's really simple and basic. Actually, I like building stone walls. It's simple, it's hard work, and it's variable enough. Little by little I'm building a wall around the garden.

I'm lucky in that I have a lovely home, a lovely wife, lovely kids. . . . I live by the seashore. Sometimes it's just amazing to open the door and look outside.

1: DESIGN THESIS

With your project in mind, answer the following questions with *as much visual material as possible.* If you can't find a single image to back up your thinking, either create the same effect with more than one image or sketch what is missing. Create a collage of words *and* images that addresses the following:

1.1: What will you design?
Describe the physical product as succinctly as you can.
  Examples:
- *I intend to design a chair for home-office use.*
- *I intend to design a jacket for bicycle messengers.*

1.2: What is its nature?
Describe its function and the components of the design: materials, colors, mechanics, and so on.
  Examples:
- *The chair will have the comfort and adjustability of an office chair and the styling and feel of a home environment. It will be made of materials that are easy to clean and that come in an array of colors and are adjustable to a range of body types and sizes.*
- *The jacket will be of a durable, easily cleaned, waterproof, and lightweight material. It will have multiple pockets in various sizes. It will have add-on options for different seasons and climates (e.g., hood, lining, and face mask). Colors will promote high visibility. Reflective materials will be incorporated. All fasteners, zipper-pulls, and so on will be large-scale to facilitate operation while wearing gloves. Styling will be led by the aesthetic of the bike messenger culture.*

1.3: Who is it for?
Describe an end user and the environment to which he or she belongs.
  Examples:
- *The end user is a professional, working from home, who needs to spend several hours a day at a desk located in a multiuse home environment.*
- *The end user is a bicycle messenger in a large urban environment. This involves cycling in heavy traffic at fast speeds while carrying packages and envelopes in inclement weather conditions.*

1.4: Why is it needed?
Describe the problem that requires this design as a solution.
  Examples:
- *Desk chairs for office use are functional and often ergonomically designed but less than attractive and generally at odds with home furnishings. A home office that is in a family area requires furniture that belongs to that environment and that provides the comfort and functionality of office designs.*
- *The jacket must be more versatile than any standard jacket because of different demands placed on it by seasonal fluctuations in weather and different requirements of motion and effort when riding or on foot. There is a challenge in combining such a high level of functionality with a sense of style.*

1.5: What are the benefits of it?

Describe the benefits this design will bring. These should be the answers to the problems posed in the previous question.

Examples:

- *The designs will provide a choice for those with home offices, allowing them to furnish their work spaces with a chair that belongs to their homes' aesthetic. Conversely, offices can be furnished in a way that is counter to the traditional functional look.*
- *The jackets will benefit bicycle messengers, making their day-to-day existence more comfortable, functional, stylish, and safe. The pockets and fabrics will create a garment that is an essential tool for the messenger's workday.*

1.6: Why is this interesting?

Explain why this project is interesting to you and how it could be interesting to a client.

Examples:

- *Designing this chair is interesting to me as I am very interested in blending the aesthetics of "home" and "work." With new materials and CAD/CAM technologies, I believe that the functional can now be subservient to any desired style. I think clients would be interested in anything that increases the number of options they have for arranging and decorating their personal spaces.*
- *I am very interested in designing a garment that answers such intensely functional needs, while addressing the very individual stylistic approach of the bicycle messenger. The clients will be interested by the ease of use, the increase in their comfort, and the specificity of the garment to their situations.*

1.7: How will you proceed?

Explain how you will proceed to begin the design process. What will you do next?

Examples:

- *I will begin by researching the ergonomics involved and the issues related to the end users' comfort and desires for style. I will then examine my options for materials, taking care to acknowledge issues of sustainable design. I will visit several home offices and note their practical and aesthetic concerns.*
- *I will begin by researching the ergonomics involved and the issues related to the end users' comfort, safety, and style. I will then examine my options for materials, taking care to acknowledge issues of sustainable design. I will interview messengers and examine their workdays and conditions, as well as the sizes and types of objects the pockets could contain. I will research bike messenger styles and emblems. I will research safety issues and the related colors and fabrics.*

2: IDENTIFYING CONSTRAINTS

Ideas are often best defined by what they should not be. By examining constraints that arise through the needs of a project and the problems that need solving, we outline what form (figuratively and otherwise) the idea will take. We define as much as possible and create as much information as we can.

2.1: What are the apparent or potential problems that need to be solved?

This concept board was created to illustrate a design thesis discussing fractured surfaces and broken lines.

2.2: What do we need to know to begin? Is there research to be done? References to find?

2.3: What are the constraints that define the possible solutions?

2.4: As you begin designing, think of which of these may apply or which of these you would like to apply.

The willful application of constraints can also be helpful in that it creates support and challenges the designer to use solutions that may otherwise have never been considered.

2.5: Consider for your project as many constraints as you can, using some from the following list:
- Information
- Function
- Form
- Materials
- Budget
- Time
- Production
- Environmental impact

2.6: Rank them in order of relative importance.

2.7: Which are inherent, and which are imposed?

2.8: See the Constraint Concept Map and consider what other constraints, either inherent or imposed, may apply to your project.

3: TOWARD SUSTAINABILITY

3.1: How do products such as the ones you intend to design affect the environment? Consider the product's entire life cycle.
1. Harvesting/gathering/creation of materials
2. Production
3. Packaging
4. Transportation/Storage
5. Usage
6. Disposal/Reuse/Recycling

3.2: How could your designs minimize the environmental impact of the product? Which solutions can you implement by yourself, in your designing, and which require a larger cooperative effort?

Conceptualization

OBJECTIVE

Once you identify your design problem, you are ready to examine methods for conceptualizing your ideas to come up with a solution. You examine the nature of a design concept and how using intuition and metaphor helps you create a coherent presentation. This requires you to develop a thought structure that uses known elemental images to explain the unknown and unseen. Finally, the chapter establishes the need for you to present your concept to the various audiences involved in a clear and organized manner.

KEY CONCEPTS

- A design concept is an abstract vision that needs to become tangible.
- Brainstorming techniques allow you to examine a concept and fully explore what it contains. Brainstorming encourages you to visualize and intuit a concept's elements.
- The laws of *gestalt* perception can be applied to the examination of a design concept.
- Analogies, metaphors, similes, and intuitive thinking are helpful tools to visualize, describe, and explain nonexistent objects.
- Designers must be able to relate to designs, their end users, and the intended interaction, which allows them to be flexible when responding to problems and questions.
- Clients, fabricators, and fellow designers have different needs regarding concepts for new designs.

BRINGING THE IDEA INTO THE WORLD

The thesis from the previous stage is a good beginning, but it only implies a direction. It does not really show us the object, nor does it convey much of its interaction with the world. Conceptualizing an idea will show you how all its pieces fit together and let you visualize the final result.

During the conceptualization stage, the idea for the design takes shape in the designer's mind.

This stage answers the following questions:

- How can you describe and explain designs that do not actually exist and may never have existed?
- How can you explain this idea further, so that your clients, fellow designers, and production team can understand and relate to what you are thinking?
- How can you understand your idea to the point where you know as clearly as possible what it is and how it behaves?
- How do you know that your concept is as good as it can possibly be? Is there anything more you can do? You must explore ways of fleshing out your concept so it begins to have a life of its own, a life that you can observe and relate to, understand, and explain.

A concept takes flight and acquires a life of its own.

GESTALT PERCEPTION

Your idea is an abstraction, a mental image created by the elements described in your thesis. You have described this vision by referring to the elements of the design, to the end user, and to the needs and benefits driving the idea. The idea itself may be grounded in a practical reality or it may be driven by a fantasy. Either way, it exists in your mind.

There are four tasks that require you to conceptualize information and to project creatively onto your vision.

- You must fill in as many gaps as you can.
- You must ground your concept in a systemic, logical reality (which may actually be different from your everyday reality).
- You must be able to present your concept so others involved in the project understand it.
- You must be familiar with the inner workings of your ideas so you can change, rework, and rearrange their details without altering the core of the concept.

An essential key to productive conceptualizing lies in our innate abilities to project mental images into gaps left by partial information. By brainstorming with holistic methods of thinking and analysis, we can create a wholly formed concept from the parts we have assembled.

Gestalt is a German word meaning *shape, pattern,* or *form.* It has taken on the additional meaning of *whole* or *totality* regarding theories of perception and cognition. German psychologists Max Wertheimer, Kurt Koffka, and Wolfgang Kohler established a school of thought that argued humans have inborn abilities to organize perceptual information and experiences. This is based on the need for all humans to make sense of the world around them. The gestalt school generated a belief that the "whole is greater than the sum of its parts," which established the notion that each of us assembles sensory experiences by perceiving them in their entirety rather than as disjointed parts.

Creative work relies on our ability to perceive a totality when given only a limited amount of information.

The gestalt school formulated the Law of Pragnanz (literally meaning *pregnancy*, implying that an unfinished object is pregnant with information), which has four subsets of laws. The Law of Pragnanz states that of all possible perceptual experiences to which a particular stimulus can give rise, the one most closely fitting to the concept of a good gestalt (a good totality) will most likely be perceived. Because we have an innate need to make sense of everything we encounter, we will tend to see incomplete objects as complete and even as familiar.

The Law of Pragnanz implies that if a perceptual field is disorganized when an organism first experiences it, the organism imposes order on the field in a predictable way. This predictable way is in the direction of a good gestalt, a psychological task that does not necessarily involve a change in the physical environment but one that represents a change in how an organism sees its physical environment. A good gestalt has such properties as *regularity*, *simplicity*, and *stability*. There are five additional laws related to the Law of Pragnanz, which are as follows:

1. *Similarity.* We tend to group similar items together.

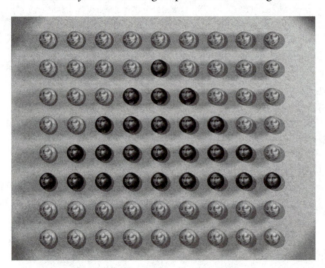

Similarity: Similar items tend to be grouped. Your mind perceives a "triangle" within the "rectangle," even though all the marbles are equidistant and the same size.

2. *Proximity.* We tend to group items according to the nearness of their respective parts.

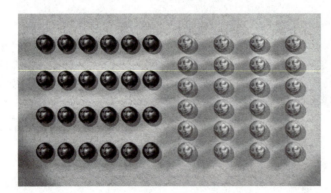

Proximity: Items are grouped according to the nearness of their respective parts. You perceive two squares and horizontal and vertical lines, though none of these are actually present.

3. *Closure:* We group completed items together.

Closure: If something is missing in an otherwise complete figure, we will tend to add it. A letter, for example, with parts missing, will still be seen as that letter. We mentally "fill in" the missing pieces.

4. *Continuity:* We see as complete shapes that are implied, by bridging the gaps.

Continuity: If you can see a shape as continuing through another shape, rather than stopping and starting, you will do so. You will very likely see the "x" as a continuation of two straight shapes, rather than a set of inverted angles.

5. *Membership character*. We define a single part of a whole according to the context in which it appears.

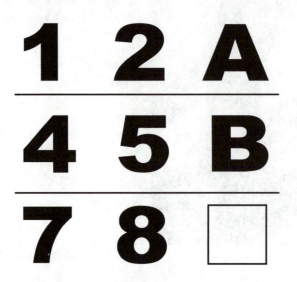

Membership character: A single part of the whole is defined by the context in which it appears. When we encounter stimuli or information, we try to make sense of it. What is the missing alphabetical character, and which number does it signify?

Pattern recognition is what allows us to fulfill the Law of Continuity. When we encounter a pattern that is incomplete, we can still recognize the object because we use our prior knowledge to close the pattern and create a whole.

Pattern recognition: If we encounter an incomplete pattern, we can fill in the blanks using previous knowledge. Your knowledge of letters allows you to understand the word in the image, despite the missing structures.

An "open" gestalt means that you have enough elements to suggest a whole, but not enough to create the entire design. There are wholes in which all the significant elements are in their appropriate places or positions and in perfect accordance with the system principle; however, there are also wholes in which only a limited number of elements are in the correct positions, sufficient to suggest the system principle, while other elements are out of position. These two examples represent "good" and "bad" gestalt, respectively. The various degrees of Pragnanz, which a gestalt may have, express how well the various parts correspond to the intended whole.

There are also cases where a sufficient number of positions are occupied in a whole to indicate the system principle, while the other positions are not filled. These are "open" gestalten as opposed to "closed" ones, in which all significant positions are occupied.

Open and closed gestalt: An open form, like an open thought, tends to change toward a good totality. When it does this, it achieves "closure." In this way a nearly circular set of forms (thoughts) may achieve closure by being interpreted as a circle.

Humans have innate abilities to create good gestalten, as good as the conditions, including the amount of information they have, allow them to be. All creative work, whether it is artistic or scientific, relies on and benefits greatly from this ability. Artists and scientists can assemble mental models and by analogy and intuitive thinking perceive the whole (the gestalt). This is how we can begin to sense things that are unknown and how we can create new concepts, theories, and knowledge by describing them. By trusting this ability, we can focus inward to fill in the gaps of our concepts and then outward to give direction to our presentations so our ideas are coherent.

BRAINSTORMING

Although many think of brainstorming as a group activity, it can also be a very effective tool for people who work alone. It is a process of spontaneously thinking and sharing as many ideas as possible about a topic without being judgmental. When we brainstorm, we take all the ideas and thoughts we have and look at them, play with them, and freely create connections among them, without having to worry about making mistakes.

Brainstorming: In a large group it is often beneficial to divide into smaller groups to brainstorm and then compare notes.

PREPARATION FOR BRAINSTORMING

You will begin to get ideas right at the outset of a project. Capturing these ideas is important. First impressions count; these are the seeds from which the project will grow. Make a habit of carrying around a notebook, tape recorder, or PDA, so you can scribble down your thoughts.

Record everything; even irrelevant or bad ideas can serve a purpose later. They may lead to questions that produce better ideas. Any organization at this stage is better than none. Even a shoebox that you throw all of your notes into at the end of the day is better than having nothing and actually quite effective if you go through it every now and then to gather the good stuff.

The most ideal thing, however, is to keep a design journal and sketchbook.[1] This should be a comfortably sized sketchbook for your day-to-day thoughts and discoveries and a folder or loose-leaf binder for a more methodical arrangement of individual projects.

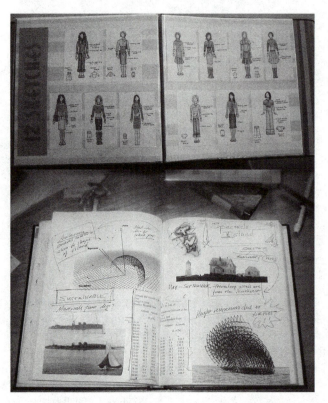

A sketchbook and its tidier cousin, the design journal. The sketchbook is a working tool, not a work of art. Better that your sketchbook be chaotic and messy than your brain. The journal, however, is presentation material.

In the sketchbook you should doodle; sketch; write down thoughts and observations; and collect images you find, copy, or photograph. It should be the net that catches everything that flies through your mind. This will only work if you have it with you all the time. Remember that it is a working tool, not a piece of artwork. While I was in college, I had the hardest time putting anything in my sketchbooks because I felt that everything had to be perfect and artistic. Once I got over this notion and began to use the books as visual notepads as well as diaries and to-do lists, they became essential and very helpful—if chaotic and messy—tools.

The design journal is the sketchbook's more mature, tidier sibling. In it, you collect and organize the material relevant to your project. As you may possibly want to be categorizing it as you go, it makes sense for the design journal to be a loose-leaf binder so that you can insert things and move them around. The journal entries may actually come from scraps of paper kept in the shoebox. You may be organizing by materials, concepts, a time-line, or whatever system seems relevant. But don't wait for the perfect system to show up by itself. Begin putting the journal together, and worry about rearranging it periodically. It is there to help you organize your thoughts, not just for show. The more elements you assemble, the better the gestalt.

RULES OF BRAINSTORMING

Brainstorming by yourself is sometimes easier because you don't have to wait for others and you're not restricted by the rules of a meeting. What makes it difficult is that you don't have others to offer input when you are stuck or with whom to share ideas.

You *can* brainstorm by yourself.

The rules for brainstorming either by yourself or in a group are very much the same.

- *Have an agenda.* At the beginning of the session, review the questions you have. What? Why? How? Be as clear as possible in describing the objective of the session.
- *Define success.* A brainstorming session may be successful even if you don't find the perfect solution. It may be enough to know in which direction the solutions lie or to have produced a set of options. This is also a good way to keep negativity in check. It is enormously liberating not to have to be perfect.
- *In a group, appoint a facilitator.* If you are brainstorming in a group, have one person be in charge of calling on speakers and recording and organizing the information that is flowing. Ideally, this should be someone with a lot of knowledge about the project. It's essential for the facilitator to prepare a list of questions, exercises, and reactions to pos-sible scenarios. If possible, the facilitator also should be familiar with the participants. When trying to solve a very specific or complex problem, the facilitator should provide the necessary information to participants in advance. However, if the group is trying to achieve a new approach or vision, it may be best to have the participants come in unin-formed, so they don't come in with preconceived ideas. The facilitator must be a neu-tral party, able to relate to a variety of personality types, and able to control a situation in which one individual is overly influential.
- *Write all ideas down.* All ideas are valuable. The whole point is to gather as many ideas as possible. You can edit once everything is done.
- *Don't criticize ideas.* Include your ideas and other people's ideas. Be respectful and

allow everyone to finish their suggestions or statements. This is not a forum for discussion or debate.

- *Deal with doomsayers immediately.* If the dreaded "it will never work" chorus begins to make itself heard, the facilitator must turn it around. "What will it take to make it work?" is a good question to ask to get back on track.
- *Focus on having many ideas.* The more ideas the better. Make sure everyone gets a say, and better still, make everyone speak twice.
- *Welcome hitchhiking or piggybacking.* After each suggestion, allow time to see if one idea sparks another similar idea or enhances an idea given by another. If ideas are flying around, make a quick note and come back to each one.
- *Encourage freewheeling.* The sky is the limit; outrageous and humorous ideas are accepted. This is a perfect time to be silly. If a spontaneous atmosphere is created, then the ideas will be even better.
- *Set a time limit.* When brainstorming sessions go well, they go really well. It's a good idea to set a limit (20 to 30 minutes is usually good for a group of 7 to 10 people) so that there is a definite cut-off point. The time limit helps to keep people engaged.
- *Edit and consolidate.* When all the ideas have been recorded, combine ideas as much as possible, taking care that nothing gets lost in the process.
- *Revisit.* Give everyone some time to digest the results, and follow up to review the information.

BRAINSTORMING AS INSPIRATION

Brainstorming is an inspirational exercise as well as a focusing activity; all the points discussed in Stage 1 are relevant. Let's revisit.

- *Don't wait for the Muses.* Brainstorming is a structured activity that should not be rushed through. You must know when you are good at it. The luxury of brainstorming is that sometimes you can set the schedule and the pace. Perhaps your flow of ideas is better at night. Whatever the framework, recognize and use it. You may have to be creative at a specific time (I have had some of my best brainstorming moments while sitting in an airplane for hours with nothing else to do). Anticipate moments (such as traveling or waiting rooms) where you'll have enforced quiet time and bring your sketchbook.
- *Be careful when letting the genies out.* When you are brainstorming, *all* the genies should fly out, but you must still be careful to spot the ideas that are relevant and let go of the ones that are not. Since you have already set up some constraints in the thesis, this is easier than when you're starting out with nothing. Use the constraints to keep yourself on track.
- *Play outside your own backyard.* If there is one principle of creative brainstorming that is above the others, this would probably be it. It is absolutely imperative that you allow strange thoughts and new connections to be made. Include the obvious, but move on to the not-so-obvious and even to the obscure and beyond. Brainstorming is an opportunity to explore possibilities. You have your constraints to keep you from going completely off the map, but even then you may find that there are interesting territories at the uncharted edges.
- *All work and no play does not work.* Brainstorming is a game; it should be fun and exciting. You should stop as soon as you feel that it is becoming a chore. Occupy your mind with something else and come back to it. It is almost pointless to brainstorm unwillingly. This results only in ideas that are forced and probably substandard. Reconnect and move ahead.

SIMILE, METAPHOR, AND ANALOGY: A POETIC TOOL KIT

In discussing inspiration, it was noted how the Muse could focus the world and cause poetry. The focusing of the world allowed the poet to see things in a new way. We can use the same tools the poet used to communicate our vision, whether it is to ourselves or to an audience.

Simile, metaphor, and analogy enrich concepts. By appealing to known elements and things that are familiar to your audience (and yourself), you can create a mental/emotional resonance that creates new connections. These can then lead to still new concepts.

Simile

Simile is the comparison of two unlike things using the words *like* or *as*.

> *My pen moves along the page*
> *like the snout of a strange animal*
> *shaped like a human arm*
> *and dressed in the sleeve of a loose green sweater*

This is as effective as it is simple. The comparison allows us to visualize the intended meaning and give it the added dimension the signifier allows. The added dimension allows us to step away from the surface and see things in a new way. The pen and the writer's arm have a life of their own; an image that becomes only too clear in the following lines:

> *I watch it sniffing the paper ceaselessly,*
> *intent as any forager that has nothing*
> *on its mind but the grubs and insects*
> *that will allow it to live another day.*

Having set us up with the image of the pen and arm as a animal, the poet broadens the image, and eventually separates himself from his writing arm altogether.

> *It wants only to be here tomorrow,*
> *dressed perhaps in the sleeve of a plaid shirt,*
> *nose pressed against the page,*
> *writing a few more dutiful lines*
> *while I gaze out the window and imagine Budapest*
> *or some other city where I have never been.*
>
> —"Budapest" by Billy Collins [2]

"Budapest."

You can approach your concept and describe it using a simile. The simile leads to questions that give rise to constraints. These can then be explored in a brainstorming session. So if you decide that your concept is like a leaf, then you ask how it will be like a leaf, what kind of leaf it will be, and how large it will be.

Metaphor

In the poem "Budapest," Collins shifts quietly from simile to metaphor, when suddenly there is an animal, rather than something *like* one. In presenting a concept, this kind of shift is extremely effective. It brings us into the world of the idea.

A metaphor sets up a more immediate relationship between the concept and its description. It omits the like, instead equating the subject directly with the signifier, as does the extended metaphor in a verse from W. H. Auden's "Funeral Blues."

> *He was my North, my South, my East and West,*
> *My working week and my Sunday rest,*
> *My noon, my midnight, my talk, my song,*
> *I thought that love would last forever: "I was wrong"*

Consider the difference between being someone's working week and being *like* it. If you say, "The building is an organism," we would be able to discuss what its skin may be, what its bones are, and how its organs function. We begin to delve into its nature. Discussing your designs using metaphor allows you (and your audience, if there is one) to begin to inhabit the idea rather than observe it.

A poem is a communication of a vision. It is energy transferred by the writer to the reader. The writing of it is not only an act of creation, but also a presentation of a vision.

By using metaphor, you set up a mental image and, in doing so, create a resonance between the unknown that you are introducing and the known. The familiarity allows you to understand the concept on your terms and begin to claim ownership of the images and ideas.

Analogy

An analogy is a comparison in which different items are compared point by point. Extremely common in science, as well as art, an analogy is usually used to explain something unknown by comparing it to something known. Scientists have compared atoms to billiard balls, brains to computers, and the underlying structure of the universe to vibrating string.

An analogy can help our understanding of structures and systems by pointing out similarities. Traffic analysis in civic planning uses analogies between the flow of gases in closed environments and traffic on highways. The rules that have been clearly demonstrated in one area are used to infer the behavior of the other.[3]

Analogies can point out relationships that may not have been visible, but they have their limitations. Analogies can "break down." That means that they are only suggestive and do not follow in every detail. In other words, analogies and metaphors don't prove anything, nor are they "rules." They are merely useful in helping people see similarities that are not otherwise apparent.

In the early days of flight, designers modeled wings on the wings of birds, following the assumption that the analogy would hold. (Da Vinci actually did some of this as well.) It does, but only up to a certain point. The shape works, and with modification and design applicable to the scale needed, aircraft were developed.

When you present a concept, set up an image of known relationships and elements.

Then attach the whole mental framework to a known element: "The curvature of a wing sets up drag and lift allowing the bird to glide easily. I will base my design on a bird's wings . . ." From this starting point you and your audience can create a good gestalt.

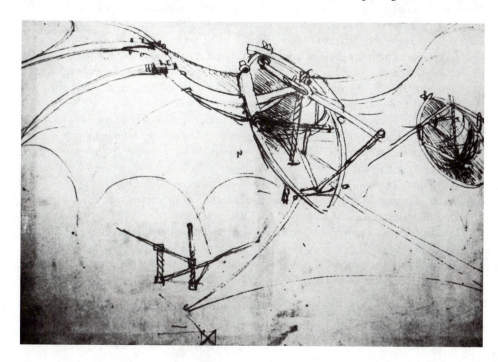

Da Vinci based his designs for human propelled flight on the wings of birds.

BRAINSTORMING TOOLS

Cubing asks you to examine your concept from six different perspectives. Like webbing (see page 82), it is an excellent tool for rapidly describing a design. It reveals quickly what you know and what you don't know, and it may alert you to decide to narrow or expand your topic.

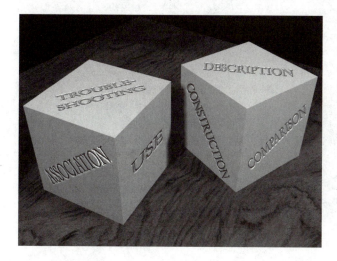

Cubing: Write and sketch from each of these perspectives. Start from what you know and identify areas that need further thought. Don't dwell on what you don't know; there are no wrong answers in a brainstorming activity. Look for surprises, unexpected insight, and connections.

Give yourself three to five minutes to sketch and write notes from each of the perspectives listed below. Start from what you know, and identify those areas that will need further thought or research. Speculate about where you will discover this information. Don't dwell on what you don't know; keep going until you have written about your design from all six perspectives. Remember there are no wrong answers in a brainstorming activity. Look for surprises, unexpected insight, and connections.

- *Description*: Physically describe your design. What does it look like? What color, shape, texture, and size is it? What are the major components? What are the significant details?
- *Comparison*: How is your design similar to other topics, things, or designs? How is it different? How is it better?
- *Association*: What other design or thing does your design remind you of? Can you compare it with anything else in your experience? Use simile and metaphor.
- *Construction*: Look at your design's components. What purpose do they serve? How are these parts related? How is it constructed?
- *Use*: What can you do with your design? What purpose does it have?
- *Troubleshooting*: What are the pros and cons of your concept as it now stands? Consider budget, ease of manufacturing, and marketing.

Concept maps are tools for organizing and representing knowledge. They include concepts, usually enclosed in circles or boxes. These are called nodes. A connecting line between two nodes indicates relationships between concepts. The connectors often carry labels that describe the relationship.[4]

On the right is a concept map related to the idea of "a leaf." It illustrates the thought connections to a leaf. It could be continued to several more levels. Try adding to it. Below it is Tapio Wirkkala's "Leaf dish" (Finland, 1951, laminated birch, 13.5"w x 7.5"d x 1"h). Which conceptual aspects of the leaf did Wirkkala focus on in his tray design?

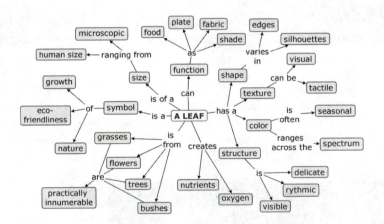

Begin by identifying the central word, concept, research question, or problem around which to build the map. Create your first node, and write this identifying information inside it. Then consider what concepts, items, descriptions, or questions you can associate with this node. Create new nodes and draw connections to them. If you can, add labels to the connections.

Concept mapping: When mapping or webbing, be informal and let the thoughts flow. You can always clean it up later.

The following are some suggestions for creating concept maps:

- Approach from top to bottom, working from general to specific, or use a free association approach by brainstorming nodes and developing links and relationships.
- Try to avoid writing entire sentences in nodes. A sentence usually indicates that there is more than one concept, and therefore mores nodes, involved.
- Conversely, don't force yourself into a bulleted style. Don't sacrifice elements of your thinking to pare down your word count. You can always edit later.
- Use different colors and shapes for nodes and links to identify different types of information.
- Use different color nodes to identify prior and new information.
- Using Post-it notes for nodes can be helpful at the beginning if you are very tentative. Just move the nodes around.
- If you have a question, create a node and mark it. (Use a cloud-shaped node or a question mark.)
- Gather information relevant to a question in the question node.
- Look into the available software for concept mapping. The Institute for Human and

Machine Cognition (IHMC, University of West Florida) has excellent software on its Web site[5] that you can download free. The beauty of creating concept maps on a computer is how easily you can move things around and add new ones.

Webbing is closely related to concept mapping but is concerned only with connections and not direction or hierarchy. Place a topic of interest in the center and draw connections to supporting details or related ideas. This is a good way to quickly assess how much you know about a given topic. Webbing is not as structured as mapping and can be a good way to begin a brainstorming session or to think on the run.

Webbing: This is the center of the web from the brainstorming that resulted in the concept map for constraints (see the image on page 81). The aim was to get as many thoughts on paper as possible and then connect them, without worrying about logic or order.

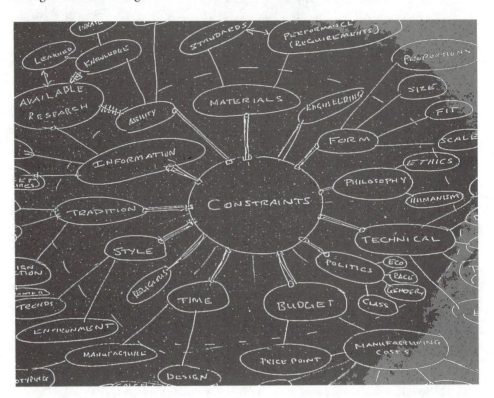

ANALYSIS

Clearly, there is more than one way to discuss a concept, even if we agree on the interpretation of the initial idea. In presenting a concept, we must be aware of the language, vocabulary, and voice we are using and who our audience is. A reference that is very clear to you may go straight over your audience's heads. Things you find stirring or interesting may not have the same effect on others.

You need to be the conductor, teacher, guide, and entertainer, all at once. The language you use, both spoken and visual, must be appropriate and clear. Say what you need to say: no more and no less. Be aware of what information each presentation is meant to give. The client may not want to hear minute details of research or production planning. The production team may be only mildly interested in trends and artistic visions but excited about a new material or worried about scheduling. Knowing as much as you can about the different constraints and how they apply will allow you to address the design from every angle.

After the concept comes into focus through brainstorming, it is a good idea to go over it again with more analytical methods to solidify the thoughts involved and understand the various facets of the idea. You need to be as clear as possible on what you have just discovered so that you can react to changes and problems without losing sight of your concept's core.

LISTING PROS AND CONS

Simply list the pros and cons of the ideas and suggestions you have brainstormed so far. This is also a good backup plan if you can't come up with any ideas during the brainstorming session. This list will either get you started again or lead you to a conclusion. By listing pros and cons, you can choose between options, if you have any, or determine that your ideas are desirable. This can be a good way to wind down a brainstorming session. But be careful; if opinions are strong, this can turn into a very lively (and time-consuming) discussion.

VISUALIZE AND SKETCH

Words and logic can take you so far, and visualizing will take you even further. Follow up your brainstorming by sketching and collecting images related to the ideas. Whether it is in the form of diagrams, technical sketches, doodles, or illustrations, the visual element of the project must come into play as soon as possible. The design in question may be a highly visual project, but we must also allow for the kind of thinking that visual stimuli and feedback bring us. An answer to a problem that cannot be stated in words is often easily conceived in a sketch.

Creating concept boards and tear sheets of found images is a very effective way of getting your message across. This can work both for actual visual elements as well as more emotional effects.

SCAMPER

A very effective tool for gaining insights into a developing concept is the SCAMPER process. It has you transform your concept in various ways, test the inherent constraints, and determine the strength of the concept's nature. The SCAMPER technique also highlights the fact that you should never take anything about your concept for granted. There is always another way of doing something. Not every part of the SCAMPER process may be applicable every time, but the exploration will enhance your knowledge of the project and expand your vision. If the results do not fit your purpose, it is good to know they are there for the next round.

The steps represented by the acronym are as follows:

- *Substitute*: Replace something with something else. You may change the materials or any of the components. Try making subtle changes, and try something completely unorthodox, extravagant, or even ridiculous. *A rubber teakettle or a rough ceramic finish rather than china? Plywood pants or just a slightly thicker fabric?*
- *Combine*: Blend or add elements together. Can something serve two purposes? Can two forms be fused? Can a contrast be eliminated? *Can the fabric of the upholstery also be in the curtains? Continue the handle of a knife so that it becomes the blade.*
- *Adapt*: Make adjustments to create something different. What else can it be? By examining and playing with its inherent functionality, change it into something else. *Make the jacket's design become one for a dress. Redesign the gym bag to become a laptop case.*
- *Minimize/Magnify:* Reduce or increase the shape or form. Play with proportions and scale. *What happens to a car if you put oversized wheels on it? What if you make the win-*

dows as small as possible? What elements of a couch can be huge? Put gigantic buttons on a shirt; now make them as small as possible.

- *Put to Other Uses:* Modify or create new ways to use something. What else can your design do? What inherent function can be put to more uses? Do you need to add something for this to happen? (This is not the same as adaptation because in this case it is still the same thing.) *Can the door handle also be a light switch? Can the roof tiles also be solar panels? What needs to be added to the jacket to make it be an all-weather garment?*

- *Eliminate/Elaborate:* Strip the concept down to its most basic state, and build it up until it is beyond overload. See where the lines are drawn.

- *Reverse/Rearrange:* Swap or interchange something to see what happens. *Try changing materials, textures, or colors.*

SCAMPER: Substitute, combine, adapt, minimize/magnify, put to other uses, eliminate/elaborate, or reverse/rearrange. Put your idea through the grinder and see if you like what comes out.

PRESENTING CONCEPTS

A concept is usually presented in an atmosphere of anticipation. Everyone involved is at least curious, if not excited. The client will see a plan for a solution of the design problem. The production team will see what they will be working on in the near future. Your design team will see the fruits of their brainstorming and what the next set of problems is.

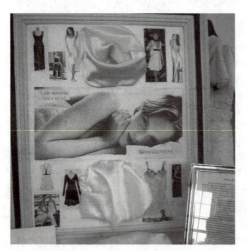

A concept board.

Therefore, the presentation (and the concept) will be perceived in a number of different ways to a number of different audiences, each with different (sometimes competing) concerns and questions. Some of the questions may be fairly simple and easy to answer. What may be clear as day to you may be completely obscure to those who have not been involved in the process so far. If your vision is clear, you have no problem. Some concerns may be more complex and related to issues that were already problematic during brainstorming. Once you analyze the outcome, you may be able to address those issues.

You must summarize the concept as well as explain it in complete detail, wrapping up what may be days (or even weeks) of work into a 15-minute presentation. If your audience is unfamiliar with the concept, you must explain it and educate them until they understand. Presentation and communication skills are discussed in more detail at Stage 6, but here are a few do's and don'ts.

DO'S

- *Practice your presentation.* Even if you are presenting to your colleagues, you are still "making a sale." There are probably many points to cover and many questions to anticipate.
- *Cover all the bases.* What are the elements of the concept? Make a checklist of all possible constraints: form, function, color, line, scale, materials, textures, fabrication, and so on. Make sure your presentation addresses all the constraints you can think of. You should also mention the ones you can't address and explain why you can't. These "problem areas" often turn out to be the most interesting parts of the project, since this is where something new has to happen.
- *Speak to your audience.* Consider who is listening and what they need and want to know. All audience members are interested in their own "bottom lines," whatever that may be. Production is interested in production issues, design is interested in design issues, management is interested in budgets and scheduling, and clients just want to know that the concept works.
- *Be enthusiastic and excited.* If you're not, how is anyone else going to be? You have to interest everyone in going ahead with the project and make them understand why it is worth doing.
- *Welcome all feedback.* Look at it as an extension of brainstorming. Even those who assisted in the development of the concept may already have new thoughts now that a little time has passed. The concept is now presented as a totality, which may bring new things to light. Criticism at this stage should always be taken in a constructive way, no matter how difficult it may be to hear.
- *Present options.* If there are several equally possible solutions emerging, show all of them. The feedback you get may determine which is the very best. If you don't feel comfortable about showing more than one, then the options may not be as equal as you think. If you favor one option over the others, you have a choice: Either present it as the only option, or build a strong enough case for it in comparison with the others.
- *Bring samples and as many visuals as you can.* Words are never as effective as things we can touch and see.

DON'TS

- *Assume knowledge on behalf of anybody.* Better to give too much information than to leave your clients or colleagues in the dark or confused. Cultural and scientific references should always be clarified. If you must go into complicated issues, consider preparing a handout. If you are worried that you are boring your audience with information they already know, you can simply ask them.

- *Assume that anything is obvious.* Murphy's Law is in full effect here. The one thing you neglect to cover will be immediately misunderstood in direct proportion to the cost of the resulting problem.
- *Gloss over gaps or problems.* If your brainstorming and analysis have not solved something, the gaps or problems are probably greater than you think. It is better at this stage to highlight the gaps and let everyone know where matters stand. No one will appreciate the buck being passed, and clients get very upset if they think they are being kept in the dark. If you must admit to a problem, do so in a constructive way, by asking for a brief dialogue. The audience may even volunteer a solution.
- *Present filler.* Keep your presentations to the point, and don't spread on the frosting just because you have it.
- *Spend more time on the presentation than on the content.* Unless the gilded frames, papier-maché boxes, and fireworks are directly helping to explain the concept, leave them out. It is very embarrassing to see a concept be outperformed by its frame. It is also distressingly easy to spot when someone is hiding behind slick technique.
- *Present inaccurate or half-finished models or drawings.* No matter how often you say, "This isn't finished" or "Oh, that'll be different," the clients will take away the image of what they saw, not what you explained. If you have to present a half-built model, don't paint it. This is why it is good to present elements and not whole images. The gestalt is coming together in the audience's mind; showing them things that are wrong could fundamentally confuse their understanding of your concept.
- *Assume that presentation technology will work (especially if it is not yours).* Test, retest, and have backups of all digital media. Allow for time to hook up equipment, boot up laptops, and so on. If you are the least bit unsure about the reliability of the digital equipment, have physical backup material.
- *Panic.* The fear of public speaking is the fear of making a fool of yourself. When giving a concept presentation, be aware that your audience is there because they are interested in the project, not in your performance. As long as you know what you need to know and have a good grasp on the ins and outs of the concept, you will be forgiven for not being a star of stage and screen.

TOMOKO MITSUMA,
ARTIST/INSTALLATION DESIGNER

Tomoko's work is composed of plants, mosses, and other living, temporal beings. She is active internationally, creating exhibitions, including three-dimensional installations, most recently in Stockholm and Paris. Tomoko also works in interior design in Tokyo, developing products for the original brand melon.

Fragments of ideas come to me from everyday life. When a few of these start to indicate a grouping or direction or when I feel that these ideas are starting to mature, then I start producing them. In other words, in my work it is very important to value the small inspirations and fun moments of day to day existence.

I'm often most inspired by taking the time to look really carefully at what's around me. For example, the shapes of leaves, plants, the rows of goods on display at the local hardware store, the dry cleaner's, a local construction site, oversize objects discarded on trash days . . . or I might take a walk in the older sections of town and see how people are resourceful with old or previously owned objects and take inspiration from their ideas. For example, someone using a tire as a pot for plants, a dumbbell for a door stopper, or rows of PET bottles filled with water to keep cats at bay.

I think that daily life is filled with things that mean something particular to me. I try to keep in mind that taking the time to actually observe things you might otherwise just pass by means that you have to be in a relaxed state of mind. I am able to switch my concentration on and off, just as I do when I'm creating artwork, and then creative ideas come when I'm not focusing on productivity. It's really quite simple.

When an idea won't develop the way I thought it would, I take a second look at my original notes or rough sketches and verify within myself the place I was at and what it was that I wanted to express. I can also depend on my husband for a solid and objective opinion. I'm cautious about asking opinions though because the timing is so important; you mustn't ask too early or too late. When I'm thinking about a work or [an] exhibition's theme, I'm probably somehow anticipating what people might think. To the extent that I'm interested in exhibiting, I think that this is important, but being overly aware of this will dilute the individuality in the work, so I try to be careful about striking the right balance. In other words, if I take in others' opinions early on, my own sense of direction becomes

blurred, and if I don't act on this early enough, I can find my work endangered by a reliance on such views. Of course, if my will were firmer perhaps I wouldn't ever have those moments of indecision.

When I have time, I often go to cafés to relax by myself—it can be morning or evening . . . whenever—and I find that this is the place where my imagination takes flight. Cafés are just enough removed from my life to let me feel completely free from it. A stream of people I don't know comes in and out; there is a buzz; it is never too quiet. This is ideal for me.

I guess I'm always learning from, and being inspired by, my previous pieces. Even though all my work looks different, each piece tends to be an extension of previous pieces, so there actually is no point at which a work is "finished." Just as I am always changing, so does my relationship to every piece that I've ever done.

1: BRAINSTORM

1.1: Apply the brainstorming and analysis techniques to your idea, and rewrite your design thesis to accommodate what you have learned.

1.2: Use concept mapping or webbing to examine your concept. Consider as many of the constraints listed below as possible and add others if necessary.
- Form
- Function
- Materials
- Texture
- Color
- Fabrication

1.3: List the pros and cons of the design solutions you have outlined.

1.4: Apply the SCAMPER method to your concept, and make note of any new insights (positive and negative).

2: CONCEPT BOARD

Assemble downloaded images, newspaper pictures, magazine pages, samples of materials, sketches, and any other visual to illustrate the results of Exercise 1. Create a collage on a presentation board. Add text as necessary to explain the concept you have created.

Guidelines for creating concept boards
- Assemble all your materials before you begin attaching anything.
- Lay them out on a table, and rearrange them a few times until you have found a good layout.
- Glue it together.

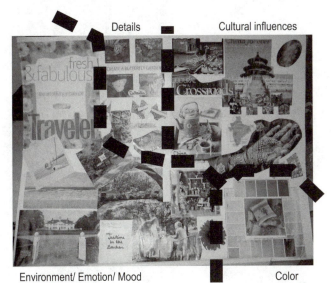

Details   Cultural influences

Environment/ Emotion/ Mood   Color

Concept board: This student's concept board is organized into four main areas, identified by my dotted lines. The viewer reading the thesis accompanying the board would have no problem in understanding the meanings and relationships of the images.

A good layout is one that does the following:
- Groups together images and samples that explain one particular element of the design
- Uses text primarily to work with and back up images
- Does not rely on an oral presentation to be understood
- Can be viewed (but not necessarily read) with relative ease from a distance of 10 to 12 feet
- Is controlled by an aesthetic that corresponds to the design concept in question. Think of your design's "look," and consider whether your board can reflect that. In the least, make sure your board does not contradict the direction of your design's aesthetic.

It is a good idea to get used to standard presentation-board sizes and begin to learn what you can fit into that format. Anything too large for the mode of transportation you are using (larger than the back seat of an average car) is clearly not a good idea. Consider also that anything smaller than 11" x 17" becomes tricky if you are relying on images from magazines and newspapers because your board will get filled up very quickly.

Exploration/ Refinement

OBJECTIVE

This chapter explores the basic methods for exploring and refining concepts so they are clearer. This chapter helps readers understand that their choices of methods and media affect the development of ideas and they can use their choices to their advantage. Finally, this chapter shows how a concept benefits from being examined and tested to its limits.

KEY CONCEPTS

- A concept for a design contains many unexplored possibilities.
- These possibilities should always be explored, no matter what the outcome.
- Drawing is a language. Your drawings are a personal method of communication that you can develop to be effective and clear.
- The methods and media you use will influence the development of a concept; therefore, you need be fluent with many different media.

PRACTICING ALCHEMY

Think of the alchemists of old as your mentors when you begin this stage. Their search for the universal elixir that would, among other things, convert base metals to gold and bestow immortality involved a variety of techniques. Alchemists blended superstition and folk medicine with mystical religious practices and emerging sciences. Anything and everything was worth studying, and no method of inquiry was too bizarre. Nothing was assumed, and they attempted everything at least once. To determine the true nature and basic essence of things, they would dissect, dissolve in acid, and otherwise reduce the object of their study to an elemental state. Their experiments often involved large quantities of mercury and phosphorus, which put them at risk for blindness, poisoning, and even death. That was, of course, if they weren't first beheaded or burned at the stake by those who were offended by their ideas. Despite all this, their search for the essence of things continued.

The methods *you* use should also be a strange blend of the practical and methodical with the esoteric and impulsive. Transmuting a basic idea into a golden one may not be quite so fraught with danger, though losing your head is a common occurrence, and things can metaphorically explode. The analogy, however, is sound enough: When exploring and refining your concept, you must examine and question everything, try everything, test everything, and risk everything. If the idea is worth pursuing, it will stand up to any test.

The alchemist-designer.

OBSERVING AND TESTING

In this stage, the brainstorming process segues into a more focused and solution-oriented state, and the tools you use become more tailored toward creating a specific result, such as a sketch or a technical diagram. By carefully exploring the possibilities an idea contains, it becomes possible to both expand and refine it at the same time.

It is important to proceed without rushing. It becomes very tempting to begin producing a finished product, and indeed, the pressure may be on to do so. However, by rushing you can miss less obvious but possibly more interesting areas. You can certainly create a design that efficiently meets all the criteria in the thesis and concept board, but the challenge is to do something other than the obvious. You can make a larger statement with more impact only by determining what the idea is capable of and pushing it to its limits.

Insight, although it can arrive in a flash, is usually built on knowledge you acquire and digest over time. By brainstorming, you should be well situated to peer at the inner workings of your idea, and by observing it from various angles, you can begin to see it in ways that you initially did not.

Apart from such concerns, there is also the task of testing a concept's viability before you commit to specifics. By visualizing your design, you can observe its interaction (or collision) with reality. As your idea takes shape and becomes more concrete, you can question its behavior and in such a way determine that you have made the right choices, be they practical or aesthetic. Focus your vision and refine the idea until it is exactly what you want it to be.

Your methods can be as diverse as your average alchemist's. You proceed with a wide ranging inquiry, relying more on intuition than logic, until you have discerned your idea's essence and recognized the laws that control it.

EXPLORATION AND REFINEMENT

Whether it's with a ballpoint pen on a napkin, computers, or traditional media, the stereotypical image of a designer is of a person sketching. For once, the stereotype is true. Finding, approaching, understanding, and explaining ideas requires reflection and dialogue, but sketches and illustrations are the most important tools, in that they can quickly show things that do not exist, and in doing so flesh out the ideas and explain them to the clients and collaborators.

The most recognizable method of exploring a design is to visualize it through sketching and modeling. With all the visual prompts available from the concept boards and brainstorming, the obvious thing to do is to begin sketching what is in your mind's eye. To use your sketches and illustrations most efficiently, clearly, and consistently, you must develop a visual language.

In sketching, we develop a visual language.

SKETCHING AND ILLUSTRATING: TOOLS AND LANGUAGES

The idea of a language of sketching and illustrating becomes important when you consider that sketches are used for two primary reasons: to explore the possibilities inherent in the idea and to communicate the idea to someone. These two reasons can be seen to be two sides of the same coin, if you consider that the exploration through sketching is essentially a dialogue with yourself. A dialogue requires language.

We effortlessly develop basic communication skills as children. In our second and third years, we begin to make our thoughts and wishes known in words, codifying our thoughts through examples we learn from the people around us. This language gets reinforced through daily interaction and then established firmly in school as we learn to read and write. Because of the emphasis on spoken and written language, the realization that we develop another language as well never tends to materialize.

But we learn to recognize and create pictures as representations of objects, and we learn this to an astonishing degree. A two-year-old child who has been introduced to elephants will recognize a hastily sketched outline as an "elephant" and will recognize new versions of it as the animal, even if those versions look nothing like anything the child has seen before. Elemental features become quickly established in children's drawings, and the rest is just refinement over the years.

This is not an elephant. But it is clearly an elephant.

Our brains are constantly trying to make sense of the cacophony around us. As you saw in the discussion of gestalt perception, we arrange things into recognizable arrays of meaning and fit unknowns into previously categorized groupings. This is a survival mechanism from way back in our existence, and we have become very good at "reading" our surroundings. Indeed, we are so good at this, that we will persist in seeing meaning where there is none. We see objects and animals in cloud formations, faces in rocks, patterns in starry skies, and so on. It seems to require very little prompting for us to layer a visual code onto random arrangements, so it is hardly surprising that we would be ready to accept a simple sketch for something far weightier.

The development of a "sketch language" relies on us establishing a "code" we can use to communicate effectively. You can create a language of symbols that has a one-to-one relationship with reality where each thing you imply on paper has a corresponding "thing" in physical reality.[1]

"Dragons," drawn at ages three, five, and nine (left to right). To the far left, dancing with the dragon is "Dad." The essential parts of both Dad and the dragon are there from the very beginning. Can you spot the elements of the sketching-language that say "dragon?" Compare Dad with the images below. What elements are already there?

"Dad," drawn by Karl, at age six (left) and by Julia, at age six (right). Notice that Karl adds a top hat and has Dad carrying a computer. These are seemingly code for "Dad." Julia, now able to depict "reality," concentrates on the face, so the head becomes over-sized. The dragon and Dad have both evolved considerably through the addition of detail and dimensionality.

We all travel a similar path at the start, and one may surmise that our capabilities to express the world in pictures is as hard-wired as spoken language. It all begins with a scribble. As soon as the motor functions are in place, usually just after the 18-month mark, a child will pick up a pencil or crayon and gleefully scribble on whatever is at hand. This is done for the enjoyment of the action and is probably not related to the expression of any thought. That follows very soon, however. Depending on the availability of materials, examples, and encouragement, children will begin to actively create symbols. They will have names for their creations and be very adamant about the "reality" of their symbols.

They develop quickly, and along with their new understanding, they seek new ways of expression, so these symbols change frequently. A year or two later, when the child reaches school age, the symbols solidify: There is now a consistent way of representing the world, usually one in which space is not illustrated and sizes of things are according to their relative importance, rather than their "real-world" scale.

Here, the seeds for a rather unfortunate series of developments are often sowed. It all begins well enough, with a need and excitement over mastering "realism" in drawing. A child becomes very proud and happy at achieving "the way it looks" and the goal of making the images look real supersedes the symbolic. Space, color, and texture are all discovered and used to this end. Being in a school environment allows children to learn from others and encourages comparison and self-criticism. An awareness of how it is done develops either from observing or from direct instruction. While this is all fine, what follows is often not.

As the child progresses through grade school, an increasing self-criticism sets in, especially in comparison with classmates and friends. It becomes clear that there are students who can draw and there are students who can't. As the child nears age 12, the goal of drawing becomes a project, and with the discovery of perspective and other taught techniques, the gap between those who can draw and those who can't widens. The natural development of drawing and perception tends to slow down or stop and an increased frustration and pre-occupation with depicting reality can lead to children consciously abandoning drawing altogether. For those who do, it is interesting to note that drawing often comes to be perceived as something for children.

We learn by experience and observation. Observation leads to challenging comparisons.

For those who continue to draw, there are hurdles to overcome in technique and expression, and discouragement is close at hand. The saving grace can be an understanding mentor. The introduction of nonrepresentational art, as well as non-fine art related applications of drawing, such as design or architecture, can also serve to get students through this crucial time.

This is key not only to the development of drawing for children but also for our understanding of how drawing works in the context of design. It is crucial not to see drawing as an end in itself. You must use sketching and illustration as a means of conveying information first, then emotion, and finally a sense of the "real," if at all. You must understand your language and develop it so you have a vocabulary that is point-to-point. You must also make sure your audience understands this language even if they cannot speak it. And it must be fun.

The language of your sketches does not have to be the language of fine art. As long as the idea is being communicated, the designer is fulfilling the mission. In fact, it may well be a hindrance to put too much store in pretty pictures early on in the process, when the energy should be going into the creation of the idea. This is why it is important to recognize the impulses of five-year-olds. Draw for expression and for fun; draw what is there to show what it is, not how it looks. If it is necessary to show an accurate detail or texture, draw the detail, get a sample of the texture, cut a picture out of a magazine, and write descriptions; don't waste valuable time on illustrations that in the end don't deliver crucial information. Pretty pictures do have their place at a later stage: They are extremely good at presentations for capturing and holding an audience's attention, they create an aura around the designs that can fuel your audience's imaginations, and they enhance the designer's credibility.

Introducing nonrepresentational art as well as non-fine art related applications of design broadens students' understanding.

At this stage sketches can clarify an idea for you and your client. By sketching the idea for yourself, you are forced to make decisions, and once the image is on paper, the idea exists in the world. It is a very powerful step, one not to be underestimated. By placing an idea in the context of an image, even if that image is a rough sketch on a cheap napkin, you have invested it with a reality that cannot be taken away again.

DO'S

*   *Sketch quickly and repeatedly.* Sketching can describe and drive your thinking. In both cases, visualization must proceed quickly to keep the idea fresh and to keep you from getting bogged down in the mechanics of drawing. It's a fine line, but if you find yourself spending more time on making the sketch look good rather than examining the idea, stop and refocus.

    Sketch quickly and sketch again to cement what you have done. This procedure also allows you to set up a quick feedback loop, in which you can look at the first quick sketch, decide what needs improving, sketch again, and so on. A good method is to first decide on the number of sketches and, when you've sped through those, pick the best.

I've become accustomed to doing 12 sketches and impulsively dismissing half of them before choosing two or three to keep. The number 12 feels right; it somehow manages to be more than enough without becoming so many that the exercise becomes tiresome. I find that the best sketches are somewhere around the three-quarter mark, so with 12, the best are somewhere around number 7 or 8. This is the comfort range of *my* sketching, but you should experiment and see what works for you. You may find that your energy peaks at a different point. Find the space between where you feel most interested in your project and where your energy begins to fail; this is where your best sketches will show up.

- *Sketch constantly.* Another reason to build up the speed of your sketching is so that you can sketch constantly. As you are pondering an idea, sketch every thought you have. Carry around a small pad and put everything in it. This frees up your brain and also makes sure you keep a record of all your thoughts. I never have my best ideas when I'm at the drawing board; I get them at the kitchen table or when I'm shopping or driving. (As sketching while driving proves to be rather problematic, I've invested in a digital tape recorder that I can clip onto my seatbelt.)

Often you start generating ideas that are not relevant to the particular project you are working on, but are perfectly viable for some later unknown project. It's a shame to let that go to waste, so put it in the sketchbook, write a note or two, and date it. Later you may want to go back and look at these ideas.

Put everything into a sketchbook and use many types of media.

Put a date on everything because you may need to backtrack, especially if an idea goes south on you. By going through the sketchbook, you can find and extract the ideas that were in action at that time, what led up to them, and determine where exactly you veered off course.

- *Sketch large and small.* Having a small sketchpad is good, but you should not limit yourself to pocket-size sketching. This can cause you to focus only on the larger forms and may habituate you to a small scale, which may cause a bit of shock later when the actual size of the object becomes significant. Make sure you change the scale of your sketches every now and again. Sketch very large to get a feel for scale and to envisage detail. Sketch small when you want to focus on the form and when you want to avoid going into too much detail.

- *Avoid limitation; use different media.* The size of your sketch as well as your choice of medium limits you. The expressiveness of crayons, pencils, markers, or watercolors couldn't be more different, and you must be aware of how each limits or expands your work. Try different media, and experiment with what suits you and the idea best. Look for the benefits of speed, color quality, and accuracy. Tailor your media choices to the character of the sketch you are trying to produce. Make a point of switching media every now and then so you don't get stuck in a certain mode, and don't be afraid to mix media if you feel the need. Later, when you begin to create illustrations, there may be certain requirements or industry standards, but by then you will have a good grasp of the character and image of your design.

  When something works well for us, we naturally begin to rely on that it will do so again. In this way we tend to get attached to certain methods and materials. We can develop a near dependency on a certain environment or tool. We cannot sketch unless we have a certain type of pencil, are in a certain place, or listening to a certain kind of music. Don't let this happen. As you practice your sketching you should not rely on the same tools or routines. Good work habits are essential, but don't build patterns that you cannot break out of at will. Purposeless habits are lethal to creativity.

- *Consider the purpose of your sketching.* In choosing the size and medium for your sketch, consider its purpose. What is this sketch to achieve? Is it for your benefit or someone else's? What is it meant to examine? What is it meant to show? These questions may seem simple and obvious, but it is surprising how often they are necessary.

- *Practice.* Sketching is, in fact, an art. The ability to quickly rough out an image that tells a story, inspires, and informs is nothing to be careless about. This ability must be nurtured in the same way a professional musician rehearses and practices constantly. The most seasoned soloist will go through a daily regimen of practice, playing scales, limbering up on difficult passages, and staying in contact with the instrument.

  Sketch something every day. Make it a habit to sketch freely for at least ten minutes. The routine is important; without it you will be overtaken by the flow of your day. Make it a habit to grab a pencil and sketch at the beginning or end of the day, just as you would brush your teeth. If you think you don't have ten minutes to spare, you're wrong. You just have to want to do it more than you do.

  Link the sketching to whatever project you have going or just play around. If you find the idea of practicing tedious, here's the good news: What you do doesn't matter as much as whether you do it. Pick something fun to practice on. If something is routinely a problem for you, such as specific textures or the human figure, practice that. If it's irritating or putting you to sleep, stop and do something fun.

Creativity needs practice, and practicing should be fun (most of the time).

Practicing involves repetition and, therefore, some tediousness, but you can at least choose a subject to sketch that is interesting or relevant. The main issue is to keep in contact with your tools and the feel of sketching. Try different media, different paper types and sizes, and levels of accuracy and speed.

One thing I found particularly helpful was to study and practice calligraphy for a while. The discipline required was difficult, but it quickly transferred to other methods and was suitably different enough to be entertaining. Also, when I got really bored, I switched and sketched with my left hand; anything to keep it challenging and therefore interesting.

DON'TS

- *Edit yourself.* When exploring an idea, don't edit it. The same rule as in brainstorming applies. Let the sketch or sketches arrive on the page, before critiquing them. If you are second-guessing as you go, you will interrupt the flow and never get anything done. There may be something in your sketches even though the entire sketch or idea isn't what you wanted. There may be a good detail or some well-formed line that you would like to duplicate. This is another reason to sketch quickly. You want to stay ahead of your critical eye by dropping the sketch onto the page as fast as you can. Let your intuition work faster than your logic. There will be plenty of time for logic later.

- *Keep your sketches to yourself.* One more reason to practice your sketching unceasingly is to overcome the fear of sketching in front of clients. A version of the fear of public speaking, this phobia has the same explanation and the same cure.

  The fear of public speaking or sketching is essentially a fear of making a fool of yourself. Make a habit of sketching as part of any discussion about your idea until it becomes second nature. Practice a diagrammatic style and use as few lines as possible so that your sketches are immediately clear to your audience.

  Get to the point where you are as comfortable using sketches as you are using words. The power of a simple visual is too great to allow embarrassment or modesty to keep you from pulling out your pen and sketching on a napkin.

FORMING

There are many more ways of visualizing a design than just sketching. Look for ways to quickly depict your design in a three-dimensional medium. A quick model can give you a feel for the form of a design, without having to go through the process of creating a fully realized sample. It can be very helpful to model before sketching; even a rough model can give a sense of space and form that is then more easily interpreted on paper.

Although speed is important at this point, you could also approach your choice of modeling material with an eye toward qualities that are inherent to your design: Consider color, texture, movement, and mass, and keep an eye on the scale you are working in.

Choose a material that will come closest to depicting the characteristics of your end product. If you are focusing on one particular aspect of the idea, such as proportions, or on a technical issue, choose whatever works best for that specific purpose and worry about the other issues later, when you build an appropriate model.

Possible materials include papier-mâché, clay, plaster, balsa wood, and paper. Be creative in your choice, and, as in sketching, don't bind yourself to the use of one specific material.

COMPUTER AIDED DESIGN

This technology [CAD] provides a way for me to get closer to the craft. In the past, there were many layers between my rough sketch and the final building, and the feeling of the design could get lost before it reached the craftsman. It feels like I've been speaking a foreign language, and now, all of a sudden, the craftsman understands me. In this case, the computer is not dehumanizing; it's an interpreter.[2] — Frank Gehry, architect

Since the early 1990s, the availability of computer technology has changed the design process in that the visualization of the design is available with greater speed and detail. Often the rough sketch is directly interpreted in a three-dimensional model or graphic illustration, allowing the designer much more control over the vision than before.

As Frank Gehry points out, this level of control has changed the way designers approach their work. The designer can interpret the vision with much more clarity than before, to the benefit of everyone involved in the project as they can be used equally well as sketching, drafting, modeling, and rendering tools.

 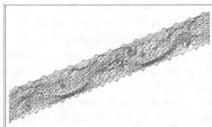 

Sketch, CAD diagram, and virtual model of "Turbulent Flow" staircase, designed by the author for the sculptor Brower Hatcher.

The increased control and clarity, beneficial as it is, has its own inherent dangers. CAD renderings and models can be almost *too* real. Textures and lighting are extremely realistic in off-the-shelf programs, and although the overall feel is still very clean and antiseptic, good renderings are almost interchangeable with photographs. This perception of reality influences the viewer's relationship with the design, mostly to a good effect, but with some side effects. Too much reality, especially at the sketching stage, can freeze the development of the idea. It becomes difficult to substitute the reality that now exists in the CAD model with another less substantial idea. A good work habit that can help with this problem is to save versions of the CAD models before making any major changes. Keeping a file of each version makes it very easy to go back and also allows for fearless experimenting. Just make sure you have a clear system for naming files, so you can find them later.

Another potential problem is that being able to visualize everything makes endless revising very tempting. More control coupled with more clarity allows more opportunities for tweaking and fixing. This is, of course, more often than not a strength, but it is important to keep an eye on the prize and not be tempted to fix it for the twentieth time at this stage. A sketch is a sketch, whether it's virtual or physical. Save the finesse for a later model.

It is a double-edged sword, when using off-the-shelf modeling programs, that environmental forces are not in play. There is no sense of having to obey physics at all. Objects can be disintegrated or embedded in one another without a problem, and gravity does not exist. With natural laws out of sight and out of mind, we are allowed to play as much as we want when sketching in these programs. If we are not careful, this can lead to sketch models that are impossible. This does not necessarily have to be a problem, and it is just as easy (if not easier) to create impossible things with a pencil and paper. The main problem is that on the screen everything has a much more finished look sooner than in a hand sketch. Thus, everything seems much more possible; our critical sense is disabled to a greater degree by the reality on the screen. This boils down to a problem that is really solved by basically getting used to it and by making a habit of performing a reality check on the model every now and then.

A sketch does not have to be "real." On the contrary, the sketches signify the vision, and the designer solves the discrepancy by bringing the idea into reality by degrees. If this is not possible, then another idea is simply sketched—yet another reason for speed and multiple sketches.

Speed and CAD sketching have a curious relationship. Although speed is important at this stage, digital sketching can sometimes be a little bit too easy. Modeling and graphics programs allow you to do the strangest of things in very little time, and there is a tendency to equate the ease with an ease of execution in the physical world. Programs are designed to allow for the ease of operation, and it is easy to add elements, colors, and typefaces and to manipulate shapes and constructs endlessly. Endless tinkering is dangerous, and the manipulation can continue way beyond any necessary or even sensible limits.

The lack of a sense of physical scale on a computer screen will also contribute to the confusion. You can zoom in and out, but little else to anchor you in the relative size of your design. Again this is a problem that tends to go away with increased familiarity. The concern until then is in the ability to add extremely fine detail and zoom and focus down to the level of individual pixels. This can lead to us working on areas so small that they have no significance. Conversely, we can neglect to go into detail and let the computer screen dictate the "frame," losing contact with the notion that the object being designed on the screen will perhaps be hundreds of times larger than the neat little model.

Again, this is also very easy to do with a pen and paper or clay model, but physically working by hand does tend to slow you down, compared with the clicking of a mouse. The time this allows you to consider your actions matters. The physical sketch and model also have a constant size, which grounds you in a fixed scale.

The solution is obviously to slow down a bit, remind yourself between clicks of the mouse that there is a reality being represented, and ask yourself now and again whether your design is at least not flagrantly disregarding it. A good safeguard in three-dimensional modeling is to place an object into the rendering that creates a reference point and a sense of scale. If you are working two-dimensionally, print a test page or make a habit of referring to the grids and rulers available.

The speed and flexibility of CAD is a great strength. Use computers as sketching tools as much as you can. Think of the software in the same way as you would any traditional media in terms of how you aim to use the results. Sketches are not ends in themselves. They are tools to aid in the exploration and refinement of your ideas.

DIALOGUE

Dialogue is of great importance. Discuss your ideas and concepts with clients, designers, production staff, or anybody else for that matter. These discussions can bring to light the needs and constraints of the idea faster than any analysis you can perform by yourself. Everyone has an opinion to share. Not everything contributed will be relevant or useful, so you must know what you are listening for. Just as in brainstorming, a lot of the work takes place afterward when you are sifting through, finding the valuable elements.

The concerns of each group are different and varied. Clients focus on the end-result (even if no one has any idea of what it will be yet) and will have numerous suggestions toward that end. They will also be very budget conscious, which may be premature at this point, depending on how clear your direction is. The production staff contribute fabrication solutions, and your fellow designers brainstorm and analyze design methods and directions. Virtually anybody you can think of can provide valuable feedback as long as you know where you are going and what you are looking for. Friends, family, and cab drivers have all served me well in finding out what an "uninformed" audience thinks. Do not assume that the expert opinions are always the best. Direct involvement in a project often creates blind spots. We want to believe in an idea and, therefore, do not see what is right in front of us. Don't forget: it was a child that pointed out that the Emperor had no clothes on.

Make sure you take in all opinions and comments, but don't fall into the trap of running after every idea thrust at you. Evaluate ideas you are offered, sketch them, write lists of pros and cons, and assimilate what you will. Don't take disagreement personally. You asked for opinions, so be grateful that you are getting them now rather than later when it may be too late to turn back.

REFLECTION

The art of reflection is one of the more neglected tools of design. The speed of the process and ever-looming deadlines contribute to methods that do not allow for much contemplation. Clients have difficulty justifying payment for "thinking time." How do you measure it? Where are the results?

It is very important while exploring and refining your ideas to take time every now and then to reflect on what you have done so far and whether this is where you want things to be. There are numerous ways to think, reflect, and meditate on your ideas, but basically your reflection can be either focused, indirect, or unconscious.

With focused reflection, you may be actively solving problems or seeking new solutions. Take time to go through your idea, piece by piece, element by element, and question it. Does this work? Does that work? If not, how can you make it work? What are the possible solutions? What is the closest you can get to a solution? Don't give up until you have at least one answer. Then visualize and sketch it.

Indirect reflection can be helpful when you are stuck. You have a feel for where you want to go, but cannot get there. Everybody has a dry spell and the way out can often be found by looking at the problem from another, often unexpected, direction. A good example of this technique is the Zen *koan*. A *koan* is a statement or question from a Zen master intended to compel a student into awareness by releasing the mind from its habitual patterns. The master introduces a seemingly absurd or impossible problem that the student is meant to solve, such as, "What did your original face look like, before you were conceived?"

or "When you can do nothing, what can you do?" The impossibility of the problem backs the student's mind into a corner from which the only escape is a new realization.

Another interesting version of this kind of thinking resulted in the artist/musician team of Peter Schmidt and Brian Eno producing a set of cards called "Oblique Strategies."[3] They had realized that their methods of creation were often similar when seeking solutions in their respective studios, and they began collecting their rules for getting out of difficult situations. This gradually resulted in a deck of cards that has now been published in several editions. Drawing a card, you will be given instructions such as "Emphasize repetitions" or "In total darkness, or in a very large room, very quietly." Clear or not, the card is to be trusted and reflected on to produce a way out of the dilemma.

Find ways to redirect your thinking when you get stuck. Learn both how your own process works and learn how others (such as Schmidt and Eno) go about it. Becoming accustomed to knocking your brain out of a rut may be the best design education you can get. Random input such as a koan or Oblique Strategy card can be exactly what you need to get past an obstacle.

This kind of thinking does not work without having the time to reflect, and you cannot expect it to work like magic. The real tool here is your brain, not the input. The input is merely the tool that creates the opening through which the light shines.

In fact, you can often trust the mind to do the work if you get out of its way. The more stuck you are, the further away from the problem you have to go for clarity to return.

Unconscious reflection occurs when you trust your instinct and previous knowledge to create a solution that will rise to the surface while you look the other way. After focusing on the problem, go for a walk, listen to some music, or look at the sky. Any activity that occupies but doesn't tax your mind will suffice. This allows the brain to process what you have been thinking about, and more often than not, this is all that is needed for an idea to appear. Sometimes just a few minutes away from a dilemma is enough; sometimes you have to "sleep on it." Don't underestimate the power of the unconscious, and give it time.

LEIFUR BREIDFJÖRD,
ARTIST/DESIGNER

Leifur Breidfjörd has been working out of his studio in Iceland since 1968 and is one of Europe's foremost stained-glass artists. His numerous commissions, both public and private, can be found in buildings, collections, and churches in Germany, Scotland, and all the countries of Scandinavia. Leifur does not limit himself to glass: He also works with oils, pastels, and various sculptural media. He also collaborates on textile projects with his wife, Sigridur ("Sigga") Johannsdottir, an accomplished textile artist in her own right.

When I create a proposal for a specific location, a public building, for example, I first go and look around the building and its surroundings to figure out what they require. Stained glass is really a rather risky material; you can quickly spoil a building by choosing the wrong colors or by creating a piece that is too dark. Stained glass can change things very radically—sometimes for the better, sometimes for the worse. It's very important, for instance, to realize very quickly how much light the glasswork should let flow into the space. Glass can actually be treated as three-dimensional or even four-dimensional, if you consider how time comes into play. The window changes its nature depending on the time of day, and whether you are standing inside or outside, looking at daylight streaming in or electric light streaming out. In addition, the light can be streaming through the glass or reflecting off it. Sometimes I will even use mirrors to reflect the space itself.

So, I look at the building from the outside as well as spending time inside it looking at the light and structures. It becomes very important to understand the space and how the work will affect it, to understand what the building needs. I also consider whether I should create an abstract or figurative work. I tend to work equally with the two, and through the years I have seen that each building has a different demand in that regard. It's also an intuitive thing. For instance, if I'm working in an older building, it might seem more appropriate to choose a more figurative style, but that's not a definite rule. It's really an intuitive response.

I also consider the scale of my work relative to the building very carefully; questioning whether the work actually fits the structure. This is especially important with figurative work where the size of the figures in the window can make the building seem large or small. One huge figure in a 30-foot window would make a church seem smaller, but putting a multitude of tiny figures in the same window would make the building seem too large for the artwork.

It really matters to look at what suits each building: figurative, abstract, modern, or older styles. I make a point of working with the surrounding structure rather than forcing some preconceived style I might have into all the buildings I create work for. I feel that to do otherwise is wrong and feel that it is necessary to create something that fits into a specific building, something that answers the building's demands. What I find very rewarding and exciting is something that I have actually achieved over the years: to create a piece for a building and hear people say, "It's like it has always been here."

I make a point of working in close contact with the architects; I will always consult with them first and show them my proposals. It's rare, but very exciting, to be included right at the start of a building being designed, although that has happened. It's great to be in on the process when the architect is sitting there with pencil and paper, sketching out things and throwing questions around like, "Where do you think the windows should be?" and "How much light should we let in here?"

Sometimes I'll spend time inside the building even as it's being built. I did that for the Icelandic National Library in Reykjavik. As it was being constructed, I sat in there for a few days, observing the space and the windows, sketching all the while. For a church in Reykjavik, I sketched the first drafts over the course of a few days, sitting in my car in their parking lot.

I've developed my use of color over the years and have no specific rules—except I think I have a tendency to not use green as a dominant color. I think that's just a personal thing. Again, I usually go by whatever the building needs each time. It can be a window without any color, just white and gray; it depends entirely on the building and the space. It depends on what I see. It's also a question of what the window should achieve. For example, is the sun to shine through it and project the colors onto the interior walls? You can change an environment by dousing the space and the people in it with color. You can do anything. Here, for example, is how you can spoil a building: I came into a church once, where someone had decided to put yellow glass in all the windows. You'd go in and look around, and everyone and everything you'd see would be yellow. However, one little window right at the top was broken; a little triangular hole through which you could see the sky. That triangle was the brightest most intense blue, contrasting with all that yellow: a strong bright blue, almost violet. It was magnificent! That's the kind of thing you can do, by controlling the light and influencing all the colors in the space, and you've got to think it through right at the sketching stage. So, I look at all the demands of the building and the site, and then look through my mind; I look through my memories and what I've learned through the years.

I think of what I've seen in buildings and churches all over the world and in my own older works. Then I begin sketching.

First I do a lot of quick pencil sketches, and then I move on to sketches in either 1:10 or 1:20 scale; these are usually in gouache. Here, I keep the scale of the work relative to the space very much in mind. I usually sketch a human figure off to one side of the drawing to have an immediate sense of scale while I'm working.

I used to make a model of the building at this point and put an enlarged photo of my sketch into it, but lately I've taken to scanning my drawings and inserting them into a photograph of the location in PhotoShop. This allows me to also simulate what it would look like from the outside looking in and is really quite good for presentation to the client. I don't do any of the artwork on the computer though. It's too slow; there's too much messing about. Sometimes I'll tweak the colors a bit [on] the computer, but other than that I find it much better to create the original by hand.

Once I've done this, I'll present the scale drawing to the client, and if everything looks good and we decide to go with it, I'll create a full-scale design in color. I've always worked this way and attach great importance to this method. I also keep all my sketches and everything. When I exhibit in galleries, I show the whole process—mounted sketches and photographs, the full-scale drawings, and the finished work.

I only ever show the client one proposal. It can get complicated, especially if there is a large committee involved, to show more than one. You might be happy with one proposal, but decide to show them three, so they can pick and choose. Then suddenly things become difficult because a third of the group would like this, a third would like that, and then a someone would say: "Could you come up with a fourth proposal?" or "Can you show us three more?" It's best to show just one that you are happy with and ready to develop. Of course I'm open to discussion later, if there are any requests for changes; you can't be so close-minded and stubborn that you can't accept requests for changes. I feel that's especially important for private clients. I might show the clients a proposal—let's say it has some red and pink in it; then I find they can't stand pink. At that point I'm perfectly willing to say, "Okay, we'll drop that." These people have to live with your work. But, it's best to show them one and say, "This is what I would like to do." However, to do that you have to have done your research and come up with something that you both know and feel is right for the location.

The key to successful cooperation is not to be too fixed in your opinions and to be open to others' views. You have to listen to people. When I was starting out, I often found it difficult to be creating pieces for specific locations. I was finding my way, trying things out, and it took a long time to figure out what was appropriate for a specific place. In time, this has become easier and simpler. I look things up in my mind and find the solution for a place. Another thing is that I like working with others. If someone brings in an idea and says, "Wouldn't this be better?" I think it should absolutely be considered. If the idea is good, then you should try to approach it. But, it's really very important to be broad-minded and listen to all points of view. As soon as you get all negative and ignore other voices, you're in trouble. It can't hurt to look at other ideas. Whether you use them or not . . . maybe you can use parts of what people are suggesting.

It's important to be working in different media and not to focus too heavily on one discipline. My wife and I have traveled all over the world and like to go to galleries and museums to see what artists in other fields are doing. She's in textiles, has specialized in woven tapestries and church vestments, so we've collaborated on that for shows and churches and such, but I also draw and paint, and sculpt, and use mixed media as well. It's hard to say why I choose one medium over another at any given time, but I find it good to give my mind a rest. After a project it's sometimes good to go and do something completely different. It also happens that after I've been working with a certain material or style for a while, that I'll just veer off into something totally different. Then I'll find my way back and wind up somewhere in between. Thesis, antithesis, synthesis, and all that . . . I'll go to extremes, and then it all flows together somehow afterward. It's another reason why it's important to work on several different things, not to be confined to one.

As far as inspiration goes, I can tell you right away what doesn't inspire me much: landscape. Whether it's an actual landscape or a painting of one . . . doesn't affect [me] at all. It's a very Icelandic thing to appreciate a good landscape, but it just doesn't touch me. Rather than look at some mountains or vistas, I'd rather take a magnifying glass or a microscope and lie down on the ground. That has a much larger impact on me. Or rather than look at some majestic mountains, I'd rather go down to the shore and look at things that have washed up; look at the rock formations, the moss, the flotsam and jetsam. Actually, what I'm looking at is their forms. They may be clearly defined and identifiable objects, but I'll be looking at them as abstract shapes.

For stained glass and textiles, it works very well to look at things very close at hand, to look at the abstract forms in nature. This goes for form, color, and light. . . . Even when I'm working with readily recognizable things, like the human body or head, I still use them in an abstract way. My work doesn't necessarily contain any narrative; these things are just forms. I'll often use text in my images, but even then that is also just form—the image of text.

A lot of people wait for inspiration in order to get their work done. They wait, and they wait, and then in the end all they've done is wait because the muse never shows up. However, it's also true that you can sometimes be less than motivated for conceptual work. That's why I also like to work on the practical aspects, like the cutting of the glass for my windows. My wife—Sigga—she does all the lead-work, but I'll be cutting glass or working on the computer or caulking or whatever comes to hand. So, say I'm sketching something, and I see that it just isn't happening. I'll just put it aside, instead of banging away at it. Just take a break from it, and go do something else. Try again the next day, and again, if it isn't working, just let it go. This is why it's good to have several projects going at once, rather than just having one and waiting around for a major flash of inspiration to get it done. Then, once you've got it done, that's all you've been working on. Just go work on something else. With two or three active, if one is stuck, then you go to the other and that works, or you go to the third, and then back. Or you just go sweep the floor. Anything will do.

Some people talk of emptiness between projects and the need to refuel. I don't really experience that; I have my different projects all around, and I just keep going. Sure, I take it easy for a bit; I go swimming every morning, or I'll watch a good movie at night, but I'm not really refueling anything. It's great, though, to travel and look at museums and architecture. My wife and I have done a lot of that. We go to a lot of museums and galleries of any kind. Paintings, sculpture, design, natural history, whatever: It all has an energizing effect; it's all an inspiration.

As you begin to commit your idea to the physical world, it is important that you understand what its nature is and how to depict it best. The following exercises will assist you in realizing what the elements of your design are and how they contribute to the totality of the concept.

1. Now that you have a more concrete idea of your designs, refer back to the SCAMPER exercise on page 89, and use it to complete the following with a more practical slant. Question all assumptions, and don't go with a solution just because it's the standard one.
   - *Materials.* Examine the materials your designs call for. What are they capable of? How do they behave? Try substituting other materials. What does this do?
   - *Function.* Confirm the functionality of your design. Look at your sketches and create a few that show it in action. Contemplate this, visualizing with the help of your sketch how it would work in the physical world.
   - *Form.* Sketch a few variations on the form. Larger, smaller, rounder, whatever you can change, change. Go to extremes and switch things around. Make short what is long. Make angular what is curved.
   - *Colors.* Sketch in color whenever you can. Examine how your choice of color influences the feel of the design. Which colors belong, and which do not? Try to minimize contrast, and create intense combinations.
   - *Usage.* How has this design been used before? What worked? What didn't? If something should change, how can you affect this? Consider ergonomic issues. What can you improve?
   - *Production techniques.* How is a design such as yours commonly produced? Is there anything in the production techniques that influences how you should design it? Are there any new technological developments or new materials that could influence this?
   - *Background/History.* By looking at the background and history of your client and design, you may find clues to changes that could be beneficial. You may also find problems that have become accepted through familiarity, such as, "This is how it has always been done."

2. By sketching or modeling, create visual responses to as many of the questions above as possible. Use different media if you can.

   Once you have 10 or 12 images, look for a common effect. What ties your sketches together? What have you emphasized? When working quickly, sometimes your unconscious mind will show you things you didn't expect. Either you are clearly emphasizing something, or you feel that something is missing. Either way, once you have figured out what's there and what's missing you can consider the following:
   - What are the main elements of your design (form, color, texture, or proportion)?
   - What is the "language" you are setting up in terms of how you sketch the designs. How do you interpret and signify the different elements you are using? Do you think your meaning is clear to others? If not, how will you make it clear?

3. Take the element of your design that you feel has the most significance. This can be chosen on the basis of visual impact or technical importance. Sketch the design, placing maximum emphasis on exhibiting the significance of this element, using three different media (e.g., pencil, markers, or watercolor). Which one serves it best? Why?

4.   Create three sketches going from small to large. Use three sizes of paper, one the size of your hand, the next the length of your arm, the third the length of your body. For the first, use pencil, for the second use a marker, and for the third use wax crayons or a thicker marker. Put as much detail as you can into each sketch. How much detail is enough to explain your thinking? How does your perception of the design change with the change of scale? Which of these three do you think is the most effective way to present the idea? Why?

5.   Take the elements of your idea and sketch them independently of one another. Create a set of sketches that address different elements of your design: color, form, proportion, texture, and movement. One way of doing this is to choose a subject at random. Create a sketch where you apply the elements of your design to that subject (e.g., a red, angular, shiny elephant). As you sketch, consider how the context informs your usage of the elements involved (how do you apply angles to an elephant?) and how the nature of the design changes by your application of these elements (what is the elephant now?). Playing with this idea, substitute various animals, people, objects, and plants, and keep sketching. This activity will connect you with the elements of your design and let you fully understand their effects, without tying you to the practicalities of the design in question. Apply what you have learned about your design in the previous exercises to one "master sketch."

6.   Use the media and scale you found best suited, and create a sketch showing your design from a few significant directions. Make sure all the main elements are emphasized (the angles of your sketch may be determined by this). Make any notes on the sketch you feel may be necessary to underscore what your audience is looking at.

Definition/ Modeling

OBJECTIVE

This chapter explains the hierarchy of needs in design and identifies the types of decisions involved in fulfilling those needs. Also discussed are the concerns of modeling designs, from both a practical and perceptual perspective. You are encouraged to explore approaches to creating models for your designs and plan the creation of a concept model. Finally, you have an opportunity to revise your design thesis with any new developments that have occurred.

KEY CONCEPTS

- A design is almost inevitably less perfect than its concept. Designers can offset this tendency by paying attention to details.
- A design must fulfill certain needs, determined by a definite hierarchy, for the design to be a satisfying solution.
- Modeling can be an efficient exploration tool and should not be thought of as an end-stage or as an end-product.
- Modeling, like sketching, is a method that conveys the effect and intent of a design; its meaning is shaped by the methods and materials used.
- The design process becomes so detail oriented at this stage, the designer may need to reinspire him or herself.

MAKING IT REAL

This chapter explores the steps you need to take to move your project from the exploration stage to a more definite embodiment in the physical world. The concept must become an object. We must transition from exploring to deciding what it is exactly and sometimes even deciding what it is precisely not, the emphasis being very much on *exactly* and *precisely*. Some people would say that this decision-making process is the designer's primary function. Indeed, the designer must make choices that keep the idea intact, while respecting the parameters and constraints outlined at the beginning and keeping in mind the possibilities and limits of the manufacturing process. Now you must make sure that the decisions you made about constraints at the exploration stage still work. You must eliminate as many unknowns as possible before you reach production or prototyping, where redoing becomes costly in both resources and time. It's time for designers to take their concepts and define their realities as fully as possible and in as much detail as they can. It is this definition that characterizes this stage and leads to the need for a model of the design.

Reality is tricky. We have conceptualized our idea so that it looks pretty solid and ready to be used in the world. But at this point, more often than not, our concepts can be seen only out of the corners of our eyes, like ghosts. When we turn to look, they fade back into the shadows.

In trying to visualize the "real" object of our design, we find that our grasp of the idea, clear as it may be, may not include enough detail or functional thinking for us to be able to fully realize its image in a physical embodiment. We must begin defining our idea in as much detail as possible and create a model to bring it into the world.

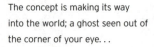

The concept is making its way into the world; a ghost seen out of the corner of your eye. . .

THE BASIS OF DECISIONS

"It is common sense to take a method and try it. If it fails, admit it frankly and try another. But above all, try something." —Franklin D. Roosevelt

The first thing to do is to look at the constraints and specifications to see that everything has been addressed. Do we have specific solutions for each problem? Do we have the time and resources to solve whatever problems remain?

WHEN IS "GOOD ENOUGH" ENOUGH?

It is important to weigh your concept on the balance of "making it perfect" versus "getting it done." Every designer must deal with the constraints and compromises of practicality and production. For example, you may want to hold out for the ideal material, but either the budget won't allow it or the manufacturer can't wait for the delivery time required. Perhaps your design requires a certain technical proficiency, and you need to figure out what level of expertise is good enough. Perhaps you are just asking for too much: You can never hope to see perfection, but rather the best possible outcome. In fact, the satisfactory completion of a design often becomes a question of defining what good enough is in terms of the overall concept and purpose of the design.

As a result, there is always a sense of regret after a design is complete, as illustrated in this description of the architect of the new addition to the Museum of Modern Art in New York.

> *Yoshio Taniguchi is a pessimist by nature.*
>
> *Each time Mr. Taniguchi, the architect, visits one of his buildings, he sees every compromise he had to make, every flaw he would like to fix. As he strolled recently through the newly expanded Museum of Modern Art, his first project outside Japan, it was no different.*

The atrium of the Museum of Modern Art in New York.

Visiting the fifth-floor painting and sculpture galleries, Mr. Taniguchi stopped and ran his fingers over a seam in one of the metal panels that separate one room from the next, mourning the undisturbed surface he said he would have preferred there.

He lamented having had to cut back on the number of skylights because of budget considerations. He worried that a wall of windows near the second-floor bookstore reading room would pull the focus away from the building's atrium. He questioned the placement of Henri Matisse's "Dance" over a staircase connecting the fourth and fifth floors, and the elevation of Claes Oldenburg's "Geometric Mouse" in the sculpture garden.

But as Mr. Taniguchi, 67, stood there surveying his soaring yet understated temple of granite, marble, oak, aluminum, and glass, he admitted to a rare moment of gratification. "I think I'm quite satisfied," he said.

"It's nearly perfect," he added. "I'm not supposed to say that because I'm Japanese. I'm supposed to sound humble."[1]

So, how good is good enough? The answer to that depends very much on the context of the needs and constraints of your designs.

THE HIERARCHY OF A DESIGN'S NEEDS

The psychologist Abraham Maslow is known for establishing the hierarchy of needs theory, writing that human beings are motivated by unsatisfied needs and that certain lower needs must be satisfied before higher needs can be.

Designs also have needs, and those needs have a hierarchy of their own, where a design will be found at a certain level depending on what needs it fulfils.[2]

Examine which needs are met by your design. If you find that you are stuck or missing a level, perhaps there is something in your concept that can change to bring it up in the hierarchy. Designs must meet these needs in succession. Skipping levels only invites a design that is less than successful in fulfilling its promise. The following needs are listed in the order of priority.

On left, Maslow's hierarchy of needs. To the right, the hierarchy of design needs.

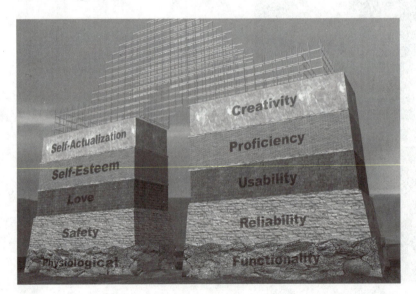

Level 1: Functionality

Does your design do what it's supposed to do? This most basic of questions may seem almost an absurd question at first. However, a quick look around will suffice to remind you that not everything that is manufactured or built does what you expect it to. For example, I purchased the Thermos on my desk to transport the liter of tea required to get me through a day of teaching, and I expect it to be a fairly well-functioning object. The functional mission is fairly straightforward: The design thesis may read, "Keep the tea warm for an afternoon. Don't leak. Be easily transportable."

The Thermos fails in two out of three respects. The interesting thing about this Thermos is that it has no insulation capabilities beyond any other metal canister. As soon as the tea is poured into it, its exterior immediately heats up to the temperature of the tea, indicating that the heat loss is enormous. This also makes it very difficult to carry until the tea has cooled down, which it does fairly quickly. One may think that someone would have noticed this at some point, but clearly the design was never tested. Worse still, perhaps someone decided that it didn't matter whether it actually worked because people would still buy it.

It may seem obvious on paper, but don't assume that your design works. Before committing to your final choices, check and check again whether your assumptions are correct. Does it fulfill the most basic requirement of functionality? A Thermos that doesn't keep anything warm is just a can. What is your design if it doesn't function?

Level 2: Reliability

Assuming that functionality is in order, the reliability of a design would be measured by the consistency of its performance. The microwave oven in which I reheat my tea, for example, is always consistent. A cupful at 75 seconds will always be comfortably warm. This may seem to be a fairly trivial example, but consider a parent who needs to heat a baby's bottle. If the microwave weren't consistent and made the milk lukewarm one night and boiling hot the next, this would cause an accident. As reliability goes hand in hand with safety, this is a very important aspect of designing. Given that the design functions, we would like it to do so consistently and predictably.

"It is wonderful, Dr. Huygens, but will it keep the tea reliably warm?"

Examine your idea by questioning all the things that could go wrong, whether they are seemingly trivial or important. Are there vulnerable points in the design? Remember Murphy's Law: "Anything that can go wrong will." However trivial the problem may seem, if the reliability of a design is in question, you will have an unhappy user.

Level 3: Usability

How easy is it for others to use your design? Ease of use is relative, of course; however, generally speaking we should not need to relearn how to use something each time we do, and we should be able to make mistakes without causing catastrophic consequences. I don't have to press a sequence of buttons on the microwave oven to make it work. The buttons are all clearly marked, and the panel is easy to read. There is no real doubt about what to do. I can still manage to push the wrong button, but I have a "cancel" button and therefore have more than one shot at entering my desired time.

In the past decade, usability has become a loudly chanted mantra in Web site and software design, but the principle applies everywhere.

> *It can be easy to fall into the trap of thinking that we are designing our site for one idealized user—someone exactly like us. But we aren't designing for ourselves; we're designing for other people, and if those people are going to like and use what we create, we need to understand who they are and what they need. By spending time researching those needs, we can break out of our own limited perspective and see [the design] from the point of view of the users.*[3]

Level 4: Proficiency

At this level, the designs actually improve the user's experience, allowing things to be done better than before or in ways not previously possible.

In 2004, both *Time* and *Fortune* magazines chose the Rheo Knee as one of the "coolest designs" of that year. The Rheo Knee is one of the first prosthetic limbs to incorporate artificial intelligence. A software algorithm in an embedded chip that learns the wearer's behavior over time manages the knee's movement. By sensing knee position and the loads applied to the limb at a rate of 1,000 times each second, the knee analyzes the user's movement and delivers the proper amount of resistance during each step.

The Rheo Knee: Both *Time* and *Fortune* magazines chose this design from Ossur in Iceland as one of the "coolest inventions of 2004." Equipped with a microprocessor, it takes 1,000 measurements a second to learn how the wearer walks. It then reacts to various different terrains and stimuli, assisting the wearer.

Users can walk long distances while expending far less energy than before and can go up and down stairs with a natural gait, as the limb learns how they move and works with them.

The incorporation of a new technology has shifted the prosthetic device from a passive object to an active participant in a wearer's motion and stance. In addition, the designers have gone outside the box and created a casing that looks more reminiscent of trendy electronic gadgets, challenging the centuries old idea that a prosthetic limb is something that should be disguised and covered up.

Find a way to improve on an existing design by adding new technology or challenging existing views of how things are and should be. Designing a new product can take years at this level, as exploration and experimentation are at the center of the activities, with many layers of problem-solving going on at once.

Level 5: Creativity

Finally, there is the level where all other needs are satisfied, and the design goes into new territory, changing perceptions and experiences. A good example from 2004 is light-transmitting concrete (LiTraCon), which is made by adding glass or plastic fibers to the usual blend of gravel, sand, cement, and water. A LiTraCon wall is as sturdy as normal concrete and as translucent as paper. Shadows seep through one side to the other, even in a thicker-than-standard wall. It is tough enough for buildings, but the glass or plastic fibers make it currently too expensive for most large-scale construction. However, this will probably change and with it the drabness of many a city street and government building.

At this level one can experience a crossover between disciplines, and we also see that designing is about much more than just making more stuff. At the beginning of his book *By Design*, Ralph Caplan writes the following:

> . . .*design at its best is a process of making things right. That is, designers, at their best, create things and places that work. But things often do not work. And making things right is not just a generative but a corrective process—a way of righting things, of straightening them out and holding them together coherently.* [4]

LiTraCon: Concrete embedded with optical fibers—another of the "coolest inventions of 2004." Shadows on the lighter side will appear with sharp outlines on the darker one. Even the colors remain the same. This special effect creates the general impression that the thickness and weight of a concrete wall will disappear.

With this in mind, it is difficult to beat the paradigm shift created by Aresa Biodetection, a Danish company. Early in 2004, the company announced that it had, by genetic modification, produced a new variant of thale-cress, a small flowering weed. The new strain turns red, not in the fall as it would normally, but only when growing in the presence of nitrogen dioxide, a gas commonly emitted by explosives. Now there is a new way to detect landmines: Seed a suspect area, wait a few weeks for the thale-cress to grow, and identify the danger zone wherever they turn red.

The sheer beauty of this design is mind numbing. Instead of using machines or putting dogs or humans at risk, the flowers identify the bombs. A killing zone is not only removed but also greened. (Trust the Danes to come up with a solution straight out of Hans Christian Andersen's fairy tales.)

Design at its most creative level crosses disciplines and changes peoples' perceptions and experiences. Thale cress, a small weed, became an elegant solution to the problem of land-mine detection.

A shift of this kind can be made by putting new technologies to unintended uses or by combining components that otherwise would not function in the same environment. What can you do to bring your idea to this level? Think of the problem you are solving with your design. How would you approach it in another way? Can you remove the problem altogether? (Don't like the drabness of concrete? Take it away.) Can you attack the cause rather than the symptom? (Make the prosthesis sensitive to its user?) Do something unexpected, and don't be afraid to be weird. (Sow flowers amidst Kevlar-clad warriors with dogs and bristling machines!)

ANATOMY OF AN IDEA

An understanding of anatomy is essential to anyone who wants to know how an organism functions. To fathom how well an idea would grow and survive, you need to approach it with an anatomist's eye before you grant it a physical existence.

By taking this approach, you will gain great insight into your idea and how all of its components fit together, which allows you to explain it to clients, manufacturers, and others and also to field their questions *or* criticisms.

Look at your idea and break it up into its constituent parts. What are they, what is their purpose, and why are they there?

Begin by asking how much of the idea deals with the actual physical representation and how much deals with philosophy or the intangible, emotional response. In other words, break your idea up into its actual physical parts and the perceived effect of these parts. For instance, you can have two fairly ordinary but highly contrasting materials (e.g., driftwood and steel). Each material has a specific quality that can be powerful and clear. Putting them together in a structure causes an effect that is greater than the effect of each individual material. Our reaction to the juxtaposition of colors and textures has an emotional quality that is created at this point. The idea contains more than just a shopping list of things; it is greater than the sum of its parts. You need to consider what the statement is in each case. What is the purpose of each entity in relation to other elements and to the whole? How do they affect, contrast, and complement one another? Then consider whether there is any way each part could be made more effective. Does it serve the idea as well as it can?

Ideas evolve, and the evolution of an idea often means that the concept has been approached several times, tinkered with, and tweaked. Things have been added and taken away, in both a physical and philosophical sense.

When complex entities evolve, parts lose their importance and perhaps even stop serving any purpose at all; yet, they remain if they are not in the way, until something—usually something problematic—draws attention to them.

Examine your idea for unnecessary appendages. Make sure every element the design contains has a purpose. Any purpose may do: Practical, decorative, humorous, or sentimental—it is up to you as the designer to make the case. But if you can look at some element of your design and say that it really has no purpose, take it out.

DETAILS

Before we look at the actual modeling of a design, we must consider the details and how they come into play. Details can be aesthetic and surface oriented as in the decorative details of apparel or interior design. They can be subtle and integrated as in the application of techniques and finishes on furniture. Details can also be functional in the sense that they can involve the use of correct specific components as in the choice of certain components, chips, or electrodes. Details may involve a choice of materials for ecological purposes or be references to other eras and art forms in their aesthetics, contexts, qualities, or material content. For modeling purposes it is good to identify details as either functional or decorative. This distinction will inform the level of functionality of the model, as you will decide how much the model needs to show of each detail.

The correct treatment of these details, whether functional or decorative, is crucial at this stage. Their definition and treatment will not only influence the outcome of the final design, but their presence or absence in the model will also present your idea in a certain context. As your model is the first impression your clients and colleagues get of the design's physical manifestation, a false or inadequate impression can be quite harmful. It will stick, as first impressions do, and when you present your next iteration of the design, there could be great shock and surprise if the implications made by the first impression were not correct.

Through sketching and concept mapping, you should now have a fairly well-defined sense of which details are important and how they come into play. Having separated them into functional and decorative, consider which are essential to the true representation of your idea. Remember that the model you are going to build is a conceptual one and should not necessarily have to arrive with all the bells and whistles of the final design. However, your model needs to tell the story, even if it is abbreviated, and the story must give all the details and hint at all the implications.

How will you create or represent functional details? Will they actually function in a way the final design needs, or will you imply and explain the action?

How will decorative details be represented? This decision may not always be easy, especially if the scale is small. Here is where you must begin to consider the language of your model, much in the same way you began establishing a language with your sketching. Regardless of how small or large it is, how functional or not, the model must be coherent and present to your audience its inherent reality, maintaining a point-to-point connection with the physical reality that the design will eventually inhabit. In other words, each element of the model has a direct reference to one, and only one, element of physical reality. Just like spoken and written languages maintain a clear individual meaning for each of their words (for the most part), the language of your model should be clear and allow for no ambiguity in terms of which model element represents what real texture, material, and so on.

How much detail do you need to make the correct statement?

CREATING MODELS AND SAMPLES

It is worth noting that I am using the word *model* in its widest possible application, meaning any kind of sample, mock-up, or attempt at physical representation of an idea, ranging from a standard architectural model to a sample garment on a mannequin. The creation of models and samples at this stage of any design is an attempt to bring the idea into the real world and help us understand how the design will function there. But why now? Why not wait until the idea is more developed and create a final model in one go, rather than one that will very likely only be a temporary representation of the design?

Modeling can, like sketching, be a very efficient way of exploring a design. There are huge benefits to making one at this point, but also dangers.

Creating a model is the best way to become acquainted with the possibilities your design contains in regard to textures, functionality, and manufacturing techniques. Not only can you use the model to show what your design can do, you can also use the model building to explore and solve issues of functionality and construction. The model will also allow you to try finishes, textures, and techniques.

There is a trap that not only student designers fall into. That is to think of a model as a sacred object, created once and observed with reverence thereafter. Realize that you can use models as sketching exercises, to experiment and explore. Make models for different purposes and from different materials. In the same way you would sketch on a napkin with a ballpoint pen, you can create sketch models from available materials and scraps.

Creating a model brings the design into the world. No matter how good the drawing or diagram, there is a different perception of an object we can touch and view from different angles. Even when viewing virtual models on a computer screen, we are still looking at two dimensions. Animated virtual models approximate the sense of space, but there really is no substitute for substance. As soon as something is in the world, taking up space, and very much there, we perceive it differently. We are beings who live in space and time and take a different view of things that share all our dimensions. Even if it's just sitting around, the model will develop its own presence and character for you to explore as well.

The Model Is Real, but It's Not the Real Thing

The realized model is extremely valuable in demonstrating the design to clients. You may have lived with the idea for some time and feel you know everything about it, but the client may not have seen anything yet and may not be good at visualizing or understanding sketches. By bringing in even a very basic model, you are essentially anticipating that problem and fixing it for your client.

Everyone enjoys a look into the kitchen. Watching someone at work is informative and often entertaining. Bringing in a model invites your client to come inside your process.

However, this may also invite some issues. You may find that the client buys the ingredients, but not the recipe. In other words, the client may focus on the individual elements of your model or your methods of construction but not approve the sum of the parts. If you create a conceptual model, the client may mistakenly believe that because the model doesn't work that the final design won't work either. Perhaps a client will expect too much because you made a model look so good and it's not immediately clear that the end result will work. This is especially problematic with computer design, whether it is graphic or three-dimensional. Graphics pop on a computer screen, as the screen is a light source, and you can achieve colors on a screen that most printers cannot duplicate. The key is to keep reminding yourself, and the client, that the model is not the real thing.

Let your clients be involved in your work process. Invite them into the kitchen.

You must be careful when presenting a mock-up that your meaning is clear. What exactly are you presenting: the look, the function, or both? Perhaps you are only presenting a part of the whole idea. Declare this up front and the confusion (yours included) will be less.

"A hand points at the moon-the fool looks at the finger"
—Chinese proverb.
Make sure your audience knows what you are showing them; make sure you know.

In addition to having to deal with the issue that the model is not the real thing, there is also the issue that the model will not actually live in the real world. It will not be subjected to the daily grind, and therefore certain problems that will develop over time are not observed.

More often than not, the model is made from substitute materials and cannot be subjected to any of the rigors of existence—a problem that becomes even more acute when dealing with virtual models. Since the virtual world does not contain any temporal or environmental forces, unless they are carefully programmed in, we may assume that the design will survive out in the real world. The better the simulation on the screen, the easier it is for us to suspend our sense of reality.

The solution is to try to envisage the object in full contact with reality. Use rough models to imagine situations and carry out as close a simulation as you can. Do the math, get the experts, do whatever you can, but above all, try *something* rather than just assuming (and hoping) that all will be well.

Scaling Problem

A very dangerous aspect of modeling is that behavior, both human and natural, does not scale well at all. Something that works perfectly well in miniature may not work at all when scaled up. The problems can basically be divided into those of *forces* and *interaction*.

Force problems are concerned with the effect of the environment on the object, most notably gravity (load) and any kind of impact (friction or stress). For example, architecture requires knowledge of what is known as the *square-cube law*. While strength is proportionate to the square of the linear dimension, mass is proportionate to the cube of the linear dimension.

A problem of scaling shown with the square-cube law: By scaling the block on the left up by a factor of two, we arrive at a block (right) with a footprint that is four times as large and a mass eight times as large.

Strength, however, is dependent on the cross-section of the object. Using the block example, a single block has a single face pressed to the ground. However, the cube two blocks high has four faces pressed to the ground. (It's composed of two levels of four blocks.) This is the cross-section, and it is the square of the linear of dimension. A building with twice the thickness of girders, compared with another one, is therefore four times as strong—but if the building is also twice as tall as the other, the weight pressing down on those girders is eight times as much. This is why large animals tend to have thicker legs than smaller animals have, and so architects need to give large buildings proportionately stronger supports.

In apparel design, if a sample is created to scale, similar rules apply to fabric and yarn. A small piece of fabric is harder to tear than a large one, as the stresses increase geometrically, and the load-bearing strength of yarn and thread is also subject to the square-cube law.

The danger in modeling is that we could happily go along and create a model using the materials planned for the finished object, and at the scale we're modeling, everything holds up. Then later we build a full-scale version and "snap!"

Beware if you are using your model to describe in any way loads, forces, and movement. The object that moves around lightly in a scaled-down version may just hang there, or worse, crash to the ground when it's created to scale.

Interaction problems come into play when a designer assumes that users and the environment will interact with the object in the same way in larger scales as they do in smaller scales. I have witnessed this problem in theatrical design on more than one occasion, especially in the case of onstage stairs. Viewing a model, no one would comment on the stairs. I learned (not too soon) to very carefully discuss possibilities of this sort at presentations, so the reality represented in the model would be clear to everyone. I would even warn the actors, "This is going to make you nervous when you see it onstage." Despite this, the full-scale reality would come as a shock to some, and the purpose of the design would have to be explained again. Be aware that this is not a problem of your audience's intelligence or the clarity of your model's information. This is a problem of perception and how people internalize information. A model is a model, regardless of how much is said. It requires a mental journey on behalf of the audience, and you, the designer, must help your audience make that trip.

Interaction can also be different for differently scaled environments. A building can be only so large before the inhabitants need elevators, scooters, and such. The maintenance required for a small garden-square, is far different from that for a large park. Maintenance crews may need vehicles, which require larger paths, which in turn lead to a desire for larger shade trees. These consequences can continue in a chain reaction far beyond any intent of the designer.

Don't get so involved in your model that you forget to make the necessary calculations, and make a point of researching any similar situations and designs you can find.

Obsession with Modeling Techniques and Methods

A variation on the above problem, and perhaps a more common one, is becoming completely obsessed with the model making to such a degree that the actual design fades into the background behind the technical and practical aspects of the modeling. This obsession is understandable but nonetheless something to avoid. We fall for the fun and charm of finally creating something tangible, and if it is a scale model, our inner ten-year-old selves take over.

On a more difficult note, obsessing with model creation is also a way of deflecting issues that are perhaps more serious. The model we can solve, the questions it raises perhaps not. Focusing on the model becomes a way of avoiding the more problematic issues at hand. It is easy to avoid this dilemma by focusing heavily on getting that texture right or making sure the scale is absolutely perfect. But the problem does not go away while you play with your model. On the contrary, it becomes worse by the fact that when you finally look up from your model, there is now less time than before to solve the problems.

If you are aware of the design hierarchy of needs stated above, you can make sure your priorities are in order, and having solved all you can, you can blissfully hyperfocus on the detailing of your model *after* you are sure you can fulfill the needs of functionality and reliability. If not, then using the model to solve these problems is the thing to do.

STRATEGIES

Dimensionality

Deciding on the presentation method of the model gives you the framework to work inside and a clear endpoint for your modeling. Your basic choices begin with making it either two- or three-dimensional. Next you consider whether you will present a functional model. Then you can decide whether you are presenting a physical or virtual model, and finally you can choose to create an animation if you have decided on functional or virtual.

In most cases, the default route for a functional model is three-dimensional, unless the project is in graphic design. However, two-dimensional diagrams can also convey all the relevant information, especially if you are modeling processes or functions over time. A three-dimensional model has the obvious advantage if depicting a three-dimensional object, but perhaps the full three-dimensionality is not the main concern of the design. Perhaps the central issues are the cross-sections, silhouettes, flowcharts, or process diagrams. Think very carefully about what exactly you are showing your audience, before creating your model.

Although modeling techniques have remained the same over the past few decades, the one change that did take place in the last decade of the 20th century is an enormous one: the rapid development of computers as tools for modeling and the creation of animations and rapid prototypes.

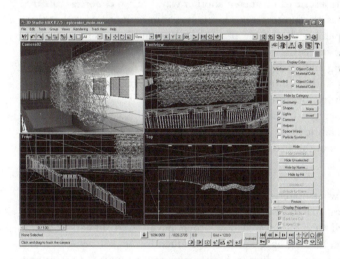

Three-dimensional design programs allow for an incredible amount of detailed visualization during the design process.

Virtual models often look fabulous and have the ability to be quickly translated into instructions for laser cutting or rapid prototyping. The inherent danger of a misperceived reality is always present, however, and I have also found that the hyperreal textures and environments in a CAD model can be distracting to an audience. The focus becomes the presentation, not what is being presented. I have found it to be helpful to include some element in a virtual presentation that "gives the game away." For example, a designer might follow a set of lifelike renderings and animations with a more sketchy set of images or wire frames. This reminds the audience that they were looking at a simulation. Sometimes less reality is better and encourages the audience to consider the designs as works in progress.

Functionality

The dimensionality of the model may be decided by how functional the model should be. Any mechanical function immediately implies three dimensions, but there are degrees of this. Does everything have to be three-dimensional? Are you modeling parts, or is everything put together? Can you model only the parts that require three dimensions?

If you are designing in two dimensions, how are you going to present? Are you printing or showing slides or projections? If presenting two-dimensional graphics, you must decide on the printing technique and medium for printing.

Choosing a Scale

If it is left up to you to choose the scale, the best way to approach this is by asking what the smallest model you can make is so that it still functions and displays the design as clearly and accurately as is necessary? Do stay within the standard scales, though. Make sure you know what scale your audience is accustomed to. It can be very confusing to be presented with a scale different from the one you are accustomed to, especially if the difference is not large. I came out of college in England versed in creating models in 1:24 and garments in 1:3 only to find myself in a theater where the rules were 1:20 and 1:4. Needless to say our scaling languages were thoroughly confused at the beginning. No matter how sure we were of the numbers we were looking at, there was an experiential threshold that could not be crossed so easily. I would read the models as if they were in 1:24 despite knowing that they were not.

The problem of choosing a scale can be taken another way. We can choose a scale that best allows us to use materials to represent our object. It is interesting to note that there seems to be a "reality threshold" in the scaling of models. It would seem that somewhere around one-twelfth scale for industrial objects and one-third scale for fabrics our brain becomes much more forgiving and ready to accept the models and anything larger as real. This is due for the most part to the scaling of textures and the material's physical behavior. Most textiles, for example, simply because of the mechanics of their weaving need a certain ratio of area to drape convincingly. Once you get below one-third scale, the thickness of the weave takes over and the fabric looks (and feels) stiff. Of course, architectural and theatrical models must, by virtue of the size of the subject matter, be at a much finer scale.

Choosing Materials

Think very carefully about what materials you will need for your model. What are you looking to represent? The real materials may not scale well, so you may have to be very innovative and allow yourself time to research how others have solved similar problems. Techniques of physical model making have not changed much in the past decades, and a quick visit to a hobby shop can give you clues on how to represent textures to scale or how to actually build objects. There you will also find softwoods, balsa, plastic clay, and other staples of model making. There is a good reason why the techniques of physical model making have not changed: They work. You may find the solutions by research, but you may have to invent your own, so allow yourself time to experiment.

Often we must substitute one material for another, so that it will "read" correctly in the scale. Wood does not scale well, as the texture is so easily discernable. A solution to this is to use another wood with a finer grain, or—if the scale relatively small—paper or plastic clay. Metals and glass scale well texturally, but not in terms of thickness. Here we find ourselves resorting to plastics, clay, or paper. The substitution then relies on a textural handling for believability, and we can apply varnish or paint and various powders to simulate textures.

Time Management

When creating a sample or model of a new design, it is very important to allow for experimentation and the redoing of things. Take a moment to think about the steps you must take to create your model, and assign time to each. You must plan time for getting materials, creating components, assembling, finishing, and preparing for presentation. Consider which elements may require more than one attempt, and multiply the time for those. Then add some time for unexpected difficulties, and you should be in good shape.

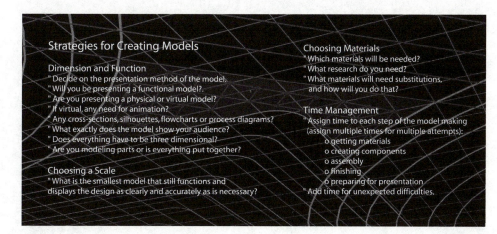

Strategies for Creating Models

Dimension and Function
" Decide on the presentation method of the model.
" Will you be presenting a functional model?.
" Are you presenting a physical or virtual model?
" If virtual, any need for animation?
" Any cross-sections, silhouettes, flowcharts or process diagrams?
" What exactly does the model show your audience?
" Does everything have to be three dimensional?
" Are you modeling parts or is everything put together?

Choosing a Scale
" What is the smallest model that still functions and displays the design as clearly and accurately as is necessary?

Choosing Materials
" Which materials will be needed?
" What research do you need?
" What materials will need substitutions, and how will you do that?

Time Management
" Assign time to each step of the model making (assign multiple times for multiple attempts):
 o getting materials
 o creating components
 o assembly
 o finishing
 o preparing for presentation
" Add time for unexpected difficulties.

Strategies for model and sample creation. Not all items on the list may be relevant at every instance.

REINSPIRE

Now that you have gotten to this point of the design process, it is very possible that a bit of fatigue is setting in. More than common, it is practically integral to the process. The initial excitement over the project gets buried in the practical details, the defining, and the planning. The amount of work ahead may be a bit daunting, and the way a studio works, you may find that now a new project has come in that looks much more exciting.

You need to remind yourself why this was a good idea and where you intended to go with it, before you make the big step toward commitment. If you don't, you may be in danger of the fatigue taking over, and the designing will become a chore since you will have to drag yourself unwillingly to do it.

Creativity is a positive act and must have a positive drive moving it forward. Doubly important, you are now at the stage of your designing where you are bringing other people into the project. Clients, colleagues, fabricators, and marketing staff will all look to you for inspiration. If you can't convincingly tell them and inspire their enjoyment, you are in for a gloomy relationship with your design. So reinspire yourself. If you are feeling a bit fatigued, go back to your sources and crank up the energy level.

IAN CUNNINGHAM, INDUSTRIAL DESIGNER

Ian Cunningham heads the design department for Rubbermaid, the food service products division of Newell Rubbermaid Inc., a Fortune 500 company headquartered outside Atlanta, with $6.75 billion in revenue in 2004. Prior to his arrival there, he had amassed years of experience as a consultant, designing in various fields.

The whole process of developing product is really exciting to me. Right from the level of understanding the design problem onward. Say you go to a dentist's office, and you see the tools they're using. A designer was employed and said, "What's a better way to help a dentist?" They've got a whole variety of tools there, and somebody was working on designing them. Design is just an easy thing for me to get excited about—I guess that's why I do it. Another thing is that it's just dead interesting to see how things are made. The way technology can help us create things is really very compelling to me. I still can't believe how we do some of the things we do in our plant in Ohio. We have some tremendous equipment there as far as automation and robotics goes. It's very poetic to watch these machines work. They're pulling 15 lids out of the cavity of this tool and stacking them up every five seconds. I just stand there and watch, and I think it's incredible.

For the most part I think industrial designers really enjoy their job[s]. I honestly don't think I've ever met one who's said, "This isn't really what I like doing." I have a lot of friends who don't like their jobs. They watch the clock, and at five o'clock they run out the door; they can't wait to get out of there. I can honestly say that I never look at the clock. It's weird to say, but half the time I'm wishing the days were longer. It's the kind of thing where all of a sudden I'll look up, and it's six o'clock—if I'm going to see my kids, I've got to get home. I think it's a matter of just doing what you love to do, then getting energized is almost easy. If you like doing what you're doing, that's inspiration enough.

Like many industrial designers, I came in through a side door; I really didn't know much about industrial design. I went through a marketing program thinking that advertising seemed interesting: a little bit on the creative side, a little bit of artistic capability. Then I started doing some work with sculptors, more in the fine arts area. During that time I found out about industrial design through listening to a radio program. One day, there was a program on NPR about a design firm that was designing garbage cans for the city of

Boston. There were a lot of constraints around the can. You had to be able to see into it; you didn't want people throwing anything into there. You had to keep rain out, but you wanted people to be able to get stuff into it easily, so it had to be covered, but not too much, and so on. All the layers that any design project goes through—that really appeals to me. Every product you look at, any product you interact with, somebody has put all this thought into it. That's what dawned on me, and I thought that this was the thing for me. So I went back to grad school for industrial design.

I wound up going to work at a consultancy and got experience in everything from consumer goods and electronics to medical equipment. I did a lot of retail and even interior work for retail spaces. That whole consultant world was a great foundation for me. You get so much variety in what you're asked to do on any given day, from toys to medical equipment to industrial machinery. Every day is a different little experiment in learning a new category or becoming an end user expert. I would advise any young budding industrial designer to jump into the consultant world first. It just gives you so much more diversity in the types of projects you see on a daily basis.

My job has changed dramatically over the past couple of years. I'm now heading a team of five industrial designers, and we do anything that deals with food and beverage that has the Rubbermaid name on it: food storage, beverage containers, and kitchen and bath accessories. So, we're in the Wal-Marts and the Targets of the world, and we also design for the more commercial or industrial user, like someone in a restaurant or hotel that needs larger volume and durability.

There really is a vast difference between the consultant's world and the corporate world. On one hand, as a consultant you may spend a week or two digging in, doing research, and really trying to become an expert in the field, knowing exactly what a person will do with the tool you're designing. Then you dive in, do the actual designing, and get the engineering portion done. Then you hand your baby off, very gingerly, to Corporate America. They take it, and you may never see it again. It may die a slow death within their doors, or it may come out the other end and not look anything like what you handed off. There's always some pain associated with that process. You're not really in control, and you don't have the ability to follow through on the manufacturing side of the business. In some cases, as a consultant, you get involved in programs where you walk things farther down the road, but it's much more the exception than the rule.

Then on the other hand, you get into a position like I am now, where you are working on a specific product category, and there's not as much diversity there. But as far as day to day activities go, there's a much broader spectrum of things that we get involved with. We're still doing all the front-end stuff, all the early conceptual napkin sketches, but we also travel to Asia or go to our manufacturing facility and work through conceptual problems with the manufacturing process. So we see many different levels and have much more opportunity for input along the way. Personally, I get much more satisfaction out of being in the corporate world. I really feel much more vested in the product. A product's success has a direct impact on my welfare and how my company is doing.

One thing a consultant background early in your career does for you is that it demands that you sketch more. I think you have to draw a lot as a designer to get good at thinking through problems; to think about three-dimensional solutions in a two-dimensional [medium]. That's very helpful. Another thing is the working in different categories. It's always amazing how something you've been working on in the toy industry or the medical industry comes back around: There was a way that something was molded, or there was a way something snapped together that applies to this food storage container that you're looking at today. It's really just exposure to different types of materials and different types of end users that adds to your experience or your knowledge base. If you focus on any one end user group too much or entirely, you don't get the additional experience that makes you well rounded as a designer. It's a critical component to my development as a designer to get to experience all those other demographics or lifestyles. You really do have to become a bit of an expert, if only for a day, on whatever product it is that you're designing. You're just not doing your job if you don't really understand how it's intended to be used or what the environmental conditions are that it is going to be used under. Those are things that are critical to being able to design new products.

As in any industry or company, our single biggest challenge is probably to have good clear communication. The industrial design team is part of the engineering group here at Rubbermaid, and we also have a marketing group. I tend to think that the industrial designers are in a gray area between marketing and engineering. I think we have to have both hats on at times, depending on what we're doing in the course of the day. We will, in many cases, be a conduit between the marketing and the engineering functions, so we have to be good communicators and be plugged into both sides.

I think that industrial designers are more focused on end user needs and that we're in charge of really establishing and maintaining the design brief for a project. We'll work with marketing at the beginning of a project to scope it out and make sure we're designing products that meet all of the key criteria for a given target market. The constraints can be almost endless. One of the things the marketing group is geared around doing is helping us establish what the constraints should be: what our target costs are going to be or how many ounces of water a container is going to hold and so on. They're going to help us make those decisions through a lot of methods. They'll use focus groups or observations, study a market, or just understand a consumers behavior through what products have historically sold.

Then the engineers are going to be more concerned about the functional side of the product, how it's assembled, and if it is cost effective and designed for manufacturabilty. Those are things that, as industrial designers, designing actual products, we have to be very focused on as well. So, there are the two very different roads that we'll go down.

Say at the beginning of a concept, we have some initial sketches, we'll take those to the focus groups. There we'll find out how to communicate the features and benefits to the end user, and we'll make sure that the participants understand all the intent behind the product. Then after that stage, we'll go to the other side, into the manufacturing facilities, and talk to the people who are actually producing the product and be very involved in that process from a functional and technical standpoint. That's the more physical link we create between marketing and engineering, but all along the way there are communication elements that the designers have to be involved with to help the other two groups work.

We may videotape people in their kitchens or go out to a commercial kitchen and watch them cook: What tools do they use, where do they store them, and how do they interact with all the products they use? Then, the way I see it, the industrial designer's duty is to make sure that those people are in mind when we are down to the nitty-gritty and making decisions. For instance, is that radius or that texture going to be comfortable for this person who's standing behind the line for six hours at a time holding a metal tong in his hands and flipping steaks? We're the only voice of the end user when it comes down to making decisions about what the product's going to be. We serve as an interpreter, making sure the needs of the end user are communicated into the product. The end users may not have the solutions, but they certainly can identify problems. We need to internalize and digest these problems and then produce solutions. And all along the way, we have to be communicating those solutions to the engineering group, the marketers, management, or whoever may be waiting for them.

As a design manager, it's a very similar experience as far as that whole process you go through, except that you're watching other people do it. Maybe I get more enjoyment out of it, in that I can contribute on a level that is more detail oriented. Making smaller contributions to the bigger picture becomes the way I get my creative fix.

I love the portion of the process where you'll be at that initial sketch-doodle stage, and the Eureka exclamation comes out. You're off on the side of the page doodling, thinking on the paper, and you hit on something that winds up turning into the end product. Then our process is such today that we are jumping very quickly into 3-D CAD systems, actually modeling the product. So in the space of 24 hours, you've gone from a little sketch on a napkin to a photo-real rendering of a product that you can show to somebody, who can understand the materials and everything you're intending to use. Computers have given us such a good tool to simulate reality. We can very quickly have some kind of representation that is very valuable in getting end user feedback or communicating internally within our design or marketing group. The marketing group is a very clever bunch of people, but they're not as visual as the engineers and designers, so having a realistic rendering as a tool to communicate with them is a great asset. There's usually this kind of 24- or 48-hour window in which an initial idea is conceptualized, and then we'll bring it into a more refined rendering level. That little 24-hour period is very exiting. You've got all the energy of this idea coming about and solving something, and then all of a sudden, you've got this visual representation of it, and you can make it any color you want and any texture and do all these exciting things to it. That's the most satisfying part of the job. In the matter of a day, you've created something.

REVISION AND MODELING

Examining the seven questions that defined the Identification stage with your current perspective, will show you where you need to bear down.

This exercise operates on two levels. On one hand, you are holding the current idea up to your thesis and revising either one. On the other hand, you are approaching the creation of your model.

1: WHAT WILL YOU DESIGN?

Here, in your design thesis, you gave a succinct description of your intended design. Most likely you can now add to that description. Does your idea, as it now stands, match the description you gave? What has changed? Most important, now that you need to create a model, what is still unclear?

1. Rewrite, add to, or edit the design thesis as necessary.
2. Create simple sketches illustrating your description with what you now know. As you sketch, keep a mental eye on the intended model, and use these sketches to help you plan its construction.
3. Consider how you will present the model and how this will affect the model's construction.
4. Choose a scale in which to create your model. Then decide whether your design is best represented in two or three dimensions and whether you should make a physical or virtual model.
5. What level of detail do you need in the model? Consider the importance of your details and how you would like to represent them.

2: WHAT IS ITS NATURE?

You described the design's function and components. There may or may not be a change in the functionality, but it is almost certain that you now know more about the design's components.

1. Is your model intended to demonstrate function, aesthetics, or both? How will it do this?
2. As it now stands, does your idea do what it was meant to do? Is there any question or problem about its functionality? How will you use your model to demonstrate this?
3. Will you need to sacrifice any capabilities or performance to achieve aesthetic goals? If so, is that acceptable?
4. Make a detailed, descriptive list of materials and components and how they contribute to the design's aesthetics and/or functions. Illustrate this list as much as you can with images and samples.
5. Consider how to represent the components in a model, and create a second list of these solutions.

3: WHO IS IT FOR?

It is possible that you can now envisage your design in a wider or different context than before.

1. Can you widen the definition of the end user?
2. How about the environment to which the end user belongs?
3. If the answer to either question 1 or 2 is "no," experiment with changing your design until the answer is "yes" and sketch out your solution. Either way, compare the previous idea with this one and decide whether your design has improved. Have you learned something new about your ideas?

4: WHY IS IT NEEDED?

As a result of the previous question, you can now examine whether your idea can be expanded to solve more than one problem or a wider concern than before.

1. Have you sufficiently solved the original problem?
2. Have any new problems surfaced?
3. If there are still unsolved issues, what do you need to do to arrive at a solution?
4. How will you present your model to best describe your design as a solution to the problems?
5. Where in the hierarchy of design needs does your design stand?
6. How can you move it up at least one level in the hierarchy? If it is already at the top level, can you make an even larger creative move?

5: WHAT ARE THE BENEFITS OF IT?

1. In light of the above, describe the benefits that will be derived from the design.
2. If this has not changed from the original thesis, consider what you could improve on to increase the benefits.

6: WHY IS THIS INTERESTING?

Now that you have been living with your ideas for some time, your perspective on the project should have widened and your vision become more detailed.

1. Reexamine why this project is (still) interesting to you.
2. How is it now more interesting to a client than before?
3. If you find that either of the above answers does not indicate enough interest and enthusiasm, what will you do to reinspire yourself?

7: HOW WILL YOU PROCEED?

Plan the creation and presentation of your model in light of all of the above.

1. Decide on a scale.
2. Plan how the model is to be presented.
3. Choose the materials.
4. Resolve how to construct the model.
5. Plan your time.

8: CREATE THE MODEL.

Communication

OBJECTIVE

This chapter highlights that a designer's main responsibility is clear communication. It reviews what is being communicated, to whom, how, and why. You will have an opportunity to explore the different venues, methods, and styles of presentation and see how a design presentation is a performance and can be prepared as such. At the end of the chapter, there are exercises that show you how to prepare a presentation.

KEY CONCEPTS

- Communication is a key factor for successful designing throughout an entire project.
- Different audiences use different modes of communication.
- The methods, media, and presentation style you choose contribute to your message.
- A presentation of designs is a performance, and a designer can prepare like an actor.

THE ART OF COMMUNICATION

Designing is the art of communicating an idea, and communication is therefore a key issue throughout the whole design process. Presentations and discussions, large and small, take place from the very beginning of your inspirational stage onward. Presenting communication as a separate stage should in no way be taken to mean that it is only important at this stage of the process. It is simply presented as the sixth stage because at this point you are ready to present the designs in its finished state. You must consider, in addition to the actual ideas and designs themselves, the best way for you to present them. You will have to see which media and presentation methods are most ideal, so you can get your design thesis's message across.

Communicating a message through media has three basic phases or moments. The first is the *encoding* phase, in which the message is created using professional and medium-related conventions of language and image use. You encoded your idea when you wrote your design thesis and created a concept board. The second phase is the *message itself*, the form and content of what is shown: a product or construct that is created through skill and technical practices. Here you fleshed out your designs with sketches, and perhaps you created a model. The third phase is the moment of reception, or *decoding* by audiences, in which the audience makes sense of the message and places it in context.[1] You achieve this with additional sketches, illustrations, and, ultimately, presenting your designs before an audience who gets your message and decodes it by placing it in a context that is relevant to them.

A designer "encodes" and "communicates" a message to her colleagues who, in turn, "decode" or make sense of the meaning and translate it into a physical reality.

Your responsibility to your audience is to make certain that they do get the message. You must present the designs clearly and without ambiguity. If there is anything unclear about your message, the reception will be likewise unclear, and your audience will be confused. You must give the audience everything they need to make sense of your designs.

Designers must communicate with everybody and therefore tend to operate outside organization charts. The designer has issues to discuss with clients, managers, budgeting departments, public relations representatives, engineers, construction crews, other designers, and assistants. The audience is very diverse and has diverse needs and a diverse understanding of the design problem. Each of the audience members views the problem from a specific perspective, and each perspective is relatively correct. After all, they want to know how your decisions are going to affect them and the jobs they need to do.

For this reason, it is crucial that designers understand their audience, what their perspectives are, what they need, and how best to deliver these needs to them. Don't take this to mean that you should just simply give everybody what they want. It is often the designer's task to educate clients, to show them that what they *need* is actually different from what they *want*. Often this involves pushing the project up a step or two in the hierarchy of design needs. To do this effectively, designers must develop clear communication between their clients and themselves. Designers must be consistent about the images, materials, and words they use.

This brings us back to the development of language and meaning, whereby each element of language, whether it is spoken, written, or visual, must have a point-to-point relationship with the world being described. In other words, you and your audience must speak the same language, where it is clear that "A" refers to "this" and "B" refers to "that."

THE AUDIENCE

The different audiences you will be presenting to have different needs and expectations. Clients, corporate officers, production staff, and fellow designers will be looking for the information they need and will present different communication challenges to you.

The Client

Never forget that clients are the people who drive the issues. Your client's needs prompted the need for your design, so you must respond to those needs (not necessarily follow them). You may challenge, educate, and surprise your clients, but whatever you do should be a result and continuation of dialogue. Talk to your clients at length and in detail. Examine their needs, and determine the constraints these needs will place on your design. Solve the problems, and take the solutions one step up the hierarchy of needs if you can.

I have recently worked with a software designer who is creating a customized CAD tool for sculpting and shape generation. In using the software, I ran into problems and found that certain things could be better. Invariably, when I gave him the problem, he presented a solution that was more general than what I had requested. He solved not only the problem I brought to him, but also eliminated the *type* of problem from the program. Although as the client I was right, I was not as right as possible.

Designer/client communication is defined by the needs of the client and the methods and techniques of the designer. This is not always a balanced mix. In the example above, my needs for the software were defined by the results I wanted and the way I wanted to interface with the software. When the designer asked me what I needed, my answers were in terms of usability and situations. He developed lines of code to fix my problem, but the programming is language I don't understand. In this case, the language of our dialogue is defined by my experience. However, the frame of reference can shift. Regarding confusion about the nature of the data I was using, our conversation began to focus on mathematics, as this was the only way he could understand how the data was meant to function. In this case, the designer's methods and his needs dictated the language.

Be careful that the flow of information between you and the client is not just one-way. If there is an imbalance in the strength of your personalities or the intensity of your discussions, there is a danger that one of you will override the other; this only leads to missed opportunities for both. You may need to show your clients where their ideas are not quite the right ones, and you may need to hear your clients' opinions and worries. Make sure you listen at least as much as you speak, and be aware that although you speak the client's design language, the client may not speak yours. Help your clients articulate their needs and desires by leading them through the project and explaining the issues and terms involved. Time spent on educating the client will be rewarded and will prevent future misunderstandings.

Corporations

If you design for a corporation, the levels of communication increase dramatically, as does the compartmentalization. There are managers, salespeople, and public relations staff. There are shipping, financial, and marketing issues. Some years ago I was working for an exhibit design firm that designed for a large industrial firm. Our client meetings were always an event, as they had to field five department heads, a project manager, and, on occasion, the head of their company. We added three to that group: the head of our company, a sales representative, and me (the designer). Ten people were sitting around a table, each coming at the project with a specific agenda. It was interesting to see the dynamics form in the first meeting: The department heads viewed the project, a 300-square-foot exhibit space, strictly from the points of view of their departments and how it would affect them practically and personally. The project manager tried to make sure everybody's needs were met and deftly compromised without stepping on anybody's toes. The head of the client's company seemed interested only in the aesthetics of the design; his concern was about the company's image, and he left the practical aspects to those who really needed to worry about them. To him we spoke about design and impact. With the department heads, we talked about practicalities of space and setup. With the project manager, we discussed logistics and deadlines. I had to be able to listen to each of these needs, translate them into design constraints, and answer each person within the relevant frame of reference. Then these discussions became material for aesthetic, spatial, structural, logistic, and time-management decisions, which could then be presented and discussed at the next meeting.

Inside a corporate structure, the dynamics of the situation above apply every day. You communicate up and down the organization chart and more than likely answer to someone and may have others answering to you. Regardless of the size or organization of the firm, you will very likely be on a level somewhere between management and manufacturing, communicating with both, sometimes even mediating their demands. You will have colleagues who will need leadership, consulting, and support.

Information becomes, by necessity, very compartmentalized in a corporate situation, which increases efficiency by not overloading everyone with unnecessary information. However, it can also lead to problems if someone is "left out of the loop." This someone could be you, of course, so be vigilant about the flow of information: where it is going, what it contains, and whether it is complete. If you miss a meeting, get all the information you can—from more than one source if you are not sure you are getting everything. Conversely, make sure you inform your colleagues, as necessary, in a concise and organized manner.

Manufacturing

On the manufacturing level, the character of the discourse becomes very specific. The language you use becomes mostly directed toward very practical matters, and the information boils down to lists of materials and diagrams. The designer's job with this group becomes one mainly of oversight, but there is also an element of being on hand to answer questions, solve problems, and guide the design back on course.

Sometimes the construction is simple, and the designer's job revolves around textures and finishes. At other times the construction is complicated and requires constant checking. Either way it is the designer's responsibility to make sure all solutions are serving the project's needs.

It is very important to respect the people who are responsible for constructing your designs, as they hold the creation in their hands. Seek them out if possible and engage them in dialogue about the project, discuss any foreseeable problems, and listen very carefully. It is very likely that you will encounter people whose experience is far beyond yours, and they may be able to teach you something new in every conversation you have. By creating personal connections you are also making everyone's life easier for future projects. They know you and how you work and vice versa. Such cooperation leads only to good things.

I was incredibly lucky to work with very experienced and talented tailors, builders, lighting designers, and photographers immediately after graduating from art school. I learned immensely from them on technical matters as well as the hands-on approach to their jobs. I soon realized that I could create the best designs under the sun, but if I did not have their talents to work with, the product of my designing would be just a pile of pretty pictures and samples. This awareness was one of the most valuable lessons I have learned.

Associates

If you are in a corporate situation, it is highly likely that at least a couple of people will be working with you. Having a team is incredibly helpful for brainstorming, sharing the workload, and moral support.

You will find yourself on a team. Often, you will be playing more than one position.

Being part of a team, whether you are leading it, means that you have to be part of the team. If you are leading, treat everyone equally and find out what each individual's strengths are. The not-so-secret ingredient is dialogue. Create and encourage an exchange of ideas, and know when to discuss and when to work. Brainstorming will help. The language of your colleagues will be the easiest one to adapt to, as you all share the common goal of getting the job done. Odds are that among you the team has a combination of talent and vision that makes you better than if you were working individually. Keep the communication open so that all members share information. Allow each team member to work and discuss things within their expertise.

Communication within a team is best when it is frequent, to the point, and relevant. (If used correctly, e-mail is a gift to team communications. Short, clear messages with good subject lines keep everyone informed in a very efficient way.) Quick group meetings on a regular basis are very helpful, as everyone should be heard and recognized, and there is a level of openness and spontaneity that develops.

INFORMATION

When you are presenting a design, there are four levels on which the information you are dealing with can be: *statement, concept, detail,* and *planning*. These correspond to an increased level of detail you are communicating. There is also clarity, a sense of purpose, and a pragmatism that increases as we move up from one level to the next. The line at which your information changes from one level to the next is not necessarily clear, but it is good to be aware of these distinctions.

Statement

When you introduce a project at the statement level, you are basically stating your matter-of-fact intent: the who, what, where, and why. You created information at this level when you prepared your design thesis. (See the exercises at Stage 2.) The aim is primarily to inform. The client needs to know where you are going, the team needs to know what it will be working on, and manufacturing needs to know roughly what is coming down the road. Management will want to know how much it is going to cost and when it will be ready. There may not be many details at this point, and discussion tends to be about large issues and general definitions of the project.

Concept

When you create concept boards and sketches during the concept and exploration stages, you investigate and flesh out your ideas. You may have done this with little regard to manageability or even reality, and the information you were dealing with would have reflected this by being nonlinear and loosely relevant at times.

The designer must ensure the team remains realistic about the project. In doing so, you will ensure the information you get at this level, through brainstorming and exploration, will feed back into the project rather than just dissipate in endless discussion. If the client is at all involved at this point, it is to be a sounding board for the various concepts being explored. Make sure you listen very well to the client, and remember to clarify any language problems. The most important thing is to treat the information that is swirling around seriously and not dismiss anything until it has been thoroughly examined. The amount of information is often immense, and you may not be able to decipher all of it at once, so keep everything. Later on, something may suddenly be very clear.

Detail

At the detail level, the idea is turning into a physical object, perhaps through modeling, definitely through more detailed sketching and illustration. Now you are in the definition and communication stages of the process and getting ready for manufacturing. All the increasingly detailed information going back and forth among you, the client, the design team, and the manufacturer needs to be coordinated and checked for accuracy. Communication is the key with information at this level. If there are any questions or problems at this point, they should be cleared up before you move on. As the number of people involved has increased, the complexity of communication is increasing exponentially, and thereby increasing the danger of misunderstanding. Make sure everything is perfectly clear to everyone. Keep the key people informed without throwing all the information at everyone. Making people wade through piles of information to find the one or two things they need to know is not helpful. Each group you are communicating with may require a different set of facts presented in a certain way.

Planning

The planning level is when we direct information about our design toward the future. In the communication and production stages of the design process, the discourse begins to turn from the development of the design itself to what should happen next and how. Practical matters may be out of the designer's hands, and the information coming from the manufacturing side becomes the focus. The designer now keeps an eye on the project to learn what could be improved for future designs. The information in question can be very practical, such as budgetary information or procedural problems; the information can also be reactions to and opinions about the finished design. This closes a circle, bringing the information back to the conceptual level. Observe people's reactions, and get technical feedback from production for future improvements. Document as much as you can. The cycle of design projects can be months or sometime years. You will appreciate having kept a journal of your thoughts and impressions.

VENUE

The venue of the presentation can affect its style and outcome, and different venues may require different preparation. Mostly, design presentations are a relatively informal affair: a meeting of people who are interested and involved in what is being designed. The atmosphere is generally calm and matter-of-fact, and time constraints are not necessarily a problem.

In formal presentations, however, things can suddenly get *very* formal. People take their positions very seriously, and there can be fairly serious questioning. In a formal presentation, such as a design competition, there are often very strict limits to the presentation in terms of time, size, and scale. The difference in preparation should really be none at all. The same rule applies as for the dress code at an interview: You should always be one stage of formality above your interviewer.

In terms of venues for a presentation, you will find yourself in one of three: You go to the client, the client comes to you, or you meet at a third-party venue, such as a restaurant or perhaps at a manufacturer's premises. Sometimes the presentation even takes place without you present. If the client comes to you, you have the home turf advantage. This can be good because you can control the level of formality, but it can also be a distraction because you not only have to prepare for a presentation but also play host, even if it's only in a small way. The home turf advantage comes in the form of you having everything you need right at hand. You don't have to pack anything up or risk leaving anything behind. However, depending on your situation, you may not be in premises suitable to receive the number of visitors you are expecting, so make sure you know how many people are coming and who they are. Make sure you have a minimum amount of space to comfortably show your designs, and if your studio is busy, make sure there will be no distractions while you are with your clients.

If you are going to the client's place of business, you do have to prepare for the traveling and create a transportable presentation. You may be going into a situation you are unaware of, so try to be ready for various eventualities. It is perfectly acceptable to ask your hosts what kind of meeting arrangements they will be setting up, such as what type of venue, how many people will be present, and so on, so you can gauge how easily visible your images and text need to be. If you are using presentation equipment, such as projectors, easels, and so on, try to be completely self-sufficient. Bring your own equipment if you can, even if they tell you that they have what you need. This has saved me on several occasions, where I have been told, "No need; we have all that" only to find that the equipment is incompatible, not working, and, in one case, not even there. Check all your equipment the day before to be sure that it works, and double check that all cables, remotes, batteries, and other accessories are packed and ready. Allow for setup time in your planning, and when you get to the venue, if you have setting up to do in front of the audience, don't be embarrassed and pretend its not happening, while you fumble with your cables. Just announce, "I need a moment to set up, and we'll begin. Thank you."

If the meeting is at a third-party venue, such as a restaurant, factory, or conference, it is likely that this will be the least accommodating option. You will find yourself presenting at a small, cluttered, café table, on a noisy factory floor, or in a hotel room that doesn't even have a table. In preparing for this scenario, the obvious choice is to create presentation materials that are small and easily passed around. Mounting everything on small boards (for example, 9" x 12") is often a good idea, as they are then easily held and passed around and will fit on an 8.5" x 11" sheet of paper and in a briefcase. Meeting in such locations holds its own set of terrors, such as spilling coffee, industrial solvents, or worse on your designs. Traveling also implies lost luggage, folders left at check-in counters, and other such issues. For these reasons make sure you have copies of your work, and mark all your work, folders, and portfolios with your name and address. These situations also allow for many distractions, and you assume a great degree of focus. On the flip side, they can have about them an air of informality that is very beneficial to client relations and serves as an instant ice-breaker.

Finally, there is also the possibility that you are not presenting at all. Either the presentation is being delivered to the client for them to view at their leisure, or someone else is presenting it. The preparation in both cases is about the same. The exception is that if someone else from your company is presenting, then you have a chance to help them prepare. Either way, you should prepare a presentation that has all the information readily visible and logically laid out, with all the illustrations and documents numbered and captioned, so there is no danger of things being missed or misconstrued. Try to imagine any questions that may be asked and preempt them. Then test your presentation by showing it to someone, preferably with a similar level of knowledge as the future audience, and see whether everything is clear.

ORGANIZATION AND QUALITY

Whatever situation you are presenting in, the information needs to be organized. You must make sure your language and facts are directed to the audience, and for this reason, it is necessary to know the audience and what its demands and expectations are.

First, you must determine the *relevance* of your information. The audience has its needs, and those needs can be aesthetic, conceptual, technical, organizational, academic, or any combination of these. You must make sure whatever information you are giving them fulfills this need for relevance.

Second, you must determine the *immediacy* of what they need to know. Are you addressing current concerns, are you planning for the next stage, or is the discussion going to be about a future vision? Perhaps it is all of these.

Third, you must be aware of the *scope* of your information. How wide is your focus? You can be *specific*, focusing on details or singular issues, or your scope can be *broad*, ranging over the entire project. You can also be *universal* and connect your project to a wider context and relate the design's solutions to a larger concern.

LANGUAGE

Language can be either *emotional* or *informational*. Either you are appealing to the intuitive and visceral or to the tangible and logical. There's nothing to say that you can't do both, but you should have a handle on which you are doing. This will give your audience a much clearer frame of reference. We tend not to shift too easily from emotions to logic, so help your audience by not veering too dramatically from one to the other.

Make sure your language has a *point-to-point relationship* from its frame of reference to the designs. Check your descriptive vocabulary and make sure a word or phrase is not used to describe one thing in one context and another in a second context. For example, your presentation probably has enough information for the audience to deal with, without them having to parse every sentence, wondering whether "rough" was now being used in a tactile, visual, or emotional sense. Be as specific in your word choices as you can, and be careful about descriptive words that require judgment on behalf of the audience. If, for example, you were to ask five people to describe a "cool" shape, you would probably get five different descriptions.

Also, when considering language, you must be aware that your presentation contains language in three different modes: visual, written, and spoken. A visual statement may not be able to stand totally on its own and may require additional written or spoken information. Conversely, the images you use can also illuminate your word choices.

The rules of language differ from visual to spoken to written, but in all cases you should be clear and consistent. Make sure especially the written and spoken languages are each distinct in form. Written language has a more formal structure, and in the case of presentation boards, you are probably dealing with very factual information, bulleted lists, and "impact words." Don't speak in lists, and don't write in speech form.

THE ART OF PRESENTATION

Each stage of the design process, from Identification onward, usually involves a presentation of sorts. Certain projects I work on require large-scale presentations of posters, models, slides, and talks. Others only require an e-mailed image or two. It's difficult to tell which is more difficult—or more fun. It can be just as challenging to fit an entire idea into two pictures as it is to create an hour-long slideshow.

Either way, this is what it comes down to: You work for weeks or months on a project, and it all comes down to a presentation that is measured in minutes, megabytes, or numbers of images. Wrapping up a project often comes logically; the task is not difficult, since you have been presenting in one way or another throughout the process. At other times, a presentation will require a lot of work. There is an art to a good presentation.

Knowing how you are going to present a project ahead of time can be very helpful because you can tailor your work to the presentation. But this will vary, not only from discipline to discipline but also within industries. Even within the same company, I've experienced different members of the marketing staff requiring different presentation formats, depending on their methods and comfort levels as well as what their own clients need. Most often you will know what kind of presentation is required, and if not, odds are that you can do whatever you prefer. But never assume anything; look before you leap.

THE TAILOR'S RULE REVISITED

Before we go further, I would like to revisit a topic discussed at Stage 2: "The Tailor's Rule and Principle". I will justify the repetition by saying that the need for designers to plan time becomes increasingly greater as the details they are working on increase. Preparing a presentation is a double layer of scheduling, as you are planning for the time the presentation itself can take, as well as planning to get the presentation done before the deadline.

The Tailor's Rule.

The tailor in question, my former student who is a genius in the field of tailoring, follows this mantra when planning anything: "Everything takes at least 15 minutes." If everything takes at least 15 minutes, then you can plan to do only four things in one hour, 12 things before lunch, and around 30 things in one day. Give this some thought. It's like driving to a distant location on secondary roads. No matter how hard you try to sneak over the speed limit as often as possible, you find that your average traveling speed usually comes down to about 60 miles per hour. The explanation for this is that you don't account for the slow spells, the traffic lights, or the stops here and there. It's the same with getting anything done. You really have to be hyper-effective to get more than 30 things done in one day.

Now, you may say, "It depends on what you mean by 'things'," and you're right. "Things" refers to anything that really *requires* being planned. These are the things you would put first on a list: You don't write: "Sharpen pencils" unless you have a lot of them. In planning anything you must account for all the steps and do the math allowing for each step to take some time. Allow for downtime, mistakes, and unexpected occurrences. You will average out to "just above the speed limit." If you try to break the speed limit at all costs at all times, you will find that accidents do happen.

PRESENTATION METHODS AND TECHNIQUES

When planning a presentation, at whatever stage your project is in, you must be aware of structure, illustration techniques, and graphic design. Giving even just a little thought to these can make all the difference. Considering structure will allow you to shape the narrative of your presentation to your purpose. Being aware of multiple illustration techniques is essential, as you should like to tailor your technique to the project and not the other way around. Graphic design and layout allows you to create a presentation that not only looks good, but also influences how the audience approaches and experiences your designs.

Structure

A presentation most often follows one of three basic patterns, which are described using the following classical musical terms.

Andante

Andante is Italian for *moving* (literally, *going*). In terms of tempo, or rhythm, it is to go at a steady, moderate pace. This is a presentation that does just that. It has a beginning, middle, and end. You have an introduction, where you tell us what you are going to show us. Then you have a middle where you show us. Finally, you have an end, where you tell us what you showed us and ask for questions.

This is the "standard" for presentations. It lets everyone observe and absorb; it is logical and not showy. It is well-suited to audiences who want just the facts and need minimal prompting to sustain their interest.

You could, for instance, begin with an overview of the project, where you outline the needs and constraints. Then you could proceed through your process, show your designs, and finish up by tying your designs back into the needs and constraints, thereby making your case for your solutions.

Crescendo

This musical directive instructs the performer to gradually increase the volume to a climax. Your presentation would start in a low register, perhaps with an introduction to the design and the process, and gradually increase the pitch with more impactful images, saving the very best until last.

This is effective for an audience who needs to be sold on the idea. Perhaps the idea is unorthodox or has developed in a different direction from what was expected. By starting slowly and factually, spelling out what happened, you give the audience a chance to accept the underlying premise.

Crescendo: "Increase the volume." Your presentation would start in a low register, building to a strong finish; saving the very best until last.

Forte-Piano

This musical directive, which means "strong-soft," tells the performer to accent strongly, then diminish immediately to a softer delivery. Make a grand entrance with an impressive piece of work or information. Follow up with a swift "sell" of what you just showed. Once you have everyone's attention, tell the rest of the story.

A grand entrance is fun and should be used on an audience who is willing to be entertained. The ideal audience has perhaps had some indication of where the work is going and already has high expectations of the results. If they want a show, give them a show. However, a skeptical audience (there are plenty of them out there) will always ask, "Will it fly?" no matter how much you dazzle them.

You must also be very sure of your decision. Promising your clients an earth-shattering, world-altering experience, only to have them say, "Is that it?" is not where you want to find yourself. If you don't feel that you can really take your audience's breaths away, play it safe and avoid the grand entrance. Better to be safe and successful than disappointing.

A grand entrance is always fun, in the right crowd.

Illustration Techniques

It is very important for a designer to feel comfortable working with several different artistic media. The media you elect to work in help you to tell the story of your design and create an impression of its effect. For this reason, it is very important to choose the right media for illustration. The impression created by a pen-and-ink sketch, for example, is entirely different from that of a rendered CAD model. In addition to the choice of media, the layout and other graphic design elements of your presentation also add to its impact.

Pencil

I am always surprised by how many of my students do not initially realize the full potential of a pencil; they have become used to it as a tool for writing. It is, in fact, a very effective tool. You can create very deep and detailed sketches with a small collection of pencils. Pencils are also cheap, readily available, and easy to carry around. The pencil sketch reveals an artist's hand as clearly as handwriting, and has a characteristic earthy charm. Pencils respond very clearly to the hand holding them, as the technique requires only what the user is willing to put in. The overall effect of pencils can be used to create a sense of immediacy to a presentation, as well as an overall look of speedy efficiency. However, because the pencil is delicate and can be worked as slowly as you wish, a very elegant and studied look can be produced. In either case, the pencil connects with a viewer on a level of familiar artistry, and as a medium therefore tends not to get in the way.

Practice pencil sketches with the same attention you would give to practicing hand-writing: Pay attention to your posture and the weight of your hand. Experiment with different types of pencils and paper and how each responds to the other. Practice speed sketching with pencils to get to the point where you can, without hesitation, drop an image onto a page at a moment's notice. Do this by choosing a common subject, say the human figure or a teapot or anything that is close to the designs you will be working on. Sketch it repeatedly, always referring back to previous sketches to see what can be improved. Alternate a very light hand with a very heavy hand to explore the extremes of what your pencil is capable of. You'll be surprised at how much breadth there is in a simple pencil. Practice an economy of sketching. Try to work with as few lines as you can, letting every line on the page count.

Colored Pencils

There are colored pencils and colored pencils. The good ones are great and the others should be ignored. Colored pencils have been underestimated; they have been generally rel-egated to wax-crayon status. If this is your experience, get a good brand (Derwent, Faber-Castell, Prismacolor, or Staedtler) and your opinion will change. Experiment with the pen-cils both in terms of sketching and fine illustration. Use them in layers with a very light hand to mix colors, going from a light base color to darker shades. Try using a 6B graphite pencil to shade and outline with (this will add a sense of depth to the color.) A fine tip marker (e.g. 0.2 mm) can also be used to good effect in outlining and "cleaning up" a col-ored pencil sketch. I prefer the kind of colored pencil that is water-soluble, but never use water with them. I like them because they are softer and respond better.

Pens and Inks

Discussing inks, one must also realize that it is not only the ink but also the pen or brush that is the issue. Ink can produce very strong and clear illustrations and a wide variety and combination of textures. The range of inks is way beyond the scope of this discussion, but it would suffice to say that inks range in quality (and price) from the ink in a ballpoint pen to Chinese ink sticks sold for hundreds of dollars. Inks come in many colors and can be divided into inks for painting and inks for calligraphy.

For illustrations, the most basic form would be black ink and a nib pen. Calligraphers endlessly seek and quarrel about the perfect pen, and no one seems to have found one; therefore, I would suggest you experiment and find one you like. The things to look for in a good pen are how it sits and balances in your hand, how smoothly its nib interacts with the paper, and how well-regulated the flow of ink is. All of these contribute to the quality of the sketch.

A good pen-and-ink rendering can have a classical aura about it or emulate cartoonists and comic-book artists. Look at ink renderings from the Renaissance onward and examine comic books and graphic novels (high-end comic books) to find a style you like.

There is one danger to be aware of when using inks with brushes for creating washes and blocks of color: The pigments and dyes in different brands of ink may not work together in the way you expect. You may, for example, find that a wash that goes over another may turn into a muddy brown when you were expecting green or purple. Before you ink any of your drawings, experiment, especially if you are using inks you have not used together before.

Ballpoint pens have a unique feel to them, and quick pen-and-ink sketches illustrated with ballpoint pens on cheap paper, say newsprint or napkins, can be used to create a look and feel of effortless speed and urgency.

A pen, brush, and ink sketch.

Markers

The industry standard in design illustrations used to be markers, and they are still heavily used, although programs such as PhotoShop and Illustrator are gradually supplanting them. Markers are extremely convenient and can be bought in colors that match industry standards for prints and dyes. Markers should not be used for archival renderings, as the color fastness of a marker's dyes is not good. ("Permanent" on marker labels refers to their solubility in water.) To archive marker renderings, consider scanning them and having a print made using archival ink.

Markers have nibs of various shapes and thickness. They can be used as sketching tools along with pencils and inks to great effect, especially for outlining and shading. Experiment, for example, with a gray or blue marker on a pencil drawing to very quickly increase its depth and contrast.

A sketch rendered in marker.

Pastels and Crayons

Renderings in pastels and oil-crayons have a loose impressionistic style and are a quick way to convey a sense of motion and air in a presentation rendering. They can have very vibrant colors despite the popular notion of "pastel" being synonymous with "pale." Pastels require no drying time, and their colors are true and durable as they are made of almost pure pigment. Usually a fixative is necessary if they are to be used in a presentation as they smear easily. (Normally they would just be placed under glass.) This can be a problem as the fixative soaks the pastel and allows it to seep into the paper and other colors. Before embarking on a large project with pastels or crayons, you should experiment with the textures, paper, and fixatives.

The choice of paper or board is also important here because it has to be rough enough (called "the tooth" of the paper) to receive the pastel properly. Too smooth a surface doesn't grip the pastel stick and doesn't hold the pigment well. Try different types of paper and board until you are happy with the result.

Watercolors

Watercolors are a wonderful media to work with and can be used to create very detailed and colorful images. The one drawback is the drying time necessary, and I have often found myself aiming a hair dryer at a last-minute watercolor. Another thing to bear in mind is that each company has its own formula, and brands do not always mix well.

It is important to recognize that watercolors require care and proper materials. There is no point in using cheap watercolors at all, and no point in using good watercolors unless you are also using good paper and high-quality brushes. These things tend to be pricey, but as far as paints go, watercolors are far less expensive, as a rule, than oils or acrylics and a little watercolor goes a long way.

A painting rendered in watercolor.

CAD programs

There are a number of computer programs in use that are increasingly taking over the space held by all traditional media. For technical issues AutoCAD is the industry standard and deservedly so. Despite how heavy it is to steer at times, it is an enormously powerful tool. This is especially true when it is used in conjunction with a modeling program that can take over where AutoCAD leaves off in terms of rendering capabilities and creating environments. 3dMax, Solidworks, Rhino, and FormZ are all currently popular, but these and AutoCAD are generally expensive and therefore not available to the casual user. This means that for the most part you will be trained to use these on the job, unless you studied them in school. I have been able to train new users to become independent, if not highly proficient, users of AutoCAD in about 36 hours (one work week).

Rendering of CAD model created in AutoCAD and 3dMax.

PhotoShop and Illustrator

This software from Adobe is now nearly synonymous with "digital image editing" and a standard requirement in most design job descriptions. In allowing us to manipulate digital images to our hearts' desires, PhotoShop has completely changed how images are approached and treated for printing. Colors can be altered and matched, images edited, combined, and merged. Then there is the entire panoply of darkroom tricks and the ability to create Web-ready images.

Preparing for printing can be tricky, as the resolution of the original can be too low, and print speed at high quality can be infuriatingly slow. However, printer technology gets better every year. To print entire boards or large posters it is necessary to go to a professional printshop where the price will be calculated by the square foot and can go up very quickly, but the resolution will be better and the quality of the ink can be archival if necessary.

Remember that the computer screen can show far greater color variations than a printer can produce. If your print is larger than the screen you are working with by (roughly) a factor of two or more, a "scaling problem" occurs. It becomes difficult to have a sense of the impact the full-sized print will have. The perception of spatial relationships in the image can change once the print is created. This is especially true where there is a high contrast of colors. In the same instance, an image that scales largely upward from the screen to the print will magnify all inaccuracies. Create a test-print for cases like this well before you are ready to print finals to try to spot any problematic areas.

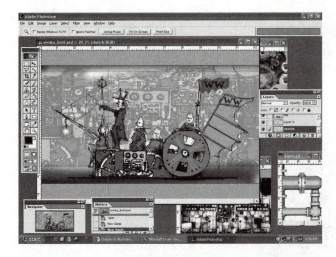

PhotoShop can also be used as a sketching tool, as it allows you to combine and layer images quickly.

Books and Boards

The most common method of presentation is to create a book or a portfolio-style binder containing text and images. This is extremely convenient and transportable and allows you to determine the order in which the audience views your information. Boards of text and imagery are also very commonly used, often in conjunction with books. The board becomes the focal point for the audience and speaker, and the book contains further, perhaps more detailed information and imagery to be passed around or viewed after the main presentation.

A presentation board is still the standard method in all design disciplines.

PowerPoint

Largely replacing the 35-millimeter slide as a format, Microsoft PowerPoint is encountered everywhere presentations are being held, whether it is in the classroom or the boardroom. Extremely easy to use, it can help even the most amateurish user create a clear, effective presentation with minimal effort. However, it has some very serious problems. PowerPoint is essentially a low-resolution format. It is good at showing images and creating the ever-present bulleted slide. It does not suit the presentation of highly detailed information, and you must fight the tendency to let the medium (PowerPoint) dictate the message (your designs).[2] Be very careful of editing your information to fit the slides. If you have a lot of text to convey to the audience, by all means summarize on the screen, but create handouts with the full details.

A portfolio book presentation.

Web Pages

The creation of Web pages for presentation purposes can be very convenient for a client who lives far from you. You can post your images, text, and journals online, and the client can peruse them at will. This suffers from some of the drawbacks mentioned for PowerPoint. There is only so much information that will fit comfortably on a screen, and people have limited tolerance for reading great amounts of text on a computer. You also have to be very aware of the navigational possibilities of your site. Make sure your viewers see everything they are meant to see and do not get lost or distracted in the process. Be also very aware that what looks good on your screen may wind up looking very different on someone else's, as their browser defaults may be different, or they may be viewing on a different monitor with a different configuration or aspect ratio.

Web pages are an excellent way of presenting designs to distant clients or when designs are being continually updated.

CDs

For digital media, such as Web pages or PowerPoint files, the possibility exists of burning the presentation onto a CD you can deliver to your client. Before you do this, try to make sure the client does not have any problems in accessing and viewing material on a CD. Check compatibility and platforms and try running your CD on a couple of different machines and different browsers before you send it off. The easier and more straightforward you can make this access, the better. Create folders and place files in such a way on the CD that the viewer will have no doubt about where to go. Burn an extra copy for your files so that if the client calls with questions or problems, you can look at the same thing on your respective screens.

Models

Just like the 35-millimeter slide, actual models are slowly but surely being supplemented, if not supplanted, by the virtual world. However, nothing beats reality, and the presence of a tangible object is a great way to connect the client with your work. It can be problematic, if creating a model to scale, to depict detail accurately, so consider more than one model if accurate representation of detail is required: One model can depict the entire object, and other models can depict detail at a larger scale.

The artist Brower Hatcher contemplates a quarter-scale section model. (See his "Perspective" in Stage 2: "Identification.")

Choose your modeling materials with care, as they will project their reality onto your design. Clay will look like clay; paper looks like paper. Unless you can use modelers' tricks to texture and disguise the materials accurately, perhaps you shouldn't even try. Just bring in what is called a "white model," such as architects often use. The model is then not textured or colored and is meant to illustrate only the spatial qualities of the design. The textures and colors are then presented in renderings and samples.

Virtual models and animations can be very arresting in a presentation for the level of detail and simulated reality they can bring. Be careful. Don't promise a reality you cannot achieve.

Use models mainly for the information they can bring, not as pretty props. Unless there are requirements from the clients about this, choose a scale and materials that best suit your purpose, then plan enough time to create a clean, accurate model.

Graphic Design

In Appendix 1, there is a more detailed examination of the elements and principles of graphic design, but it's important to note the importance of layout in a presentation. By your choices of typeface and colors and size and placement of text and images, you can control your audience's eyes and how they perceive your presentation. Your choice of paper or boards and the method of printing will speak of the quality of the presentation and, by extension, to the perceived quality of all your work, as well as of yourself as a designer.

When putting together a presentation allow for enough time in its creation that you can use your intuition as well as learned principles. If it feels right, it is very possible that it is right. Look for happy accidents in your presentation preparation, and keep your eye on the big picture while paying attention to the details. Both scales of perception will be important to your client.

A DESIGNER PREPARES

A presentation is a performance. To consider how to go about its creation, it is good to take our cues from those who do this for a living: actors. When preparing for a performance, there are a number of things actors must consider. They must be completely familiar with the script, learning the text and the actions as written; they must work with a director to establish physical and emotional movement, and they must establish an inner connection with their roles to create three-dimensional, believable characters.

A presentation is a performance. A designer can prepare in the manner of an actor preparing for a role.

Know Your Lines

A script is the basis for any performance, and a script's length is a matter of degree. Some performances have every word and movement spelled out; others leave much room for interpretation. In a good presentation, like a good acting performance, there is a certain balance between the scripted and the spontaneous. Certain things come from the script; the actors can then add emotional and physical aspects from their storehouse of talent. In learning the lines and actions and internalizing them, the actor understands the course the action will take and the meaning that must be delivered.

In a presentation of designs, this translates into knowing precisely what it is you are presenting and what you have to say about it. This comes back to what you can consider the outline for your script: the design thesis. What is it? What is its nature? Why is it a good idea? How did you get here? It is also good to realize at this point to whom you are delivering this. Some scripts are written for a knowing audience; some are not.

You, as a designer, do not have to know lines in the literal sense, but you do have to know the information that you are conveying to the audience. Your script is your knowledge of your work, and you can know those "lines" in the way an actor studies, learns, and internalizes a script. Look at all the information you have. It is good practice during a project to keep a journal of sketches and notes. Go through all this and revisit your process. Be able to discuss the choices you made and field any questions about options and possibilities. Know all you can about the material choices and manufacturing issues.

Know Your Props and Setting

An actor must know the lines, but as anyone who has seen a poorly acted play or film knows, the text is not everything. A good performance requires more.

Some years ago, I was working on a production of *Who's Afraid of Virginia Woolf?*. At the beginning of the technical rehearsal, something needed fixing, leaving the actors with little to do for a while. I was at loose ends myself, and as I sat in the auditorium, I saw the actor playing the lead male role of George walk onto the stage. Alone there, he proceeded to go through his first moments of the play repeatedly. He would enter through a door, flip a light switch, and go directly to a bar-cupboard on stage right. There he would, without really looking, pick up a bottle and glass and make as if to pour a drink. He would then put back his props, reset the light switch, go out, and repeat his actions. He did this oblivious to the machinations going on around him. Later that evening, when he gave the stage manager extremely specific instructions on where the bottle and glass should be placed for the top of the show, it occurred to me that I had been watching a masterful act of preparation. The actor was habituating himself to the environment and props to a degree of total naturalness.

In the play, the character George has been living in the house the set represents for more than 20 years and drinking quite a bit, it would seem. The actor, putting those first moments into physical memory, could be completely on autopilot. He could make it look as if numerous times over the course of many years, he had done exactly this: He enters and automatically flips the switch as he heads for the bar. His hands find the glass and bottle simultaneously; then, breaking out of automatic mode with a quick quizzical glance at the level of whiskey, he pours. The actor has told us an entire story without uttering a word. He sets the stage for his character's existence and informs us of his relationship to the surroundings. The audience is pulled into his situation as they unconsciously register his familiarity with the surroundings and his surprise at the level of whiskey. "Okay, he lives there; there's less whiskey than he expected." Then the question forms: "What's going on here? Did he drink it earlier? Did someone else?" One minute into the performance and already the audience is intimately involved.

Now, this level of sophistication may not be *de rigueur* for your average design presentation, but an approximation may be worth the effort. It is very important that you know exactly where you are going and to what end. The purpose of your presentation is to show and convince your audience of the viability of your ideas and to draw them into your sense of excitement about them.

You can prepare for this by repeatedly going over your idea until you are completely familiar with its nooks and crannies. Know the materials, techniques, methods, and finishes involved in the construction. Know exactly how it works, what it does, and how you feel about it. Be clear on where there are gaps in your knowledge and how you will approach filling them.

Do the same with your presentation materials. Be completely familiar with every element of your presentation, and know how you are going to use these and in what order. If there are technical procedures to display, make sure you have complete mastery of the tasks involved.

Know Your Direction

An actor is not alone in making decisions. A play will have a director making suggestions and decisions on approaches to characters and their actions. In a performance a story is told, or at least a point is made. The story is outlined in the script, but it is not fully told until it is put into action; the text is not everything. The actions and how they are carried out will tell the rest of the story and at the same time fill it out and give it life. How the arc of this story develops is a result of the collaboration between the director and the cast. The instructions given can range from simple movement, such as "Enter. Go stage right," to timing, such as, "Don't say that until you are halfway out the door," to more subtle motivational instructions: "How do you feel when you see her?" A director will also monitor the progress of the actors' interactions and the arc of their emotions, either heating them up or cooling them down, depending on how the story should unfold. It is also important to read between the lines of the script and uncover subtext; the director works with the actor to uncover this and bring it to the stage without words. In your presentation, you are both actor and director. You must decide where you are going and what you will do when you get there. You must also decide what to emphasize and what you can speed through. Furthermore, your inner director must know your inner actor well enough to know when the actor can wing it and when it's best to stick to the script.

Again, the method is for you to be thoroughly aware of the story you are telling. What is the information you are trying to get across? What is in the words? What is in the objects? What is in the actions? Know where to go quickly, where to pause, and where to be absolutely sure your audience is getting the message. For this reason, it is always a good idea to practice a presentation out loud and have a dress rehearsal. And if at all possible, practice with someone who can tell you if you are making sense and help you find the points that are not as clear as they should be.

Finally, the end result is to tell a story. It is the story of your idea: what it is, how did you came about it, and how it will develop from here. Tell the story in order; don't skip to the end until you have told the beginning and the middle.

Know Your Motivation

An actor will prepare for a role by creating an inner version of the character with a back story. The actor will create a past and inner life, motivating the actions, making them truer to life by adding *why* to the *what, how,* and *when.* The actor can thereby "live" the character, creating a much more identifiable person on the stage or screen. These back stories can be indicated in the script or totally made up by the actor. As long as the actor believes, so will the audience. Just as a salesman who doesn't believe in the product will not sell very much, a performer who doesn't approach the performance with motivation and energy will fail to hook the audience. When presenting a design, you will be both selling and performing. You must be inspired, or you will not be inspiring.

Just as the actor may need to spend an inordinate amount of time on the hidden work of motivation, you must find the time to connect with your idea on an emotional level.

Revisit the back story of your design and once again remind yourself of why this is a good idea, what its benefits are, and why you are happy about it. Connect your design with the world of the audience and let them feel how interested you are.

Do this by truly believing in what you have done. Now, it may just happen that you see "every compromise [and] every flaw" in your design. As you can well imagine, it will not be helpful to your audience's appreciation of your work if you spend your entire presentation pointing these out. Don't hide anything, but use these as a basis for constructive dialogue and perhaps your audience will brainstorm with you about a solution. Emphasize what is good and what works; be solution-oriented toward the rest. In this way you will create an atmosphere in your presentation where everyone is ready and willing to believe in the viability of your design.

PERSPECTIVE

MARK ZEFF,
DESIGNER/ARCHITECT

Mark Zeff is the president of Zeff Design, a multifaceted New York–based company working in architecture, interior design, furniture, graphics, product design, and marketing. Mark comes from South Africa via England, where he studied architecture and furniture design.

I think probably the most important component in the design world is the ability to communicate with your client and hear what the client wants. Then you must be able to translate that into an understanding between the client and yourself—of what the client is expecting and of what you can deliver. You must show that when a client gives you a budget or style parameter, you are able to move with it. The most important part of listening is being able to accurately turn what you hear into a working process. We've developed a series of processes that we take our clients through, and there are always checks and balances along the way, to weed out all problems, keep the project within budget, and deliver the expectation in terms of service and quality.

Sometimes, based on education or background, a designer or design firm becomes stuck in a certain style or genre or in a style of working. What happens then is that the communication with the client is manipulated into something different—not what the client wants, but what the design company can actually offer. What we try to do is to listen very carefully, so that after, or at, the first meeting, a design brief is set up. Here we say things like, "It's my understanding in this first encounter that this is what you want, this is what you don't want, this is how big it is, this is how much it is, and is this true?" "Have we forgotten that?" and "I have been reading your letter, and there were some other things you brought up," and so on. We always get this done first. Then, in my company, I have a weekly session at which my project managers talk to me about every single project we are working on. We go through them alphabetically, item by item, problem by problem, solution by solution, per job for the entire job. We'll identify what the problems are this week, and everybody in the room hears the same thing. This is neither one on one, nor is it a team thing. This is a company meeting, so someone who is not involved with the job in question still hears what the problem is and also hears the solution from me. The hope is that they will take that lesson and apply it to similar problems that come up in the jobs they are working on.

This takes three-quarters of the day, and by that time, we are up to speed with where we are with our projects and where we're going for that week. After that, we move into an inspirational discussion about new jobs, new ideas, or new things that are coming up, so everybody gets a sense of what I'm thinking, and we get a sense of what they're thinking. This builds strength in terms of communication.

Externally, what comes out of that meeting is a White Paper that's sent to the client, giving the status of the job at that particular moment. We also have online development sites, which a client can enter using a password to look at something that we want them to see. We have on our Web site a section called "Client Love," and it's really about communication and interacting with our clients. We have used the Internet not as a gizmo or as bells and whistles, but we've really used it to keep the communication channels up. People are sometimes fearful to communicate if there is a problem; that's the worst thing.

When interviewing new hires, I always look for somebody who really understands these communication skills. Can they listen to what is being asked of them and hear what the nuances are? That's really important when you have an office and you have several jobs going on. When you're explaining something to junior designers or to intermediates, they must get it—and get it immediately. You don't have time to go back and forth. Going through that learning curve is not always easy for us.

Another thing I look at is obviously the ability to communicate through drawing by hand, rather than computerized technology. I think that if you can draw, that's the most important thing to being a designer. If you can draw, then you have the spirit in your head to be able to take an idea and put it on paper in ten seconds. I had a teacher once who said that if you could draw upside down for a client, then you'd get 99 percent of the jobs that come your way. I believe that to be true. It certainly works for me.

With new hires, I'll also look for someone who's tenacious and brave. Being brave is really about having confidence and being able to overcome all the things that go against a young person, like being intimidated by your boss or being intimidated by a whole new environment—from school to an office in New York and all the things that come along with that. I look for somebody who is able to stand up for himself or herself and be brave in terms of pushing forward a design or an idea. Out of that comes a tremendous amount of interaction with a client. Sometimes a client can be very powerful and intimidating, and you can end up listening only to the client and just following the client's direction, which is sometimes not good for the client. Being brave is about being able to say, "You know what? Try this" or "I don't agree with what you said because of this and that." I say it the way it is, and that's good and bad. But, in the end it's worked very well for me. I think you can lose all of that in school, depending on the environment. I think when somebody comes out of school, they've either been good, so they are brave and they have confidence, or they haven't done well, but will still come to the interview. They're talented, but they're not brave because they've been consistently put down. They've been critiqued constantly, and they come into the workforce timid and fearful.

There are two things that make a job attractive to me. First, I'll consider the people I'll be working with or for. That is extremely important, since it's a minimum of a year that we'll spend together, and we have to connect in a lot of different ways. Secondly, it's important that the project has a sense of newness for me, which is why, if you look at my body of work, you get a sense that it's quite different from one project to the next. That's why I like doing what I do because I can do somebody's home or somebody's restaurant or design a piece of furniture—and we do a lot of that—it's like going from one personality to another; it's almost like each job has it's own brand. That's what I look for. If I would go to fourteen interviews and they all wanted a striped sofa . . . I don't know if I would do that.

The good thing is that being the creative director, I don't have to be immersed in every part of a project all the way through. I have people [who] help me with that. So I'm lucky in that I can move from one creative process to the other. In between, I strongly believe in taking time off, going places that are totally different from where I live or what I have experienced. I like to travel to places that are both brave and challenging in terms of what they offer. I also get away from my work in other ways; for instance, I do different kinds of work—I'll do a book project, or I'll design somebody's brand or build somebody's home. I like a change of geography and scale; it gives me a sense of being able to breathe between projects. If I have four meetings in a row—which often happens—and I'm going from one architectural project to the next, by the end of the day, I am finished. But if I have the four meetings, and one is a branding meeting, and one is a creative meeting for a piece of art for an installation in a restaurant, and so on, then it's no problem; I could do that for days.

Someone said of me—this was a client speaking to another potential client in front of me— "Listen, if you want to hire Mark, the best thing you can do is to visit his home. If you like the home, you have an insight into his world. If you like that world, he's the man for you. But if you go to the home and you don't like it, he's not your guy."

I have two homes; one of them is in the country, and one is in the city, and they are very,

very different. In each house I have these bowls, about 24 feet in diameter; sometimes I have two or three of them going at the same time, but generally I have one in each home. I have a bowl of ocean stuff, and I have a bowl of earthbound stuff. It's just a collection of things: seeds, and pods, and bits of bark, and rocks, and stones. The ocean one obviously has seashells, and coral, and bits of anemone . . . whatever I have found that visually intrigues me.

I do look at little things as well as big things, and I like to put little things inside big things so that you can get a sense of their scale and of their importance, even though they're small. I just found a beautifully articulated Japanese silver beetle, and I made a stand for it, so it stands in the middle of the room—it floats. The sun catches it, and it glitters, and it's all about that detail . . . and then you've got the inside of a building and how that articulates itself.

What's great about collecting this natural bric-a-brac is that it comes in wonderful shapes and sizes, and there's even the way things are positioned in the bowl. They start to get a textural tapestry going on, and it's always changing. And not only that, but then you also decide "No, I'm tired of having it on this table; I'm going to move it to this room," and then you change its position, and the whole room has changed. So this bowl is probably my favorite thing in the whole house. I'll always walk by and look at it, and it gives me a sense of where I come from.

Also, I guess I always return to my roots: the wonderful country of South Africa. Every time I go back, I take a deep breath and walk away from the experience thinking, "This is really what has inspired me." The colors, the texture, and the lifestyle of that country and that beautiful space are inside of me; I don't have to dig deep for it. I love innovation, so my real theory is to take the beauty of nature, meld that with the latest, greatest technology, or innovative material, or invention; bring them together; and mix them with the past. It's the colors and the textures and all the influences from South Africa melded with all this new stuff—that's really how I create my palette: There's beauty in the past, and there's beauty in the future.

1: DESIGNING A PRESENTATION: LAYOUT AND GRAPHIC DESIGN

Before you put your presentation together, sketch a layout for the presentation as a whole, as well as for individual boards, slides, or pages, assuming there are more than one. (See Appendix 1 for guidelines.)

Consider how many illustrations you will need, what they will show, and how large they need to be. Then think of what needs to be explained in printed text. Finally, how will you apply the text and in what kind of typeface(s)?

2: A STYLISTIC EXPERIMENT

Now experiment with your presentation style by sketching a new layout in which you apply different styles and graphic languages.

Play with the balance of text and imagery. Depending on how your sketches look from the exercise above, turn the emphasis around. Make one much larger than the other, then reverse them or try to balance them. As you go, consider the background color of your pages or boards and try two or three possibilities. Now review and decide which layout to use.

3: ILLUSTRATING THE DESIGNS

Create finished, annotated illustrations for your presentation. Using the medium of your choice, create a series of illustrations to depict your design. Make sure you describe everything that your audience needs to see to understand. Create as many views, sections, and diagrams as are needed, but assume a presentation where you will be present and speaking. In choosing your size, format, and color usage, make sure you keep an eye on the design and layout of the presentation as a whole. These should be consistent and have a unifying purpose.

4: DESIGNER'S NOTES: PLANNING FOR THE AUDIENCE

Consider the various members of your intended audience. For each of the following, write a short memo, listing the information that is particularly relevant to them:
- Client/End user
- Fellow designers/Associates
- Production staff
- Management
- Financial representatives
- Publicity and salespeople

To whom of these will you actually be presenting? Where are overlapping areas? Is there any information that is missing? Is there anything that is specific to only one group?

This will help you script your presentation.

5: DESIGNING A PRESENTER: ASSEMBLING THE PRESENTATION

Now that you have your illustrations, notes, and layout, print the text and assemble your presentation. As you put it together, consider how you were going to speak of it, in what order; what points you will make, and what kind of presentation structure you will use. Make notes to yourself and practice as you go.

Production

OBJECTIVE

At this final stage, it is important that you understand the interaction between designers and their production teams and see the benefit of feedback. This chapter reviews prototyping as a way of finalizing ideas before they are ready for production. It then examines decision-making in terms of budgets, schedules, materials, and sustainability. Lastly, the chapter highlights the documentation that should result and lessons that should be learned from the end of a project.

KEY CONCEPTS

* A designer must be a leader *and* a team player.
* The production team has knowledge and expertise that a designer should make the most of.
* Feedback, both positive and negative, is valuable information.
* Creating a prototype is a good way to finalize any ideas that still need exploring.
* Designing is always about making choices and decisions but never more so than at the point of handing final decisions to production.
* Every project is a learning experience and can leave you with fuel for your next projects.

IT'S A WRAP!

Congratulations! You have created your designs from a solid concept and presented them to all concerned with great results. Your responsibilities are fulfilled. The production team takes over from here and sees your designs through to the end. But don't think you can pack everything up, hand over the designs, and fly to sunny climes for some well-earned rest.

Now is when some would say the work begins in earnest. It may certainly feel as if you are done, and you are partially justified in feeling so, since you have completed the crucial stage of getting the idea into the world.

Actually, at this point, life is not yet a beach.

However, the job is not done; now the idea must become the object. Tempting as it may be to hand the job over to production and skip off into the sunset, you will need to be available to answer questions and address concerns. Sometimes designers are commissioned to bring the idea only to this point; but even when that is the case, it rarely turns out that way. Things go wrong, and you are needed. Things are unclear, and you are needed. Changes are needed, and you are needed.

Production issues do not, of course, appear out of nowhere at the end of the design process. The concerns of this stage are active from the very beginning and loom larger as you progress toward your finished designs, becoming your main concern as you prepare to hand your designs over to production.

MEETING YOUR MAKER: THE PRODUCTION TEAM

Bringing a design to production requires that you interact with that production team. Depending on the scale of the operation and the discipline you are working in, this can involve a number of levels. There could be stages of engineering and prototyping; there could be numerous stages of production from the procurement of materials to the "roll-out" on the shop floor.

The designer, as team member and leader, creates a lot of interesting social patterns within a workplace. Because the designer communicates with so many people on so many different levels, good work habits in terms of relationships with the team are paramount. The virtues that combine the characteristics of a good leader with those of a good team player are essential, since the designer must very often make a seamless transition between the two.

First and foremost, working with a team requires you to have respect for the people you are working with and respect for their abilities, experience, and opinions. Working with disparate groups of people, you will learn very quickly that everyone has an opinion. It is very important for you as a designer to listen and respond, as often these opinions will have been based on experience. Some of your collaborators will indeed know more about the subjects at hand than you do. They will have more experience than you and perhaps even have encountered similar projects (and similar designers) before. It is very important not to be taken aback by this. An unfortunate side effect of the culture of art colleges is the distancing of design from shop-floor experience. Having spent a lot of time successfully navigating projects in studios, newly graduated designers can perhaps take themselves a little too seriously, not realizing the enormous amount of knowledge and information to be had from carpenters, welders, seamstresses, painters, and so on. This was certainly true in my case; it took me more than a year on the job to understand that by graduating from college, I had only begun a new phase of learning. Listen to opinions, ask advice, but keep your vision intact by reminding yourself continually of where you are going. Refer back to the beginning of the project and keep the conceptual material in plain sight. Your concept board, sketches, and other material will serve as your navigational tools when a hundred opinions begin pulling your compass needle every which way. If you have communicated your vision effectively to the production staff, they will understand and respect it and help you achieve your goal. Be aware that respect works both ways: You earn it by giving it.

Motivating the team requires a lot of time spent on communicating correctly. No one likes to feel as if he or she is "just working here," and the more creative the project, the more people like to feel that they are actively involved. By understanding each person's talents and methods of contributing, even in small ways, you can find a way to involve each of them personally, and thereby significantly, in the project. By acknowledging the importance of their contributions, you will bolster the pride they feel in their work.

The following description of the efforts of a brilliant architect shows this respect for teammates well:

> Santiago Calatrava, the Spanish architect, may be best known for his flying buttresses of cable and steel, but at the Milwaukee Art Museum, his design also included intricate concrete work of almost weblike delicacy. "At the beginning I was told that doing concrete in the U.S. is impossible," Mr. Calatrava said from his office in Zurich. "There's no tradition for form work. I thought it cannot be true. Look at the old T.W.A. building; it is a most exquisite example. Look at the Salk Institute." So he chose to work closely with local carpenters, teaching them exactly how to achieve the results he desired.
>
> "The team spirit in the U.S. is exceptional," he said. "Once they are in front of a challenge, they rise to it. It was a pure American effort." But to help them get to that point, Mr. Calatrava invited the local construction managers to Europe, where they stayed with him and his family for 10 days of bonding.[1]

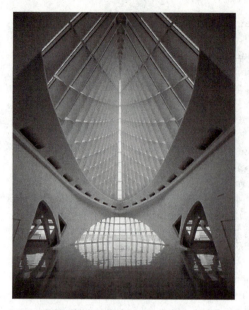

The reception area of the Milwaukee Art Museum, designed by Santiago Calatrava.

In teamwork, whether you are a leader or a team member, diplomacy goes a long way. Your goals are important, and you should not compromise your vision. Then again, there are degrees of compromising. We looked at the question of "how good is good enough" earlier, and now we are back to another facet of that question: "How much compromise is too much compromise?" If you must adapt to someone's practiced technique or allow an artisan's style to influence your design, perhaps you are not compromising at all. Perhaps it is more than just diplomatic to say, "You are right; your way is better;" perhaps you are enhancing your design by admitting another's talent. Again, the key is to know your design inside and out. Know what is at its core, and if the core is intact, you can afford all the diplomacy in the world, and your design will be the better for it. You have to know enough to be able to explain why *your* approach has to be the one followed. Diplomacy is politics, and workplaces are political places. This does not mean that you wear masks all the time and produce empty flattery. This means knowing what you want, knowing what everyone is capable of, and knowing how to make sure everyone gains something professionally. You cannot be arrogant, and you cannot badger people. In teamwork, nobody likes a braggart or a whiner. When working with a professional team of people, be professional and stick to facts. Praise a job that is well done, and accept praise from others. But when it comes to public relations and self-praise, be very aware of the audience you are facing. Your communication should be clear, to the point, and relevant to your audience. Everything you say to the production team about the design influences the design one way or another. If you are unprofessional and disrespectful about the work, then that feeling will spread. If you exhibit enthusiasm and curiosity about the process and the work of those around you, you will generate a good atmosphere of collaboration. Generating a positive atmosphere to all involved is half the battle in successful collaborative designing.

WORKING WITH FEEDBACK

A benefit from following your design through the final stages toward production is the feedback you pick up. Feedback can come from different sources: the client, the production team, or even yourself. Feedback can even come from someone who has no involvement with the project. Wherever it comes from, let it inspire and energize you. Positive feedback will do this easily. Negative feedback may be more difficult to handle; but if treated correctly, it can energize you even further. Let the entire process be a source of feedback. As you go through your designing, take a moment every now and then just to reflect on what you are doing and what you have done to get to where you are. For this process, it is good to keep a journal for each project. Keeping track of reflections by writing and sketching builds up an interesting collection of notes and images. Looking back over the journals at a later date can be extremely energizing and sometimes pleasantly surprising.

Positive feedback is easy; we all like to hear good things about ourselves and our work. It is an excellent motivator. Because it is most often a pleasure, it is all too easy to just bask in it and not look at it closely to learn from it. When you get positive feedback from your designs, at whatever stage of the process you are in, stop and consider what it means. What *exactly* was being praised? Whatever it was, was it something you actually put into the design or something perceived by the viewer that you hadn't really planned on? Either way, whatever worked requires closer scrutiny to resolve whether it can lead to success in a new design. Perhaps it was something that resulted from your production methods, in which case, you must see whether it can be duplicated. It can also be reinforcement for the idea as a whole, in which case you may justifiably feel proud. Don't forget to give credit where credit is due. If the positive feedback is due to work from others on the team, letting them know is good for morale and reinforces the team spirit.

Unfortunately negative feedback is probably the more common kind. People not only have an opinion, but also feel obliged to have one; it is usually easier to formulate a negative view. Difficult as it may be to hear someone criticize your work, you must view this as positive. By listening to criticisms, you have the opportunity to learn how to improve your design. It is therefore a good rule to not only listen to all the negatives, but also always to assume that they are true and correct until you can prove them otherwise. Sometimes you cannot do that because matters of taste are subjective. In that case you can equally impulsively either agree or disagree, only keeping in mind that if there is one person who thinks this, then there are sure to be more out there who think the same. Should you do something about that? Maybe you should; maybe you shouldn't. Chasing after everyone's opinion will drive you crazy, and you must understand that you can never please everyone. View the criticism in the light of how it connects to the needs of your clients and end users and whether it may be valid from *their* points of view.

Negative feedback will usually prompt an immediate reaction of some kind. Often, this will lead to changes in your designs, requiring the recreation of models or even finished products. In a theater I used to design for, the word *changes* was spoken with dread. The overtone was similar to the phrase *dead fish*. Difficult as this was to hear, it was done, I might add, with some justification. Changes, at the production stage are often costly, as things have do be redone, thus delaying production plans at a point when deadlines are looming and actual, and they can be purely irritating to the production team who see their hard work go up in smoke. However, if brought on for the right reason, changes are worth the occasional bout of disdain and irritation, the right reason being that the changes are beneficial to the design. In any creative atmosphere, there will inevitably be changes due to feedback. You cannot collaborate with creative people without a concept evolving. Creativity breeds creativity, and the clearer the result of a project becomes, the more ideas will be generated. Use this energy, but don't let it get out of hand. Your job as a designer is to decide when to say "enough," often contradicting even your own desire to continue experimenting.

One thing to be very aware of (something that often is not clearly understood by those outside the creative field) is this: Any unexplored territory will have areas that will not and cannot be clearly defined until you get to them. You simply cannot see what it is until you see it for yourself. The same holds true, on the technical side, for unproven technologies. It is not until you get to the final stage, where you can build a prototype and test it, that you know for certain whether things work. Clearly, the universe and Murphy's Law being what they are, it is almost inevitable that something will go wrong under such uncertain circumstances. There you are: *changes*, as welcome as dead fish.

Will there be any changes to the design during production?

If negative feedback, whether yours or someone else's, has brought you to a standstill where you don't know exactly what to do, go back to the beginning of your design process and figure out where the problem came about. Reevaluate your design from that point on to see whether you can steer it back to a good place. Ask for advice from anyone who may be able to give you an insight, whether it is technical, practical, aesthetic, or philosophical. Whatever you do, do it as quickly as you can. Odds are that you have a production team waiting for your decision, and if they have nothing else to do, you are costing someone a lot of money for nothing by keeping them idle.

You must keep in mind, however, that you should not let the thought of people waiting for a decision pressure you into making one that you are not happy with. If you must take your time to redesign and ponder for a bit, do so. But don't do so without informing those who are waiting on your thoughts that you are going to take a while. Most professionals know that this happens and will know that it is usually worth the wait. It is a large mistake to pretend that the pause isn't happening or to try to hide your hesitation by not discussing the problem with your associates. Designing feels like a solitary job at times and especially so at times such as this. However, it only seems that way because the designer is, as we have seen, not permanently placed, but operating on many levels of discourse and collaboration. Not being on a fixed level, and therefore not permanently part of a group, creates an illusion of solitude that can be dispelled by realizing that the communication and interaction, over all the levels involved, is an integral part of the job. As a designer you are the connector at the center of a very large group that is looking to you for answers. Although some of the answers may have to be found by you alone, most can be obtained through collaboration and discussion.

PROTOTYPING AND TESTING

Prototyping is the creation of a model or mock-up of a design to test various aspects of the idea. The prototype is usually one of three types,[2] depending on what use it is going to be put to. It can be a *concept prototype*, a *throwaway prototype*, or an *evolutionary prototype*. In each case, examined further below, there is valuable feedback to be had from the exercise, and there are benefits to be had from the three-dimensionality of the object. Three dimensions will show characteristics of your design that rendering never can, no matter how realistic that rendering is. Human perception is very much geared toward objects, and we are much more able to accept an actual three-dimensional representation as "real," even when its level of accuracy is far less than that of the printed or digital image. Prototyping is about more than the *look* of the design, however. It is also, and primarily in most cases, about the functionality and construction of the design in question.

Often during the prototyping stage, a bit of quality control is in order. This is a good time to try out finishes, materials, textures, colors, and whatever manufacturing techniques you may need to explore. You may need to be sure that the accuracy of detailing will be what you want it to be. There may be questions about the soundness of construction, especially if you are using unproven, adapted, or improvised technology. Finally, a prototype can be useful to test the fidelity of the engineering. You may have not created the diagrams from which parts were made, or the actual structural elements may have been designed outside of the range of your oversight. A mock-up would be helpful to make sure the specifications are true to the original concept.

A prototype should be full scale if at all possible. This allows you to make sure that the elements being tested approach their true functionality and that there is no danger of unforeseen scaling problems. The benefit is clearly that in having a workable 3-D representation, you can actually see and feel the function or interaction being tested, minimizing the risk of reality doing something unintended or unforeseen at a later date.

If the scale of the model cannot be close to reality, it is important to decide where the priorities lie in representing the design. If creating something that is at less than full scale, the careful relative scaling of materials is necessary, but may result in materials in the model being weaker than they will be in the final result. Some materials lend themselves to scaling better than others.

Concept Prototyping

The concept model is a model or representation of the idea that can be very rough and thrown together, mainly for the purpose of communicating the basic concept to the team and client. The benefit of this kind of representation is that the whole team can get a quick sense of the object that is being created and connect with its reality, even though the idea is still in its early stages. Often this is done very close to the beginning of the design process to evaluate the idea before too much time and money are spent. Remember that when you create a concept prototype, you must not begin to get ahead of yourself and finalize your design before its time. When preparing for the presentation of an idea, it is always tempting to go a little further, and a little further still, but you must bear in mind the purpose of your model. It need not necessarily function or even be of the correct materials, but should at least imply all the function and nature of the design.

An apparel designer may create a concept garment that is made of substitute fabrics and with nonfunctioning closures. This model gives the designer and production team a three-dimensional representation of a finished garment, and as such, provides enough information for the creation of a functioning sample made of the correct, usually more expensive, fabrics. Often concept garments are exhibited on the runway, and the reaction to press photos may be "who would wear that?"—missing the point entirely. Automotive designers create concept models of vehicles that are sometimes just shells on another vehicle's frame. These are created to exhibit the direction of the company's design sensibilities and get a reaction from future buyers.

Before creating a line of clothing, designers will pull together a concept garment, exploring their idea in three dimensions and in fabric. These are not necessarily wearable.

Throwaway Prototyping

A throwaway prototype is a model created for the purpose of testing a particular aspect of the design, most often a functional element, such as the workings of a moving part, the interaction with environment, or an exploration of scale. It is called a throwaway because a prototype of this sort will be created for the purpose of a single test before being discarded. It may be intentional to damage the prototype as a result of testing, as when a garment or piece of furniture is tested for wear and tear.

When using a throwaway prototype, make sure you get all the information out of it that you can. If the test will destroy it, is there more than one result that can be observed?

Another point to consider is that the creation of a throwaway, although technical in its purpose, may give you an opportunity to discuss the design from various angles with your clients and team. Before you embark on the tests that will destroy the model, consider whether it also can serve the purpose of being an introduction to the design's three-dimensionality. Be careful, again, that there is no confusion about the nature of the model.

Evolutionary Prototyping

Evolutionary prototyping is useful when design specifications are uncertain or need further exploration. In this case, the prototype serves as a work in progress with changes being made as you learn and make new decisions. This can be very inspiring and fun. However, as is true of the conceptual prototype, the evolutionary prototype also carries with it the danger that you will focus too early on details and essentially finish your idea too soon, before you have explored all the possibilities your concept contains.

"Reality"

In all of these cases, the creation of a prototype can actually influence the design to a very large degree. The idea shown as a three-dimensional object will often result in your perception either changing or refocusing: You may see things that you hadn't thought of before. Sometimes because you are working with an incomplete or rough model, a prototype will result in a "happy accident:" something will go wrong, be incomplete, or just unexpectedly different, and you will decide that you actually like it that way. Be vigilant for these possibilities. Designs have a way of taking the reins and showing you where they are really going if you let them.

Be very careful not to confuse your prototypes with reality. These are models; do not focus so hard on what they do at this stage that you forget to translate the experience into what could happen later on. Also, beware of a tendency to start "protecting" your models from the forces that you should be testing them against. If your prototype is intended to explore the interaction of your design with reality, then give it the full reality. If you were testing a toy design for two-year-olds, you would want to give the mock-up to an actual toddler, who would randomly do something impulsive that you wouldn't expect.

DECISIONS

The designer's job is mainly about making choices. Some of these decisions may be clear and based on parameters that are known well beforehand; others are not. Sometimes you have very little choice; the decision is dictated by circumstance, such as budgets and scheduling. At other times the choice is entirely yours, perhaps when choosing materials or making aesthetic decisions. More often, there are constraints of differing degrees, which place your range of choices somewhere in between, for example, when making choices for sustainable design.

Budgets

As mentioned at the Identification stage, it can be difficult to accept that often your designing will be dictated by a budget. It is, of course, possible to see this as being as challenging as any other constraint, by treating the budgeting as one more piece of the complex puzzle that your project has become. The budgeting of a design is a puzzle within a puzzle, since the components of a well-planned budget are many and diverse, and the budget is often the first thing that is definitely known about a project. It is unlikely that a designer is in control of every aspect of the budget, and therefore financial constraints are, in most cases, the least flexible.

For example, it is possible that the actual cost of having you design the product may be a factor in the budget. There may be a limit on how much time you can spend or the resources you can use. You may have to choose between time and resources if things come down to the wire. The trade-off between time and money is all too common.

Make sure you know as much of the budget requirements as possible right from the beginning, and keep track of them throughout. You don't want to find yourself at the end-stage of the process and be told that you need to stop because there is no more money.

The requirements can be of all sorts. Often the maintenance of the operation as a whole has to be taken into account. There are bills to pay and perhaps rent. There may be payroll, which could be part of a bid, and you become responsible for the inclusion of this line in the budget. Then, there is the actual cost of building the prototype and final design. You need to budget for materials and resources, tools, technology, and expertise. Perhaps you need to hire someone for consultation. Finally, you have to factor in contingency planning in case there are surprise costs or unexpected problems that require money to solve. Even without major problems, it's fairly certain, especially if you are designing an untested product, that there will be something you didn't think of or something that costs more than you were led to believe. Adding an extra 10 to 15 percent to your budget is a good way to temper such situations and is common practice in budgeting, especially when bidding on a project. In most cases, it is the designer's decision-making that causes the pieces of the budget planning to fall into place and the puzzle to be completed.

Scheduling

The same attention to disparate detail as in budgeting holds true for scheduling. You must decide the pace of the project, at least up until the point where the shop floor takes over. Can you create the designs in a given timeframe? How long will the model take? When should you have the first, second, and third meetings with the client? Each of these meetings will probably include a presentation by you, so you must factor the creation of these into your schedule.

You must also outline the priorities in terms of getting things done. What needs to be available to allow the project to move forward? Where is the information coming from about this and that? Who needs to make which decision about what? Whom should you call and when? It goes on and on. Suddenly you find yourself stuck to a desk and a phone. It is somewhat disconcerting to first realize that scheduling is a large part of your job. Not much time goes into the organizational side of designing in school, but it is inevitable in the workplace and requires attention. Get help in the form of a spreadsheet program and a large calendar. These can be lifesavers when dealing with budgets and schedules. The time spent learning how to use a spreadsheet is time well spent, especially if you have long-term scheduling and budgeting that will need updating or you are running multiple projects, where one can benefit from the core planning of another.

Whether you want to be on a virtual or physical desktop, the main thing is to organize your planning so that it is always visible. Don't ever try to keep things in your head. Have your calendar where you can see it, write *everything* on it, and look at it often.

There may be an art to using a calendar, but the main point is to use it.

Materials and Aesthetics

Materials were very likely already defined in the earliest stages of your project, so by the time you get to production, things are likely to be clear; definitions have been nailed down and materials procured. However, even at this stage, decisions about materials may need to be made. The production methods may require changes. For example, machinery may require different thicknesses of material than you intended, or there may be feedback from the production crew that suggests alterations to the choices you've made. Also, feedback from prototyping may influence your choices or confirm ideas that were not yet fully clear.

Where there is a collision between the needs of manufacturing, it is often because the decisions you have made are defined not by a practical, but rather an aesthetic sense. At this stage you may be required to defend your decisions or make compromises. You come back to the point of deciding whether the outcome will be "good enough." Think back to the architect Yoshio Taniguchi. Just as he found himself looking wistfully at seams in a wall that he would have had perfectly smooth, you need to decide that you cannot have everything be exactly the way you envisaged. Your role at this stage becomes one of defending your vision from deterioration, utilizing the production crews' knowledge to enhance it, and deciding how good "good enough" actually is.

Sustainability

Issues of sustainability come to the fore during production, where the environmental impact of a product is often the largest: in the delivery of materials, actual manufacturing, packaging, and transportation to market. Designing for sustainability requires vigilance over the entire life cycle of the product, and you can make a difference here by influencing where materials are purchased, to minimize the amount of transportation necessary. You may also be required to justify design decisions that do not, perhaps, make immediate economic sense. Your product may, for example, require a slightly more expensive material or manufacturing process to minimize pollution, but the expense will be recouped in the long term through increased loyalty from your clients or through reaching a market that the product would not appeal to otherwise.

The environmental decisions may come at you from the other direction as well. You may find that there are production parameters that can minimize waste if you make changes to your design, such as substituting natural dyes for chemical ones or by eliminating the need for a process that is very energy consuming. Such decision-making may then again require that you educate the client in the issues involved. As mentioned before, communication is the primary issue. Educate and inform your team and your clients as much as you can, and make sure you have all the information you need to impart. The more you involve everyone in your thinking regarding sustainability, the likelier you are to create a ripple effect that will benefit everyone in the long run.

DOCUMENTING

Don't forget to document your projects. It should be extremely easy to keep a record of each project, given the ease that scanners, CD burners, and digital cameras have brought to the game. Resist the temptation to put the documentation on the back burner. Especially when projects overlap, the time it takes to archive portfolio material seems like time you would rather spend on something else. Make it an integral part of your projects to store images, digitally or otherwise; safely and in an organized manner; and with descriptions, dates, and names affixed. Years from now, when you need a portfolio, or want to revisit an old idea, you will appreciate the effort. Again, any organization is better than none at all.

REVIEWING THE DESIGN PROCESS

This book presents the design process in a much more organized manner and drawn with much clearer lines than happens in reality. The order of the stages is most often as clear, but their division is not. They may dovetail, and you may find yourself looping back. However, in one way or another, you will visit all the stages between the time you are given the project and the time when you deliver the finished product. You will even find that you are working on more than one stage at once, as chances are that you will have more than one project running at once. Most designers do not have the luxury of putting each project to bed before beginning the next one. You should be able to let the overlapping help you, as each stage has its own set of priorities and mental states, and you can allow each project to inform the other by looking from one stage to another as you go.

Finishing a project is seldom as easy as you would hope. Details multiply at every turn. For every solution you come up with, ten new questions surface, and they may require backtracking and revision. Even during manufacturing, your oversight may be needed, and, even if it isn't, you're at least emotionally invested in seeing the project come out well. So until it is actually in the world you are not able to leave it be. It is only then that you can be sure you don't have to make any new decisions or revisions and only then that you can look at it and see it for what it really is.

As we have already seen, things are seldom what they were first meant to be. Your final designs will be different from the initial image in your mind, and it is hugely beneficial for a designer to keep track of the trajectories of projects. This way you learn what to expect from your process and how to direct the arc of your creativity as close as possible to your intended target.

Treat the end of each project as a learning opportunity. What worked? What didn't? What surprised you? What do you know that you didn't know before?

What you have created in response to the exercises in this book, if kept in an organized fashion, can constitute a record of your progress through the project; even if you can't see it immediately, you will eventually see the arc that you traveled. You can use this information to repeat what worked and avoid what didn't. Consider the interviews with the different designers and artists in this book, and emulate their approaches, which they have acquired through their years of experience. Realize that this process does not end: It flows back into itself and always leaves something to be explored further. Using the knowledge of the stages and the thoughts and approaches suggested here, you should be able to design with energy, interest, and, most important, with joyful inspiration. Have fun!

PERSPECTIVE

PÁLMI EINARSSON,
DESIGN DIRECTOR, OSSUR GENERATION II

Pálmi Einarsson is the design director at Ossur, an international manufacturer and leading innovator in the field of prosthetic and orthotic devices. He led the team responsible for the Rheo Knee, which was chosen by both Time *and* Fortune *magazines as one of the best products of 2004.*

The design process at Ossur has been very much the same since 1998. We have five basic gates [that] all our designs must go through.

The first gate entails a very brief introduction of the general concept and basic financial numbers, pitched to the directors of the company. If they find the project interesting, a collective decision is made to formally accept it, after which we can begin to use time and resources for further development.

Second, all the numbers are presented in detail: development costs, projected sales, the definition of the target market and its size, and production costs along with a definitive concept and the technical platform for the product. Everything is put into one document that gives us the net present value of the project, which tells us what the profit from the product should be five years after its introduction to the market. If the directors are happy with the project "as is," it is approved, and we move on to the design and prototyping stage of the project.

When we get to the third gate, all the designing has taken place, and the product has gone through the necessary testing, and risk assessment has taken place. At this point all the alpha (prototype) tests are complete, and the product should now function according to the premise of the design. The designing of the product is now suspended, and the product is formally handed over to production. As the product comes out of production, a previously determined number of pieces are put into beta (market-ready product) testing in the market for about two months, and if everything is in order, a meeting is called. This is gate four, where the designing is formally over. The product cannot be sold until it has reached this point.

When the product has been in the market for six months, a final gate, the fifth, is set up to review the project's budget and see whether the response to the product has been as expected, and if not, why? If there are problems, projects are created to find solutions. If there are no problems or once the solutions are in place, this chapter is closed, and the project is now formally over in all aspects.

Of course this is just a short summary, but the process is very well organized with much paperwork at each stage. This guarantees that everything has been done, done correctly, and prevents problems from emerging.

The design of the Rheo Knee is the widest-ranging project our company has ever been involved with, and it took place more or less along these lines. The idea for the design of the knee came from the Massachusetts Institute of Technology. There, the prototype of the hardware and the highly sophisticated software was developed, and a team at MIT created all the original models. When a functional prototype, which could be fitted to a person, was ready, the project was moved to Ossur in California, where we had a team of six who were originally only meant to take the project and wrap it up. They soon found that there was more to it than that. As they began to polish up the design, various problems came to light. The biggest obstacle came from the technical platform the product is based on, the Rheological fluid technique. To understand this, you have to realize what a knee actually does. A knee is basically a brake, if you think about it. Its function is mainly to keep you upright. You only exert muscular energy in the knee to get up from a seated position or to walk up stairs; 90 percent of the time you are only using it to arrest the motion of your legs.

As a brake, a prosthetic knee has to be very intelligent, and our knees' abilities are based on complex algorithms designed at MIT. There are various types of brakes, and the most common in prosthetic knees, until now, has been hydraulic systems. The problem with using hydraulic systems is that you need to control the size of an opening through which the hydraulic fluid flows. If the brake must move quickly, the opening must open wide so that a lot of fluid can flow through in a short time. This, however, is difficult to make happen quickly enough. Imagine you're walking, and your leg swings forward in smooth but rapid motion. As soon as the foot begins its downward motion, the knee must begin to brake, but not lock. We essentially have built-in shock absorbers in our knees. As this is extremely difficult to control, MIT began to look for alternative options and found a result using the Rheological fluid, which consists mainly of a suspension of microscopic metal spheres. The joint is built up of many thin layers with the fluid between them. The fluid responds to a magnetic field with increased viscosity, thereby increasing the resistance between the layers and slowing down the movement. This technique makes the Rheo a very special knee, as the response using the fluid is much faster than in a traditional hydraulic mechanism.

However, at the time we began this, the Rheo fluid technology was completely new,

and there were only a few versions available. The biggest challenge in this project was related to the further development of the fluid. Standards dictate that a prosthetic knee must sustain one million steps a year, but the original fluid lasted for only 5,000 to 40,000 steps, as the metal spheres began to break down and flatten. This resulted in the knee stiffening, and eventually it would stop functioning as required. It took us almost two years to develop the fluid, as this is a new technology and nothing available off the shelf. The fluid is now a mixture of different substances that prevent it from breaking down, and its lifetime is close to three million steps.

A great deal of work also went into perfecting the software, which is extremely complicated. The knee must sense, as soon as the foot touches down, whether you are walking on level ground, or going up or down stairs or an incline. The knee does this by incorporating a microchip, which receives a thousand readings a second from two pressure sensitive cells and a sensor measuring the angle of the joint. The information streaming in is stored and continually compared to new data. The knee therefore has the capability to learn from—and constantly adapt to—the wearer's gait.

The original project team consisted of eight people. There was an electrical engineer who directed the project and created the software, two mechanical engineers in charge of hardware, two technicians in charge of static tests and prototypes, a chemical engineer, who designed and created the fluid, a prosthetics specialist who fitted the limbs to people and analyzed their gait, and finally, an administrator. This group was entirely responsible for the functional design of the knee, and when I came to be in charge of the project on the California side, the design looked too, well, functional. I realized that we were working with the newest technology in the field of prosthetics and that this knee would get a lot of press, so I decided to bring an industrial designer into the group to design the product's look to reflect the cool modern technological aesthetic.

I contacted the Prologus Design Factory in Iceland and enlisted Gudmundur Einarsson. We gave him the framework, and he began working with materials that would be both practical and visually pleasing. He wound up using very anatomical forms, and you can clearly see a calf and knee implied in the Rheo knee's outer casing. He also chose a fairly soft polymer for the cover so that the tactile sensation would not be cold metal, as is so often the case, but rather a soft and comfortable texture. The soft polymer also functions as a buffer when the user kneels down. Prologus sent us a drawings and a model that was presented to the engineers, [who] then proceeded to create rapid prototypes using [the modeling software]

Solidworks. Now, engineers do not always have the same understanding of details as industrial designers; they would change a radius here and a curve there to make it easier to create the concept model in the software.

I had to be bit diplomatic to achieve the look we wanted, as the first Solidworks renderings we received from the engineers didn't even resemble the designs from Prologus. So I called a meeting and said, "Yes, this is fairly close, but could you change this radius?" pointing to just one of ten forms that needed correcting. "No problem," they said, and this is how it went ten times—one detail at a time. Finally, it wound up being 100 percent what the industrial designers had intended. It was all rather tricky because the industrial designers were very attached to the lines they had created. I guess there is something in the training of industrial designers that allows them to be very confident that their design is the exact solution to a design problem, without perhaps being able to explain exactly why. This, on the other hand, is something engineers often have a difficult time working with.

What gets me excited about design projects is that I feel there are always so many possibilities in everything we do. I have been designing and leading design projects for Ossur for almost ten years, and what I always enjoy is seeing the product making a person's life easier after what has sometimes been a very difficult time. For example, when the first ten users we recruited to test the Rheo Knee had worn them for one month, we had to take five back. They worked very well, but we didn't have the manpower at that time to follow so many test subjects. It was tough to take back the knees because the people had begun to live their lives in a different way than they had before; there was so much more they could do with this device than with their old prosthetic. The five were almost brought to tears. However, this tells me that we are on the right track and makes us even more determined to move forward (not that we get any kicks out of making people weep). When a project concludes, we hear through our sales force that our end users are enormously happy—that's our goal and that gives us all the inspiration we need. Nonetheless, after a long project winds up, I personally like to turn to something else for a while and, on a regular basis, enjoy going out into nature, fishing, or golfing, just to empty my mind.

1: PROTOTYPING

Design and create a prototype or sample of your designs from the previous chapter. Consider the following factors:

- *Emphasis*: What important features must you emphasize? What is essential to get across to the audience?
- *Functionality*: How much functionality will be built into the prototype? What do you need to see work?
- *Scale*: Consider the scale of your model; can you create a full-scale prototype? If not, how will you represent the design as truly as possible within these restrictions?
- *Materials*: What materials will you use? Can you use all the materials that will be used in the final product, or do you need to substitute?
- *Testing*: What tests does your prototype need to undergo, if any, to ascertain the design's viability? How will you make this happen?

2: PLANNING

- Considering the prototype you have created, do you think any changes or adjustments are necessary? Where in the hierarchy of needs do these changes fall?
- Break the design into production elements. Create diagrams and annotated sketches of details for each element. Include all information required for their construction.
- Set up a timeline for the procurement of materials and the construction of your design. Where are there possible bottlenecks, and how may they be resolved?
- What could go wrong in the creation of your designs? How will you avoid these problems?
- What are the issues related to sustainability in your designs? Where can you improve on them to lessen their environmental impact?
- Create an illustrated "memo" to the production team: It will be helpful to imagine that you are working with a team in a design studio.

The team may involve the following:
- Assistants
- Buyers
- Detailers
- Engineers
- Production crew
- Budgeting managers
- Public relations personnel

What information does each section of the team need to help move your project forward? The following could be addressed:

1. The overall purpose and aesthetic of your design. Consider
    - *functionality,*
    - *style, and*
    - *current trends to follow or contradict.*

2. What is needed in terms of
    - *materials,*
    - *structural elements,*

- *detailing,*
- *decoration,*
- *color,*
- *budget points (high, low, or danger zones), and*
- *sustainability.*

3. Who should be told of changes and adjustments, and what do they need to know?

3: WHAT NOW?

- Given that you have completed your designs, what would your next round of designs be?
- What will inspire you to begin the next project?
- How would you use your experience from this project to gain a better experience from your next one?
- Reconsider your designs, and design for maximum sustainability. What changes? How would your initial approach be different on your next project?

Appendix 1

ELEMENTS AND PRINCIPLES OF DESIGN

The following is to be considered a quick refresher of the topics involved, for the purposes of outlining vocabulary and creating points of discussion.

COLOR

The current form of color theory was developed by Johannes Itten (1888–1967), an art theorist who taught at the Bauhaus School in Germany from 1919 to 1922. Itten modified the color wheel, from models previously created by Isaac Newton (1643–1727) and Johann Goethe (1749–1832), basing his wheel on red, yellow, and blue colors as the primary triad and including 12 hues. His approach to color theory was revolutionary because he looked at color not only in terms of the physics of how light is absorbed or reflected by matter and not only in terms of how one color looks when situated beside another, but also at how color affects a person psychologically and spiritually. Itten believed that there were certain characteristics inherent in particular colors that would have a direct influence on how the viewer felt. These views are very much a result of the early 20th-century views in psychology and human behavior, but are nonetheless an interesting study. His books, *The Art of Color* and *The Elements of Color,* are still in full use in art colleges all over the world and considered definitive works.

Hue

When we speak of hue, we are basically identifying the color itself, as it would appear on a classical color wheel (i.e., red, blue, yellow-green). In discussing color, this is the least amount of information we can give. In the absence of a color swatch, this is too loose a definition and requires more information for your audience to understand precisely for what you are aiming.

Value

This is the relative lightness or darkness of a color. On a gray scale, the lightest *value* is white, and the darkest is black. The terms tint, tone, and shade are also used in this context when dealing with paint, where a *tint* refers to white being added to the color, a *tone* is when gray is added, and a *shade* is when black is added.

The value of a color refers to its relative lightness or darkness.

Intensity

The intensity of a color refers to its saturation and is traditionally used in terms of paint, although lighting designers will also refer to saturation for the amount of color generated by gels. Paint is made of binder and pigment, and saturation refers to how much pigment is in the solution. Paints straight out of a tube are highly saturated, and liquid paints are less so.

A color's intensity or saturation refers to the amount of color or pigment present.

Temperature

Of all of these ways to discuss color, this is probably the most subjective and visceral. There is in us a natural response to color in terms of a temperature sensation, although the precision of this will vary from one person to the next. However, for discussion and definition it serves well to refer to colors in terms of their temperature, where red-orange will be perceived as hottest and blue-green as coolest.

Light Versus Pigment

Color requires several frames of reference when being planned or discussed. Generally, color is spoken of in terms of light, but for the designer the more important system would involve pigment. This has become very pertinent now that most design specification involves visualization on a computer screen. The computer monitor exhibits color in RBG (Red–Blue–Green) mode, whereas printing will utilize the so-called CMYK model. This stands for the four inks used in the printing process: cyan, magenta, yellow, and black. Four-color printing refers to CMYK.

One of the more difficult aspects of this relationship is properly converting the RGB colors into CMYK colors so that what gets printed looks the same as what appears on the computer monitor. The difficulty can be illustrated in the following way:

- You cannot print the red you see on your monitor out in CMYK. Because CMYK red is built with magenta and yellow, a full saturation of true red is impossible.
- Look at the saturation figure on p. 186. The points on the circle represent pure saturation. Now look at the line between M and Y: You see that you can't get all the way to full saturation of R from the center. The line between M and Y intersects the line toward pure saturation and cuts off the saturation before it gets all the way.

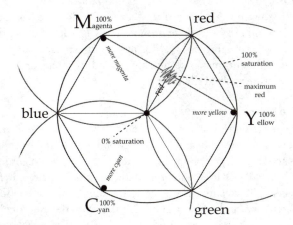

The CMYK model cannot achieve full saturation with all colors.

Symbolism and Psychology

The symbolism of color is a popular topic, but mostly it is based on pop culture and romantic notions. Many of the symbolic ideas in Western culture are left over from preliterate times in the middle ages, when color could code meaning in a painting or altarpiece, allowing the viewer to identify a figure or one of the deadly sins, for example.

Color symbolism is very culture dependent and can be influenced from year to year by media and advertising. Be very careful to research any and all such notions before venturing into unknown territory (both figuratively and literally). One example of such color usage may be the inversion of white and black as colors of mourning between Asian and Western cultures.

In Western culture of the late 20th century, there were a number of referential colors directed toward the two main Christian holidays: red and green at Christmas and yellow around Easter. But these colors have no specific significance or symbolism in the minds of most beyond the superficial and have essentially been separated from their origin. Colors in the 20th century assumed political significance, with black, brown, and red assigned to Fascists and Communists, although black has since resumed its political position as being symbolic of anarchy. For a color to assume any kind of symbolic significance, it must strike an emotional chord and relate to the viewer on a visceral level that can only be created over time. After the color orange became the color of antigovernment defiance in the Ukraine in late 2004, many seemed to think it would become so the world over. Despite its use by various groups, its lack of specific meaning (it was the Ukrainian opposition's color by default; all the other colors were taken) would seem to have stopped it from taking hold.

Color Trends

Apart from cultural context, color is also very dependant on fads and fashion. New products will arrive with a different color story, in part to differentiate them from previous versions, but also to answer trends that have been perceived and sometimes set in motion by the industries involved.

When you see a sudden influx of a "new" color in appliances, cars, or clothing, it's likely you're seeing the work of the Color Marketing Group,[1] an international, not-for-profit association of color and design professionals who identify and forecast color trends for all products and industries, usually about two years in advance. This advance time is necessary for the setting up of supply chains of raw materials, pigments, and dyes through their various stages of manufacturing.

As these decisions are made from trend analysis that may at that point have been a year or more in the making, it is interesting to note that today's "hot new" colors are based on trends that have been set in motion and observed three or more years ago. It is no wonder that color forecasting is an expensive and nerve-racking business, as much can change in three years, especially now that information moves so quickly around the globe and local trends can be easily influenced from unexpected directions.

Examining and Setting up a Color Story

When creating a color story for your designs, it is very important to be precise. Color perception varies from person to person, as does the language we use when referring to colors and their effects. It is not unfair to demand perfection in the treatment of color planning. Always include accurate samples of color with your presentations, and be extra careful when presenting on an RGB display. Make sure there is understanding of the color from screen to sample, if there is a discrepancy (and odds are good that there will be). Show color on its own, on a neutral background (50 percent gray) and in the context of the total color treatment and the color environment. This will allow your audience to fully appreciate the colors of the design, as well as any contextual effects and possible problems.

It is very helpful in the presentation of colors to consider also the scale of each color sample versus the amount of each color in the final design. The impact of a color is relative to the area it covers, so it can be misleading to have, for example, equally sized chips of blue and yellow, when the yellow would be only a small stripe on the final design.

LINE

When discussing "line," we must differentiate between a drawn line (a clearly visible geometric line) and an implied line, which exists by virtue of forms or shapes arranged to form a continuum—a result of our brains having a propensity to fill in and connect otherwise unconnected shapes into a totality (gestalt).

Direction

A line has direction, horizontal, vertical, or diagonal. Practically, this hardly requires any discussion, but the main concern would be in how our eyes and minds react to the direction of lines. As our visual perception takes place with a left-right sweep, the visual mechanism reacts to a line's direction in very different ways. A horizontal line does not create an obstruction and allows the eye to sweep from one side to the other, whereas a vertical line will stop the eye, sending it off its path for a moment. In this way it creates a sense of impediment and gives the brain something to work on for a brief moment. We perceive shapes in terms of change—one thing becomes another, so encountering a line will make the brain pause and ask, "What is going on here? Is this something new?"

A diagonal line will create a sense of motion by deflecting, but not stopping, the eye. Look out for a sense of "up" or "down" in its placement.

Clarity

A line can be obscure or well defined. Either kind will produce an almost visceral response in the viewer and can produce emotions of degrees of calmness and excitement.

The clarity of a line will also create a sense of organization and authority, as well as giving the viewer a quick understanding of the structure and purpose of the shapes involved.

Shape

A line's shape can be concave, convex, or straight in a section. The concavity or convexity is relative to the observer and can be deeply curved or very subtle. The shape of a line creates a sense of dynamic motion in one or more directions and exerts an almost physical force on the viewer.

Length

Length needs to be considered relative to the total shape as well as to other lines and shapes involved, as well as to perspective and the viewer. The *sense* of length comes from comparison, as in "longer than" or "shorter than" and not from measurement. It is perhaps obvious, but good to remember, that units of measurement are an artificial construct, and there is no universal definition of length as a value in itself.

Width

The same applies for width as for length. We must consider the width of a line both in relation to other shapes and lines. The width of a line is defined in relation to its length.

SPACE

We carve out space in two basic ways: We are either working in physical space, by filling or surrounding an area, or we are creating illusionistic space, by utilizing gestalt by implying or outlining a space. In the first case, physical space is that which is occupied by a single column. In the second case, the illusionistic space is that which is created by two parallel rows of columns. There is an outside, an inside, and a contained area. Illusionistic space may also be created by the placement of two-dimensional figures in such a way as to imply three-dimensional space.

Space can be physical as in the actual space occupied or illusionistic, as in the space created by the configuration of objects. Look at the space between as well as the space around and implied by an object.

Space is balanced by symmetry and made dynamic by the altering thereof. Symmetries are many and more than just of the horizontal or vertical two-fold kind. Classical Islamic architecture tends to favor five-fold symmetries. Complicated symmetries are becoming easier to create now that CAD-programs are everywhere, and tiling with multiple symmetries is no longer just the domain of higher mathematics and Maurice Escher. Small changes in symmetry can heighten the visual interest of a design, even when the imbalance is so small that the viewer will not instantly recognize it.

By using the direction of lines and the placement of details, you can direct your viewer's **focus** as clearly as if you placed arrows and signposts. The eye will follow line until it hits an obstruction. It will then hover over the obstruction for a while until it has figured out what it is seeing. Then it will move on. You can also place a detail on an open space, and the eye will quickly traverse the emptiness to explore the detail.

TEXTURE AND PATTERN

In considering texture and pattern, it is important to differentiate between the tactile and the visual. The two are often spoken of in the same terms and sometimes confused. In one instance, we have the experience of touch—the feeling of a surface as it presents itself via our skin. In the other, we have the information coming to us by sight—we perceive the texture or pattern as interplay of light and shadow or differentiation of color.

In a blurring of this distinction, we can experience the tactile through the visual, where experience will teach us to recognize certain visual stimuli and their corresponding tactile "feel." We become able to interpret texture at a distance, and this is indeed where the tactile and the visual begin to merge in design. We speak of the "feel" of a pattern and the "look" of a texture. Tactile terms are then often translated into visual reference, and "rough" and "smooth" begin, for example, to refer to visual experience.

It is more difficult to experience the visual through the tactile. "Reflective" does not, for instance, translate well into anything our fingertips will relay. This becomes more a question of language than actual sensory experience. (What would you need to understand *a texture* described as "red?")

Patterns are essentially the repetition of an element and can be inherently textural or a variation of color. One thing to keep in mind is the natural tendency of the human brain to interpret stimuli in terms of patterns. This actually makes avoiding patterns difficult, as the viewer will supply them for you. True randomness is, for this precise reason, also very difficult as patterns tend to crop up under random generation (giving rise to the occurrence of truly random events being perceived as clusters).

When discussing texture and pattern in design terms, choose your words carefully and provide your audience with a frame of reference that allows them to differentiate between the tactile and visual and gives them a starting point from which to gauge the relativity of your terms. How rough is "rough"—as rough as concrete? How about rough silk?

Harmony

Harmony is generally achieved by arranging parts into a unified whole in the same way that a musical harmony is produced from many separate voices or instruments. If the unity is too great, then the harmony becomes overwhelming, as in the uniformity of the uniforms of a massed band. If there is enough variety, it makes the total interesting. This is a balancing act. Harmony is often considered an end in itself in design, but just as a painter or composer, a designer can use discord to heighten the impact of the design. A carefully placed "sour note" can bring the whole smooth harmony that follows into relief and cause a sensation of pleasure in the audience.

Proportion

Throughout history there has been an effort by architects and artists alike to find the rules underlying "pleasing" proportions. The Golden Section and the Fibonacci sequence seem to hold a part of the solution.

The Golden Section is the ratio often denoted by the Greek letter Phi. It is the number that satisfies the equation

$$Phi2 = Phi + 1$$

Since it is a quadratic equation, it has two answers. These are

$$1{\cdot}6180339887 \ldots \text{ and } -0{\cdot}6180339887 \ldots$$

As you can see these two are separated numerically only by one, and the best part is that they represent the larger and smaller ratio of the sides of a so-called golden rectangle. Given a rectangle having sides in the ratio 1/*Phi*, the golden ratio is defined such that partitioning the original rectangle into a square, and a new rectangle results in a new rectangle that has sides with a ratio 1/*Phi*.

The Fibonacci sequence is formed by starting with zero and one and adding the latest two numbers to get the next one.

$$0, 1, 1, 2, 3, 5, 8, 13, 21, 34, 55, 89 \ldots$$

If we take the ratio of two successive numbers in Fibonacci's series (1, 1, 2, 3, 5, 8, 13 . . .) and we divide each by the one before it, we will find the following series of numbers:

$$1/1 = 1, 2/1 = 2, 3/2 = 1{\cdot}5, 5/3 = 1{\cdot}666 \ldots, 8/5 = 1{\cdot}6, 13/8 = 1{\cdot}625, 21/13 = 1{\cdot}61538 \ldots$$

In other words, the ratio of Fibonacci numbers tends toward *Phi*.

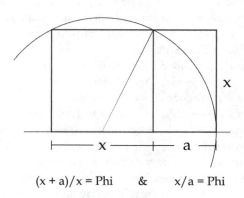

The Golden Ratio appears in both the large and the small rectangles.

(x + a)/x = Phi   &   x/a = Phi

Fibonacci numbers are found in numerous places in nature, such as the numbers of petals on flowers, how leaves are arranged on plants, and so on. It is important to note that there are other sequences that can be found in nature. The Lucas series begins with one and three and progresses in the same way as the Fibonacci sequence: 1, 3, 4, 7, 11, 18, 29 . . . .

An interesting fact is that for all series formed in this manner, the ratio of successive terms will always tend to *Phi*.

It is the ratio that matters. The reason this ratio is "pleasing" is perhaps not as clear as the fact that it is in many ways the easiest way to go in nature, where things have to pack efficiently and line up in the most cost-effective way possible between material and form in space. It is not unlikely that humans have an innate sense of natural proportion; on some level we sense when things are aligned with natural processes and see that it is good. This ability gives us a sensible strategy for dealing with proportion in design. Use mathematics and ratios as much as you will, but in the end follow the architect Le Corbusier's advice that "your eyes are your judges."[2]

In general, proportion and scale are elements best judged by your eyes. Consider the environment of your design and its scale relative to the people and the intended usage. Experiment and try extremes to get a feel of what your design "wants." Whether your designs are extremely practical or tilting heavily toward the artistic, you will find that your prime measure of proportion is the human who will use or inhabit your work.

ERGONOMICS

Ergonomics is unfortunately in very many cases more spoken of than understood; it became a buzzword in the 1980s. People know that it has something to do with office furniture and posture but not much more. Indeed, furniture is sold with the "ergonomically designed" sticker slapped on, when all it means is that the furniture is adjustable to the user's size and shape.

Ergonomics is the application of scientific information concerning humans to the design of objects, systems, and environments for their use. It concerns itself with both the physiological and the psychological. Ergonomics is the discipline that examines the capabilities and limitations of people. The term *ergonomics* is based on two Greek words: *ergos,* meaning work, and *nomos,* meaning the study of or the principles of. In other words, ergonomics refers to the *laws of work.* The goal of ergonomics is to design the workplace to conform to the physiological, psychological, and behavioral capabilities of workers.[3]

The branch of ergonomics that deals with human variability in size, shape, and strength is called anthropometry. Tables of anthropometric data are used by ergonomists to ensure that places and items they are designing fit the users.

According to OSHA guidelines, "ergonomic hazards refer to workplace conditions that pose a biomechanical stress to the worker. Such hazardous workplace conditions include, but are not limited to, faulty workstation layouts, improper tools, excessive tool vibration, and job design problems. They are also referred to as ergonomic stressors."

The best method for reducing stressors is to design facilities, workstations, equipment, and apparel to comply with anthropometric data, such as that found in MIL-STD 1472D, the U.S. military's guidelines for design.[4] These aim to "achieve mission success through integration of the human into the system." Apart from the hugely entertaining military-speak, these guidelines are an excellent study for their military precision and thoroughness. Their four main goals, which can be easily translated into any design discipline, are as follows:
- Achieve required performance by operator, control, and maintenance personnel.
- Minimize skill and personnel requirements and training time.
- Achieve required reliability of personnel-equipment combinations.
- Foster design standardization within and among systems.

There are numerous sources of ergonomic data on the Internet. The military is at the top of the list, but NASA also has an excellent Web site that focuses on all things ergonomic.

Mainly, never forget who your end users are. You are designing for a world of people, and all of those people have needs that are directly related to them individually, personally, physically, and emotionally. You may not be able to meet all these needs, nor will you necessarily want to. It may even be impossible or ridiculous to attempt to do so, but never forget them.

MATERIALS

When considering the choice of materials for a design, there are three basic areas of concern. You may need to consider support, containment, and protection,[5] with aesthetics hovering around all of them, as most of your choices will influence the look of your product (depending on your form-following-function stance). *Structural materials* need to be chosen primarily for their strength and durability, but striking a balance between performance and practicality in manufacturing may be necessary. All cars could be made from totally impact-resistant steel, but this would cause them to be overly heavy and shoot their fuel consumption figures through the roof. Make them of too lightweight a material, and they become unsafe for highway driving. Flexibility may also come into play, as this could be equally important as strength for structures under duress. Considering *containment*, we go to materials that are easily formed, as they would need to enclose space. Anything that could be considered a container should come to mind: barrels, bottles, boxes, fuselages, and tanks. New ways of folding and bending steel have greatly changed how shell-structures like this are now manufactured, and many lessons can be learned from nature in creating delicate but flexible and resistant structures with minimal material use.

Finally, *protection* may require materials that are primarily strong, but protection could also be environmental and deal with resistance to chemicals and weather. In choosing materials, you may take into account how the materials are understood on an *emotional level.* This is highly dependent on the spirit of an era, culture, and location. Metals, stone, timber, plastics, and natural fabrics evoke different emotional responses, through cultural, historical, and psychological connections. We have learned associations through mythology, our environments, and experience that we attach to materials. Just imagine a simple bowl made of stone versus one made of clear plastic. Then picture it made of wood. Each bowl evokes a response and creates an environment of its own. Consider jackets made of denim, fleece, and leather. What are the associated images that come to mind in each case? How do each of the jackets make you feel?

The feel of a garment can also be related directly to our sense of touch, and we can choose materials based on how they impact the human nervous system directly in terms of texture and temperature.

Appendix 2

RECOMMENDED READING AND RESOURCES

This list should be a good start; treat it as such. With the wonderful immediacy of information available on the Web, finding resources is easy. Some of these titles will interest you immediately, and others may not.

Although many of the titles seem to be geared toward a specific audience, I have attempted to choose books that convey their messages in such a way that you can apply them to other disciplines. What works conceptually for a graphic designer should also work for a designer of apparel or furniture (which is, after all, the central thesis of this book). I have found, for example, Mark Oldach's *Creativity for Graphic Designers* to be very inspiring and helpful for any of the fields I have worked in, whether I have been costuming for theater, creating a Web page, designing an exhibition space, or anything else.

The philosophical books, as well as the artists' journals, are here because they have all in one way or another been helpful and inspiring to me as a designer and as a teacher of design. Some are less taxing to read than others, but all are valid texts that may inspire you as well.

Look up these titles online to find critiques and excerpts, which are helpful and may link you to other titles.

In addition to lining up your reading, make sure you add to your knowledge actively and visually as well. Go to museums, see shows, watch films that are acclaimed for their design work, and create images and writings of your own based on what you experience. Learn continuously and eagerly.

ARTISTS' JOURNALS

- Gauguin, Paul. *Noa Noa: The Tahitian Journal.* New York: Dover Publications, 1995.
- Van Gogh, Vincent. *The Letters of Vincent Van Gogh.* Edited by Mark Roskill. New York: Touchstone, 1997.
- Warhol, Andy. *The Philosophy of Andy Warhol (From A to B and Back Again).* Fort Washington, PA: Harvest Books, 1977.

COLOR THEORY
- Itten, Johannes. *The Art of Color.* New York, NY: John Wiley and Sons, 1997.

CREATIVITY
- Adams, James L. *Conceptual Blockbusting: A Guide to Better Ideas.* New York, NY: Basic Books, 4th edition, 2001.
- Csikszentmihalyi, Mihaly. *Creativity: Flow and the Psychology of Discovery and Invention.* New York, NY: HarperCollins, 1996.
- de Bono, Edward. *Lateral Thinking: Creativity Step by Step.* New York, NY: Harper & Row, 1973.
- Gardner, Howard. *Art, Mind and Brain: A Cognitive Approach to Creativity.* New York, NY: Basic Books, reprint edition, 1984.
- Gardner, Howard. *Creating Minds: An Anatomy of Creativity Seen Through the Lives of Freud, Einstein, Picasso, Stravinsky, Eliot, Grapham, and Gandhi.* New York, NY: Basic Books, reprint edition, 1994.
- Oldach, Mark. *Creativity for Graphic Designers: A Real-World Guide to Idea Generation—From Defining Your Message to Selecting the Best Idea for Your Printed Piece.* Cincinnati, OH: North Light Books, 2000.

DRAWING
- Abling, Bina. *Fashion Sketchbook.* New York, NY: Fairchild Publications, 4th edition, 2004.
- Chaet, Bernard. *The Art of Drawing.* Belmont, CA: Wadsworth Publishing, 3rd edition, 1983.
- Ching, Frank. *Design Drawing.* New York, NY: John Wiley & Sons, 1998.
- Sutherland, Martha. *Freehand Graphics: For Architects, Landscape Architects, and Interior Designers: A Problem-Solving Approach.* New York, NY: Design Press, 1991.

HISTORY OF ART AND DESIGN
- Banham, Reyner. *Theory and Design in the First Machine Age.* Cambridge, MA: MIT Press, 1980.
- Boucher, Francois. *20,000 Years of Fashion.* New York, NY: Harry N. Abrams, expanded edition, 1987.
- Eco, Umberto. *The History of Beauty.* New York, NY, Rizzoli, 2004.
- Hughes, Robert. *The Shock of the New.* New York, NY: Knopf, 1996.
- Moffet, Marian. *A World History of Architecture.* New York, NY: McGraw-Hill, 2003.
- Pevsner, Nikolaus. *Pioneers of Modern Design: From William Morris to Walter Gropius.* New York, NY: Viking Press, revised edition, 1975.
- Pile, John. *A History of Interior Design.* New York, NY: John Wiley and Sons, 2nd edition, 2004.
- Pulos, Arthur J. *American Design Ethic: A History of Industrial Design to 1940.* Cambridge, MA: MIT Press, 1983.
- Albus Volker, Reyer Kras, and Jonathan M. Woodham (eds). *Icons of Design: The 20th Century.* New York, NY: Prestel, 2000.
- Weston, Richard. *Modernism.* Boston, MA: Phaidon Press, 2001.

PHILOSOPHY AND COGNITION

- Baudrillard, Jean. *Simulacra and Simulation*. Translated by Sheila Faria Glaser. Ann Arbor, MI: University of Michigan Press, 1995.
- Chandler, Daniel. *Semiotics: The Basics*. New York, NY: Routledge, reissue edition, 2004.
- Dewey, John. *Art as Experience*. New York, NY: Capricorn Books, 1958.
- Dewey, John. *How We Think*. Cincinnati, OH: Dover Publications, 1997
- Frankfurt, Harry G. *On Bullshit*. Princeton, NJ: University Press, 2005.
- Hume, David: *A Treatise of Human Nature: Being an Attempt to Introduce the Experimental Method of Reasoning into Moral Subjects*. New York, NY: Oxford University Press, 2000.
- Lakoff, George and Mark Johnson. *Metaphors We Live by*. Chicago, IL: University of Chicago Press, 2nd edition, 2003.
- Royle, Nicholas. *Jaques Derrida*. New York, NY: Routledge, 2003.
- Ward, Glenn. *Teach Yourself Postmodernism*. New York, NY: McGraw-Hill, 2nd edition, 2003.

PRINCIPLES AND PRACTICE OF DESIGN

- Ashby, Michael and Kara Johnson. *Materials and Design: The Art and Science of Material Selection in Product Design*. Burlington, MA: Butterworth-Heinemann, 2002.
- Caplan, Ralph. By Design: *Why There Are No Locks on the Bathroom Doors in the Hotel Lous XIV and Other Object Lessons*. New York, NY: Fairchild Publications, Inc., 2nd edition, 2005.
- Garrett, Jesse James. *The Elements of User Experience*. New York, NY: New Riders Publishing, 2003.
- Heller, Steven and Elinor Pettit. *Design Dialogues*, New York, NY: Allworth Press, 1998.
- Heskett, John. *Toothpicks and Logos: Design in Everyday Life*. New York, NY: Oxford University Press, 2003.
- Kuniavsky, Mike. *Observing the User Experience: A Practitioner's Guide to User Research*. San Fransisco, CA: Morgan Kaufmann, 2003.
- Lauer, David A. and Stephan Pentak. *Design Basics*. Orlando, FL: Harcourt, Brace and Company, 5th edition, 2000.
- Nielson, Karla J. and David A. Taylor. *Interiors: An Introduction*. New York, NY: McGraw-Hill, 3rd edition, 2002.
- Norman, Donald A. *The Design of Everyday Things*. New York, NY: Basic Books, 2002.
- Norman, Donald A. *Emotional Design: Why We Love (or Hate) Everyday Things*. New York, NY: Basic Books, 2004.
- Pile, John F. *Interior Design*. Upper Saddle River, NJ: Prentice Hall, 3rd edition, 2003.
- Tufte, Edward R. *Envisioning Information*. Cheshire, CT: Graphics Press, 1990.
- Tufte, Edward R. *The Visual Display of Quantitative Information*. Cheshire, CT: Graphics Press, 2nd edition, 2001.
- Wallschlaeger, Charles and Cynthia Busic-Snyder. *Basic Visual Concepts and Principles for Artists, Architects and Designers*. Dubuque, IA: William C. Brown, 1992.
- White, Alexander W. *The Elements of Graphic Design: Space, Unity, Page Architecture, and Type*. New York, NY: Allsworth Press, 2002.
- William Lidwell, Kritina Holden, and Jill Butler. *Universal Principles of Design: 100 Ways to Enhance Usability, Influence Perception, Increase Appeal, Make Better Design Decisions, and Teach Through Design*. Gloucester, MA: Rockport Publishers, 2003.

- Wong, Wucius. *Principles of Form and Design.* New York, NY: John Wiley and Sons, 1993.
- Zelanski, Paul, and Mary Pat Fisher. *Shaping Space: The Dynamics of Three-Dimensional Design.* Orlando, FL: Harcourt, Brace and Company, 2nd edition, 1995.

RESPONSIBLE DESIGN PRACTICES

- Heller, Steven and Veronique Vienne (eds). *Citizen Designer: Perspectives on Design Responsibility.* New York, NY: Allworth Press, 2003.
- McDonough, William and Michael Braungart. *Cradle to Cradle: Remaking the Way We Make Things.* New York, NY: North Point Press, 2002.
- Papanek, Victor, *Design for the Real World: Human Ecology and Social Change.* Chicago, IL: Academy of Chicago Publishers, 2nd edition, 1985.

Appendix 3

NOTABLE DESIGNERS AND ARCHITECTS

The following pages contain a list of notable architects and designers in chronological order, starting with William Morris at the beginning of the Industrial Age. Please do not assume anything negative if a person is not mentioned at all. Similarly, the works listed for each person are by no means a comprehensive list; think of this as something to get you started—material for the search engine, if you will.

Take the time to look at each person on this list, and you will have added immensely to your knowledge, as well as your design vocabulary.

WILLIAM MORRIS 1834–1896
- Creation window (design by Morris and Philip Webb) at Church of All Saints, Selsley, Gloucestershire, England, 1863
- Sussex Chair, 1865
- Marigold Wallpaper, 1875

VICTOR HORTA 1861–1947
- Tassel House, Brussels, Belgium, 1893
- Hotel van Eetvelde, Brussels, Belgium, 1898
- Maison du Peuple, Place Emile van de Velde, Brussels, Belgium, 1898
- Horta House (now Musee Horta), Brussels, Belgium, 1898

CHARLES RENNIE MACKINTOSH 1868–1928
- Glasgow School of Art, Glasgow, Scotland, UK, 1897–1899 and 1907–1909
- Hill House and the Hill House Chair, Helensburgh, Scotland, UK, 1908
- Peter Behrens, 1868–1940
- Behrens House, Darmstadt, Germany, 1901
- E.G. High Tension Factory, Berlin, Germany, 1910
- G. Farben Offices, Frankfurt, Germany, 1925
- Apartments at Weissenhofseidlung, Stuttgart, Germany, 1927

FRANK LLOYD WRIGHT 1869–1959
- Fallingwater, Mill Run, Pennsylvania 1937
- Johnson Wax Building, at Racine, Wisconsin, 1939
- Boomer Residence, at Phoenix, Arizona, 1953
- Guggenheim Museum, New York, New York, 1959

EILEEN GRAY 1878–1976
- E-1027 (a house planned for her own use) Roquebrune, near Menton, France, 1929
- Tempa a Pailla, at Castellar 34

WALTER GROPIUS 1883–1969
- Director of the Bauhaus, Dessau, Germany, 1925
- Gropius House, Lincoln, Massachusetts, 1937
- Harvard Graduate Center, Cambridge, Massachusetts, 1950

COCO CHANEL 1883–1971
Coco Chanel wasn't just ahead of her time. She was ahead of herself. If you look at the work of contemporary fashion designers as different from one another, such as Tom Ford, Helmut Lang, Miuccia Prada, Jil Sander, and Donatella Versace, you see that many of their strategies echo Chanel. The way she mixed up the vocabulary of male and female clothes and created fashion that offered the wearer a feeling of hidden luxury rather than ostentation are just two examples of how her taste and sense of style overlap with today's fashion. —Time, June 8, 1998

LUDWIG MIES VAN DER ROHE 1886–1969
- Weissenhof Apartments, Stuttgart, Germany, 1927
- H. Lange House, Krefeld, Germany, 1928
- Barcelona Pavilion, Barcelona, Spain, 1929
- Tugendhat House, Brno, Czech Republic, 1930
- Farnsworth House, Plano, Illinois, 1950
- Lake Shore Drive Apartments, Chicago, Illinois, 1951
- Crown Hall, Chicago, Illinois, 1956
- Seagram Building (with Philip Johnson), New York, New York, 1958
- New National Gallery, Berlin, Germany, 1968

LE CORBUSIER (CHARLES-EDOUARD JEANNERET) 1887–1965
- Villa Savoye, Poissy, France, 1929
- United Nations Headquarters, New York, New York, finished 1953
- Notre-Dame-du-Haut, Ronchamp, France, 1955
- Carpenter Center, Cambridge, Massachusetts, 1964
- Centre Le Corbusier, Zurich, Switzerland, 1967

GERRIT RIETVELD 1888–1964
- Red-Blue Armchair, 1918

ELSA SCHIAPARELLI 1890–1973
A leading fashion designer in the 1920s and 1930s, she worked with many surrealist artists, including Salvador Dali, Jean Cocteau, and Alberto Giacometti, between 1936 and 1939. Her innovations included her use of color, notably "shocking pink;" animal print fabrics;

and zippers dyed the same colors as the fabrics.

GIO PONTI 1891–1979
- La Pavoni coffee machine, 1946
- Superleggera Chair, 1955–1957
- Planchart Villa, Caracas, Venezuela, 1955
- Pirelli Tower, Milan, Italy, 1956
- Cathedral of Taranto, Taranto, Italy, 1970
- Denver Museum of Art, Denver, Colorado, 1972

RAYMOND LOEWY 1893–1986
- Lucky Strike packaging, 1939
- Greyhound bus, 1954
- Shell logo, 1962

    In 1975, the Smithsonian Institution opened the Designs of Raymond Loewy, a four-month exhibit dedicated to "the man who changed the face of industrial design."

ALVAR AALTO 1898–1976
- Villa Mairea, Noormaku, Finland, 1939
- Nordic House, Reykjavik, Iceland, 1962
- Seinajoki Town Hall, Seinajoki, Finland, 1965
- Riola Parish Church, Riola, Italy, 1978

MARCEL BREUER 1902–1981
- Wassily Chair, 1925–1927

ARNE JACOBSEN 1902–1971
- Soholm Housing Estate, Klampenborg, Gentofte, Denmark, 1950
- Series 7 chair, 1955
- Munkegaards School, Copenhagen, Denmark, 1956
- Grand Prix Internationale d'Architecture et d'Art, Paris, France, 1960

ERWIN KOMENDA 1904–1966
- VW "Beetle" body, 1936
- Porsche 550 "Spyder," 1954

CHRISTIAN DIOR 1905–1957
Dior presented what would be called "The New Look" in women's fashions in 1947, bringing back elegance and femininity after the fashion-starved years of World War II and affirming Paris as the center of haute couture fashion. He began the practice of licensing agreements in the fashion industry.

PHILIP JOHNSON 1906–2005
- Johnson House, aka "The Glass House," New Caanan, Connecticut, 1949.
- Seagram Building (with Ludwig Mies van der Rohe), New York, New York, 1958
- Pennzoil Place, Houston, Texas, 1976
- Garden Grove Church, Garden Grove, Los Angeles, California, 1980
- AT&T Building, New York, New York, 1984

ALEC ISSIGONIS 1906–1988
- The Morris Mini, 1957–1959

CHARLES EAMES 1907–1978 and RAY KAISER EAMES 1912–1988
- Eames Lounge Chair, 1956
- Aluminum Group, 1958
- Molded Plastic Chair, 1971
- "Powers of ten" installation and film, 1977

EARL S. TUPPER 1907–1983
- Tupperware, 1946

EERO SAARINEN 1910–1961
- Kresge Auditorium, Cambridge, Massachusetts, 1950–1955
- Yale Hockey Rink, New Haven, Connecticut, 1961
- TWA terminal, New York, New York, 1962
- Dulles Airport, Chantilly, Virginia, 1962
- John Deere and Company, Moline, Illinois, 1963
- Gateway Arch, St. Louis, Missouri, 1966

HANS WEGNER 1914
- Peacock Chair, 1947
- Wishbone Chair, 1949
- Flag Halyard Chair, 1950

I. M. (IEOH MING) PEI 1917
- John Hancock Tower, Boston, Massachusetts, 1977
- Pyramide du Louvre, Paris, France, 1989
- Bank of China Tower, Hong Kong, China, 1990

ETTORE SOTTSASS 1917
- Carlton Sideboard (Mobile diviorio), 1980
- Wolf House, Ridgway, Colorado, USA, 1989
- Cofounder of the Memphis Group, 1980

CESAR PELLI 1926
- Ohio Center for Performing Arts, Cincinnati, Ohio, 1991
- Aronoff Center for the Arts, Cincinnati, Ohio, 1995
- Petronas Towers, Kuala Lumpur, Malaysia, 1998
- 20 River Terrace—The Solaria, New York, New York, 2004

JACOB JENSEN 1926
- The Margrethe Bowl, 1955
- Kirk E76 Telephone, 1976
- Beocenter 9000, 1987
- Beosystem 4500, 1989

FRANK GEHRY 1929
- Gehry House, Santa Monica, California, 1979 and 1987
- Guggenheim Museum Bilbao, Bilbao, Spain, 1997
- Experience Music Project, Seattle, Washington, 2000
- Walt Disney Concert Hall, Los Angeles, California, 2004

MILTON GLASER 1929
Glaser's graphic and architectural commissions include the "I (heart) NY" logo, which has been described as "the most frequently imitated logo design in human history," commissioned by the state of New York in 1976.

PETER EISENMAN 1932
- Bruges Concert Hall, Bruges, Belgium 1999
- Memorial to the murdered Jews of Europe, Berlin, Germany, 1998–2005

RICHARD ROGERS 1933
- Centre Pompidou, Paris, France, 1976
- Lloyds Building, London, England, 1984
- Millenium Dome, London, England, 1999

MICHAEL GRAVES 1934
- The Humana Building, Louisville, Kentucky, 1982
- Team Disney Building, Burbank, California, 1986
- Ministry of Health, Welfare and Sport, the Hague, The Netherlands, 1993

NORMAN FOSTER 1935
- Hong Kong and Shanghai Bank, Hong Kong, China, 1986
- London Millennium Bridge, London, England, 2000
- 30 St. Mary Axe ("The Gherkin"), London, England, said to be London's first environmentally sustainable skyscraper, 2004

YOSHIO TANIGUCHI 1937
- Shiseido Museum of Art, Kakegawa, Japan, 1978
- The Gallery of Horyuji treasures, Tokyo National Museum, Tokyo, Japan, 1999
- Museum of Modern Art addition, New York, New York, 2004
- Kyoto National Museum, Kyoto, Japan, designed 1998–2000, to be completed in 2007

RENZO PIANO 1937
- Centre Pompidou, Paris, France, 1976
- Kansai Airport Terminal, Osaka, Japan, 1994

REI KAWAKUBO 1942
Fashion designer Rei Kawakubo, founder of Comme des Garcons (1973, menswear in 1978), was born in Tokyo in 1942. Being untrained as a fashion designer, but having studied fine arts and literature, she conveys her ideas verbally to her patternmakers.

The Fashion Institute of Technology honored her in 1987 as one of the leading women in 20th-century design.

REM KOOLHAAS 1944
- Netherlands Dance Theater, The Hague, Netherlands, 1988
- Kunsthal Rotterdam, Rotterdam, Netherlands, 1993
- Recipient of the Pritzker Architecture Prize, 2000
- Seattle Public Library, Seattle, Washington, 2004
- Casa da Musica, Oporto, Portugal, 2005
- China Central Television (CCTV) headquarters, Beijing, China, under construction as of 2006.

BERNARD TSCHUMI 1944
- Parc de la Villette, Paris, France, 1983
- Alfred Lerner Hall, Columbia University, New York, New York, 1999
- Le Fresnoy Art Center, Tourcoing, France, 2004

DANIEL LIEBESKIND 1946
- Jewish Museum Berlin, Berlin, Germany, 2001
- Food Theater Café, London, England, 2001
- World Trade Center Reconstruction Competition, New York, New York, 2003

PAUL SMITH 1947
- Presenting his first Paul Smith menswear collection in 1976, Paul Smith has established himself as the preeminent British designer, his numerous collections of apparel and accessories consistently inspire and anticipate trends.
- "Mondo" collection of furniture, in collaboration with Italian furniture manufacturer Cappellini, 2002
- "Bespoke" upholstery textile, in partnership with textile manufacturer Maharam, 2003

PHILIPPE STARCK 1949
- Costes chair, 1982
- Royalton Hotel, New York, New York, 1988
- Juicy Salif juicer, Alessi, 1990
- Paramount Hotel, New York, New York, 1990
- Kong restaurant, Paris, France 2003

TIBOR KALMAN 1949–1999
Kalman was best known for the groundbreaking work he created with his New York design firm, M&Co, and his brief yet influential editorship of [Benetton's] *Colors* magazine. Throughout his 30-year career, Kalman brought his restless intellectual curiosity and subversive wit to everything he worked on—from album covers for the Talking Heads to the redevelopment of Times Square. Kalman incorporated visual elements other designers had never associated with successful design and used his work to promote his radical politics. The influence of his experiments in typography and images can be seen everywhere, from music videos to the design of magazines such as *Wired* and *Ray Gun*. (Based on his obituary, May 19, 1999, on Salon.com)

JAQUES HERZOG 1950 and PIERRE DE MEURON 1950
- Dominus Winery, Yountville, California, 1998
- Gallery of Modern Art for the Tate Museum, London, England, 2000

- Pritzker Architecture Prize Laureates, 2001
- Walker Art Center Expansion, Minneapolis, Minnesota, 2005

"A building is a building. It cannot be read like a book; it doesn't have any credits, subtitles, or labels like pictures in a gallery. In that sense, we are absolutely anti-representational. The strength of our buildings is the immediate, visceral impact they have on a visitor."
—Jacques Herzog

ZAHA HADID 1950
- Vitra Fire Station, Weil am Rhein, Germany, 1993
- Bergisel Ski Jump, Innsbruck, Austria, 2002
- Rosenthal Center for Contemporary Art, Cincinnati, Ohio, 2004

SANTIAGO CALATRAVA 1951
- Stadelhofen Railway Station, Zurich, Switzerland, 1984
- Alamillo Bridge and La Cartuja Viaduct, Seville, Spain, 1992
- Alameda Bridge and Underground Station, Valencia, Spain, 1995
- Campo Volantin Footbridge, Bilbao, Spain, 1998
- Oriente Station, Lisbon, Portugal, 1998
- Sondica Airport, Bilbao, Spain, 1999
- City of Science Museum and Planetarium, Valencia, Spain
- Palace of the Arts, Valencia, Spain, 2001
- Milwaukee Art Museum, Milwaukee, Wisconsin, 2001
- Sundial bridge, Turtle Bay, California, 2004

HELMUT LANG 1956
- Lang is synonymous with the cool minimalism that defined the fashion world in the 1980s.

JASPER MORRISON 1959
- Hanover Tram, Hanover, Germany, 1997
- The largest European light rail in production; it was the first vehicle to be awarded the IF Transportation Design Prize and the Ecology Award.
- Air Chair, 1999
- Furniture for the Tate Modern Museum, London, England, 2000

MAYA LIN 1959
- Vietnam Memorial, Washington, D.C., 1982
- Civil Rights Memorial, Montgomery, Alabama, 1989
- Groundswell, commissioned by the Wexner Center for the Arts, Ohio State University, Columbus, Ohio, 1993
- "The Wave Field," University of Michigan, Ann Arbor, Michigan, 1995
- Langston Hughes Library, Clinton, Tennessee, 1999
- "Ecliptic" Ice Rink in Grand Rapids, Michigan, 2001

KARIM RASHID 1960
- Morimoto Restaurant, Philadelphia, Pennsylvania, 2001
- Foscarini Blob lamp, 2002

- Semiramis Hotel, Athens Greece, 2004

JONATHAN IVE 1966

- Vice president of Apple Computer's Industrial Design Group from 1992
- iMac, 1998–2002
- G4 Cube, 2000
- iPod, 2001
- Designer of the Year, London Design Museum, 2003

ALEXANDER MCQUEEN 1969

Since leaving St. Martins School of Design in London in 1994, McQueen has become one of the most famous and respected international fashion designers in the world. He was named British Designer of the Year four times in 1996, 1997, 2001, and 2003. In October 1996, he was appointed Chief Designer at the French Haute Couture House Givenchy where he worked until March 2001.

HUSSEIN CHALAYAN 1971

- Absolut Creation Award, 1995
- Designer of the Year, British Fashion Awards, 1999
- Designer of the Year, British Fashion Awards, 2000

Appendix 4

READING THE ZEITGEIST: TRENDSPOTTING IN A DECENTRALIZED WORLD

Spotting a trend in any field is a complicated exercise. Many factors contribute to a society's behavior and trends. Often, the position of the viewer is equally important as any other factor. This will be a short overview of spotting design trends geared more toward pointing you in the right direction and giving you a sense of where to look.

Primarily it is important in any design field to be aware of not only the stylistic demands of your clients, but also their approach in general to aesthetics and technology. A designer must be aware of trends in art and design as a matter of course, but to understand the forces that shape the trends is an important edge.

Understanding the forces that have shaped a current trend allows you to anticipate movement, giving you the ability to predict what could be the prevailing trend in the near future. It is also important to understand where you stand in the context of the culture you live in, knowing what is at work affecting your clients' choices and opinions. Designers do not necessarily need or want to adhere to trends, but not adhering requires knowing what should be avoided, updated, counterbalanced, or otherwise played with. Knowing where people's sensibilities are going can also be a way of finding where you can push the envelope.

OBSERVING THE ZEITGEIST

Every era, in a given culture, has a set of characterizing attitudes, styles, and principles. This is the Zeitgeist, "the Spirit of the Time." This can also be stated as being the thoughts and feelings that typify an age or period. Understanding the Zeitgeist of any given period requires you being open to reading the signs in a culture and being able to understand how the various elements that create the unique "feel" of a period in history. With the benefit of hindsight, defining the Zeitgeist is easy, but predicting its movement can be extremely difficult. By examining the signifiers in the past, you can learn to recognize the current signs and thereby make predictions. People look to art and design to see the styles, but why they are the way they are and what it is that drives the publics' needs and tastes can be entirely remote from the world of design. Observation is key. Keep your eyes open and your ear to the ground.

OBSERVATION

Getting a sense of the Zeitgeist may involve not much more than looking around. Observation is key, and knowing what is "out there" can be very indicative of where things are headed.

Observation requires both media-savviness as well as a grasp of what is happening on the street. The media image can be at odds with the reality, as trend reporting tends toward the sensational and with very clearly defined lines, while the reality can often be more subtle and blurry. Often the media definition of what is current can be based on a certain area or economic bracket. A magazine or TV show may tell you that "everyone" is doing something, but a slightly closer look reveals that "everyone" is only a handful of ultra-rich people or celebrities in the city where that magazine is based. If they are your market, fine. If not, then perhaps more looking is required. Perhaps this handful of people is just about to be emulated by thousands more. To recognize this, you must be aware of the forces that drive such choices.

It is important to have a wide view, as styles evolve at different paces in different disciplines. Those of a longer lifetime, such as architecture and fine arts, lead the way traditionally, and other design fields track behind, with apparel revolving on multiple tracks at bewildering speed. In essence one can look to the more long-lived to influence the transitional and seasonal. Art and architecture can, for example, influence a community for centuries, whereas most clothing and small appliances will maintain their style for a year or two at most, often more influenced than influential.

However, it is interesting to note how this hierarchy began to break down somewhat at the end of the 20th century. Partly this was due to the popularization of "designer" goods and the increasing education of apparel, industrial, and graphic designers. This market was fueled with the assistance of the media saturation experienced in a large part of the world through television and the Internet, allowing the marketing of consumer goods and "lifestyle" products as never before. New things, new looks, and new ways of doing things have forever been of interest to people, and with the ability to see the new and different at all times, with marketers forever finding new hooks for us, our demand for updated versions of whatever we own has increased to the point of near ridiculousness.

TECHNOLOGY AND COMMUNICATION

Underlying this change in the transference of style is the way our culture's perception of the world has changed in the past century and is still changing with our capability to communicate and receive information. The clearest description of this appears when one examines how the dissemination of information changed with industrialization. Increased commerce and shipping required more efficient communication after the middle of the 19th century, and the telegraph allowed information to move at a speed that was beyond that at which humans could travel. Subsequent development brought wireless transmissions, telephone, film, television, satellites, the Internet, and cellular phones.

New ideas, news of events, and images of styles can be transmitted around the globe at the speed of light, allowing anyone with access to a television or computer to be as well informed as anyone else, regardless of how close to the source of the information they are. No longer do we wait for the latest film or magazine to arrive so that we can learn of the latest styles in the grand cities of the world. The images are in front of everyone at the same instant, and the notion of what "everyone is doing" acquires a new significance. The speed at which ideas travel changes our experience and perceptions of the world, as it is not just what we perceive, but also how we perceive. This is the core of Marshall McLuhan's idea, set forth at the advent of television, that our world has essentially shrunk to the scale of a village, where all information is now available instantly. Any event can now be experienced instantly and simultaneously worldwide, breaking down borders and notions of exclusivity.

Now that we have extended not just our physical organs, but also the nervous system, itself, in electric technology, the principle of specialism and division as a factor of speed no longer applies. When information moves at the speed of signals in the central nervous system, man is confronted with the obsolescence of all earlier forms of acceleration, such as road and rail. What emerges is a total field of inclusive awareness. The old patterns of psychic and social adjustment become irrelevant.[1]

MEDIA

When considering media as a signifier of the Zeitgeist it is important to distinguish between the politics of the media and the politics of the street. With the advent of round-the-clock news and Internet blogging, news has taken on a character where it is often difficult to discern what is an actual trend and what is hype, spin, dissemination, or news-cycle filler. Broadcast news media and magazines are always on the lookout for a headline, to the extent that the complex issues are often compressed into a "story" that fits the headline and the format, leaving out perhaps larger context or finer detail. To understand a society, one must therefore go beyond the news and try to look at the source, namely the people of the society. People make politics and get the politicians they deserve. People's needs and desires are reflected in their politics; uncertain times cause people to fall back on traditional values and resist change more than they do in times of security and prosperity. Social unrest can result in new styles and changes in consumption.

It is often difficult to spot the cause-and-effect aspects of society on politics for the very reason that the influence is often circular. Especially with the amplifying echo chamber of the 24-hour news media, it becomes difficult to discern the core of the situation.

However, in terms of what a designer may be looking for, you may try to limit the search for the sense of adventure mentioned above. Is the market ready for new and experimental things? Are people spending or holding their income? Are there any movements that have begun to create their own look or trends of consumption?

The media highlights a trend and thereby creates a feedback loop. We believe the trend is there because we've seen it in the media, and we emulate it, thus creating a larger trend still, in something of a self-fulfilling prophecy. However, given that the trend does not have an organic origin in any of society's needs (apart from the need for something new) its lifespan is only as long as the time it takes for the next "new thing" to come along. The opposite can also be true: A trend can be stifled at birth by oversaturation. This is especially true of youth-oriented styles, where the perception that something has "gone mainstream" will instantly cool off the desire for it. So on one hand we have the ability for the media to enhance a trend by creating the perception that it is already widespread, and on the other we have the completely opposite effect. Which way it will go can be difficult to predict.

IS IT REAL OR . . . ?

Increasingly, distinguishing between actual events and "manufactured" events has become difficult, as publicists and reality-television producers have become more adept at their crafts. It seems to matter less and less that in a scripted media event, nothing is actually happening, any more than you would say that something is actually happening on a stage during a play.[2] In fact, the scripted event has taken on a significance of its own, like ritualized theater. The invented situation of movie stars' romances or a political candidate's posturing is pored over with the intensity of courtiers deciphering the mood and health of their kings.

The significance for trendwatchers lies then not so much in the "what" that is going on, but in the "who?" and "how?" Who is being watched, by whom, and for how long can be an indicator of where our interests and ideals lie. A good early example of this may be found during the late 1960s, when marketers picked up on the baby-boomer generation's desire for distance from the culture of their parents and marketed "youth culture" and "generation gap" aggressively. A strong signifier of changes in the Zeitgeist in 1967 would have been the arrival of the musical *Hair* on Broadway. This was hippy counterculture packaged and presented onstage with the various politics and issues of the day set to music. Revolutionary and challenging as it may have seemed at the outset, it can now be seen as the beginning of the end—a pinnacle of the 1960s youth culture from which there was only going down. Picture suburban couples on a night out, buying tickets to a show to "see the hippies," and the trend comes into focus.

TRACKING GENERATIONS

Since the middle of the 20th century, the story of pop culture in the United States, and from there to an amazing number of other countries, has largely been the story of the "boomer generation." One of the more important demographical signifiers has long been age, and when the boomer generation showed up as a demographic that could be aggressively marketed to, the idea of a "generation gap" was actually productive in that the gap could become a unifying theme. This was nothing new. Older generations have complained about younger generations for countless years, and younger generations have done everything they can to avoid resembling their elders. It was therefore inevitable that in an affluent, free society, a large generation of the "baby-boom" ilk would create a cultural wave wherever it went. Indeed, the trends and demands of the second half of the 20th century can be traced more or less to the boomers due to the combination of their abundance of leisure time and money.

The youth culture of the 1960s gave way to the hedonistic 1970s, which lead to the yuppies of the 1980s, where the baby boomers officially became their parents and began the call for designer things. As the boomers aged in the 1990s, there was an increase in the demand for the health products required by the middle-aged, and in fashion the line between youth and middle age blurred as it became clear that this generation was uneasy with growing old. As we now near the time where this generation begins to reach retirement age our political discussion is dominated by talk of Social Security and pensions, and the dominant television ads are those for pharmaceuticals designed to alleviate the pains and problems of advancing age. Given that the tail end of the boomer generation will not reach retirement age, until around 2020, we may have a way to go, but the interesting trend watching will take place between now and then in the areas where the boomers will let go of their hold on popular culture, both as producers and consumers. In this way, one may predict that 20th-century trends will not fully end until somewhere around 2020, barring events that may take place to hasten or blur that shift.

EVENTS

The Zeitgeist can change very quickly if something happens to give everyone a jolt. When scouting out the path of the Zeitgeist, it is necessary to expect the unexpected. Events that jolt a society out of its path can be on the level of wars and natural disasters, but lately, with the 24-hour news cycle constantly on the lookout for a story, individuals' stories get produced and assume the same scale as natural disasters. In a way, the 24-hour news cycle has become the equivalent of 18th-century court gossip, where the smallest detail of someone's personal crisis can suddenly be all over the world, overshadowing events that in a historical sense may be far larger. News programs competing for audiences have become entertainment and thereby contributed to a decentralization of events and ideas. If everything is given equal weight, then nothing is of primary importance.

Perhaps this is not as new or strange as you may think. Perhaps it is only in contrast with the previous 100 years that it seems odd. The first century of industrialization was marked by a great seriousness of ideas and a belief in progress through technology and political idealism. Events were either serious or not, and the standard historical model of great men and their machinations was adhered to in the news, both in print and later in electronic broadcasts. With the development of the electronic global village, perhaps the trend influences have begun to return to the scale and focus of a village culture, where there are always wars and rumors of wars, but events of a personal scale have perhaps more influence than anything the outside world can deliver.

TECHNOLOGY

Technology is exciting and has forever been the measure of human progress. It also can alter a culture by what it can produce. New materials give rise to new products. New manufacturing techniques or modes of delivery change the nature of a product. Soon the new has become commonplace, and we cannot imagine our lives without it. The way we receive information and connect with the world is one thing, but technology all around will change how a society behaves and how it views itself. New exciting technologies have always prompted people to dream of the future and alter their present behavior accordingly. High-speed travel has always captured the imagination, whether be it railroads, cars, airplanes, or spacecraft. In the first half of the 20th century, the functionalist streamlining of designs owed much to the idea of speed represented in the new vehicles of the time, but also to the manufacturing processes of the assembly line. In the first decades of the 21st century, it is more than likely that new technologies will appear that radically alter our perceptions of the world and our daily lives. Computer-aided methods of designing and manufacturing and increased miniaturization of components have already begun to result in departures from the conventional forms of buildings, cars, and appliances large and small. One could imagine that soon the effect will trickle down to apparel. It has already done so in footwear.

TRENDSPOTTING IN A NEW CENTURY

Predicting trends is not as easy to do as you would like to think. The postmodern practice of referencing and mining the past may render predictions worthless by blurring the distinction between past and present style and thereby injecting an element of unpredictability into stylistic influences. Once "retro" becomes a style used to such a degree that it is no longer possible to tell which is the old and which is the new, one could say that it loses its identity. It is neither old nor new. The direction for a trendspotter to take is to wonder why this particular era, decade, or style is being referenced at this particular time and not dismiss the nostalgia, escapism, or romanticizing of the past that is implied.

The modern age is associated with the high point of the industrial age—the pre-digital machine age of the decades preceding and following the beginning of the 20th century. The rise of machination and industrialization along with the prevailing sociopolitical theories of Charles Darwin, Sigmund Freud, and Karl Marx, gave rise to the notion that human life and culture could be quantified, ordered, analyzed, and directed by regulation. Furthermore, the expansion that had taken place in Western culture since the Enlightenment of the 16th century had created the belief that Western culture was superior and should be exported and applied everywhere. Political systems right and left were under the same belief, culminating in World War II and the subsequent Cold War. Design took its cues from heavy industry and machines, creating an aesthetic of streamlined unadorned shapes, where local customs and traditions were of no consequence. An international style was to take the place of everything in the same way that the political theories of the early 20th century were to be exported and layered on top of local systems by force if necessary.

As the 20th century drew to a close, this line of historical narrative began to blur. With the previous systems of colonial empires and political power blocks gone, the idea of the historical inevitability of communism or capitalism as the ultimate victorious system became suspect and almost quaint in perception. The notion of culture as a Western construct also began to show cracks. Essentially all notions of centrality in culture, literature, and art are now debated. Even our personal sense of history has become nonlinear, since we are able to visually experience all eras at once, and our experience of history is through film, exhibits, and the contrived settings of theme parks.[3]

Our vision of the world is largely created through mass media. Our experience of the world is less from actual observation and contact than from what we see and read on television, in films, and on the Internet. Films and television programs are ever more self-referential, feeding on their own history, and the simulation of "reality" has become an art form to the point where the reality being depicted is subservient to the demands of the media, and creates a hyperreality, which is a simulation of experience.[4]

The dissolution of centers of influence through the availability of information has also resulted in the near impossibility of recognizing a trend through the observation of an upper class, as used to be the case through most of history until World War II. The new elite of actors, rock stars, and personalities do not serve as models in the way aristocracy and the wealthy used to. Fashion is no longer top-down, and high-flying lifestyles are lived in a much less flamboyant mode. The systems of class and race and the power of money are all still there, but the signals are much more subtle, and the person in the roughed up jeans and T-shirt may well be the person who has paid the largest sum for his or her clothing.

In the postmodern world, there is a dissolving of the notion of a central truth in any category, including art and design. Without fixed centers, truths that used to hold get confused and the differences between high and low, rich and poor, stylish and unfashionable, and design and kitsch become unclear. Outlines of the categories get more blurred and closer together, their meaning gradually fades and a new truth emerges.[5]

One may think that such a time would be somewhat difficult for design. On the contrary, there is a certain excitement about a time such as this. Perhaps this is exactly where we need to be. Experimentation abounds as designers and artists seek out a new look for our times. This is what is known as a liminal moment. ". . . a moment when things are betwixt and between, when old structures have broken down and new ones have not yet been created." Historically, these times of change are the times of greatest cultural creativity; everything is infused with new meanings.[6]

Perhaps the true value of trendspotting at the beginning of a new century would be in deciphering what these new meanings are.

Appendix 5

ZEITGEIST AND DESIGN: A TIMELINE

I have taken events related to technology, design, communications, and pop culture and created a chronologically ordered list. This is a grab bag of sorts, a mosaic, a collection that, in the choices it reveals, probably says more about me than it should. I made the choices of what to include based more on impulse and instinct than any logical progression of information. I see each event listed here as a building block of some large sprawling structure that is unclear and cannot be seen at all except as a sum of it parts.

A timeline can just be an entertaining collection of facts for trivia games or for whiling away the time on the Internet. A timeline can also create insights into the flow of ideas and influences and, by putting events into historical context, give us a sense of the continuity of thought in the world.

For each event registered here there is probably at least one that should be, but isn't. I apologize for any omissions, but I'll point out that an interesting way to use this timeline would be to find what you can add to it and explain why you would like to do so.

Don't read too much into the structure of the list. The fact that two events share a year does not necessarily mean anything, but taken over the course of many years, patterns emerge. You can see the shape of the Zeitgeist over the decades, forming the world we live in and the future we are approaching.

1849

- Henry Cole publishes the *Journal of Design*. Cole maintains that design should encompass more than applied ornament. He states that knowledge of manufacturing processes and materials is necessary for successful design. In the pages of the journal, manufacturers and students of design would find "something like a systematic attempt to establish recognized principles."

1850

- Adding machine employing depressible keys is patented, New Paltz, New York.
- Paul Julius Reuter uses 40 pigeons to carry stock market prices.
- First public demonstration of ice is made by refrigeration.

1851

- Great Exhibition—decorative extravagance of Victorian design—Crystal Palace.
- In the United States, paper is made from wood fiber.
- Bally begins mass production of footwear in Switzerland.
- Isaac Singer is granted a patent for his sewing machine. Although not the only one working on the development of sewing machines, he builds the first commercially successful version. He is promptly sued for patent infringement by Elias Howe, with whom he then enters into business.

1852

- Emma Snodgrass is arrested in Boston for wearing pants.
- Uncle Sam cartoon figure makes its debut in the *New York Lantern* weekly.
- Massachusetts rules all school-age children must attend school.

1853

- First major U.S. rail disaster kills 46 (Norwalk, Connecticut).
- First electric telegraph is used, Merchant's Exchange to Pt. Lobos.
- First U.S. woman, Antoinette Blackwell, is ordained a minister.
- First potato chips are prepared by Chef George Crum (Saratoga Springs, New York).

1854

- Curved stereotype plate allows for multicolumn printing of newspapers; wide ads follow, creating demand for designs.
- George Boole develops a logic system on which future computers depend.

1855

- Joshua Stoddard of Worcester, Massachusetts patents first calliope.
- Henry Bessemer patents the Bessemer steel-making process, allowing for inexpensive mass-production of steel, paves the way for the modern industrial age.

1856

- Perkins discovers the first synthetic dyestuff, manuvine, which produces violet tones that cannot be obtained from natural dyes. This leads to a mania for violet things and begins a rush toward the development of other synthetic dyes.
- A cage-like frame of metal strips, the crinoline, is patented, leading to enormous skirts becoming fashionable for the following ten years.

1857

- James Gibbs patents the first chain stitch, single-thread sewing machine. Ready-made clothing now becomes commonly available. The spread of sewing machines in middle- and lower-class households later leads to increased demand for patterns and new fabrics. This also speeds up the fashion cycle, as the high fashions are now quickly copied, requiring society women to put more effort into staying ahead of the shopgirls.

1858

- Charles Frederick Worth, an Englishman, establishes the first haute couture firm in Paris, soon creating clothing for royalty and high-class customers all over Europe.

1859

- Ground is broken for the Suez Canal in Egypt, which eventually joins the Mediterranean and the Red Sea. It opens for shipping ten years later, allowing transport between Europe and Asia without circumnavigating Africa. It has an immediate effect on world trade, increasing European penetration and colonization of Africa.
- First successful oil well is drilled, near Titusville, Pennsylvania.
- Charles Darwin publishes *On the Origin of Species.*
- Jules Leotard performs first flying trapeze circus act (Paris). He also designs the garment that bears his name.

1860

- Arts and Crafts Movement: John Ruskin, William Morris, and Gustav Stickley consider machine production degrading to both workers and consumers. To fight the deadening hand of industry on design, they advocate and put into practice an aesthetic based on traditional methods of craftsmanship.

1861

- First hostile act of Civil War; Star of the West fired on, Sumter South Carolina.
- Steam elevator is patented by Elisha Otis.
- Flush toilet with separate water tank and a pull chain is patented by Mr. Thomas Crapper
- Kinematoscope is patented by Coleman Sellers, Philadelphia, Pennsylvania.
- First public schoolhouse opens at Washington and Mason Street, San Francisco, California.
- Congress authorizes paper money.
- First transcontinental telegram is sent. The telegraph not only ends the Pony Express, but also allows large amounts of information to move faster than humans, ending the connection between information and the human capacity for travel.
- Gatling gun is patented.

1862

- U.S. Navy launches first ironclad warship (*Monitor*) in January, sinks off Cape Hatteras, North Carolina, in December.
- Adolphe Nicole of Switzerland patents the chronograph.
- Jean Joseph Etienne Lenoir builds first automobile.
- Slavery is outlawed in U.S. territories.
- In England, Lewis Carroll writes *Alice in Wonderland* for Alice P. Liddell.
- New York-San Francisco direct telegraphic link is established.

1863

- James Plimpton of New York, New York patents four-wheeled roller skates.
- Chenille manufacturing machines patented by William Canter, New York, New York.
- Thomas Crapper pioneers the one-piece pedestal flushing toilet.
- First U.S. newspaper is printed on wood-pulp paper (*Boston Morning Journal*).
- Fire extinguisher is patented by Alanson Crane.

- William Bullock patents continuous-roll printing press.
- Antidraft mobs lynch blacks in New York, New York; about 1,000 people die.
- President Lincoln issues eye-for-eye order to shoot a rebel prisoner for every black prisoner shot.
- Submarine *H.L. Hunley* arrives in Charleston on railroad cars.
- President Lincoln makes his Emancipation Proclamation speech.
- Patent is granted for a process of making color photographs.

1864
- Charing Cross Station opens in London.
- Louis Ducos du Hauron patents a movie machine, but does not build it.
- United States mints two-cent coin (first appearance of "In God We Trust").

1865
- Edouard Manet's painting "Olympia" is displayed at the Salon of Paris. A departure from the idealism of the preceding century, its realism and rough technique shocks and outrages the public and the critics. Guards have to be stationed next to it to protect it, until it is moved to a spot high above a doorway, out of reach. Some consider "Olympia" to be the first modern painting.

1866
- Atlantic cable ties Europe and the United States for instant communication.

1867
- Japanese art is exhibited at the Paris Exposition. Painters such as Van Gogh and Gaugain are heavily influenced by what they see.

1868
- The stapler is invented by George W. McGill.

1869
- James Oliver invents the removable tempered steel plow blade.
- First plastic, Celluloid, is patented by John Wesley Hyatt, Albany, NY.
- Steam power brake is patented (George Westinghouse).
- Voting machine is patented by Thomas Edison.
- Ives W. McGaffey of Chicago patents first vacuum cleaner.
- Margarine is patented in Paris, for use by French Navy.
- Waffle iron is invented.
- Baptist minister invents the rickshaw in Yokohama, Japan.
- Hotel in Boston becomes the first to have indoor plumbing.
- The Suez Canal opens (Egypt).

1870
- Brooklyn Bridge construction begins and is completed May 24, 1883.
- John D. Rockefeller incorporates Standard Oil.
- Donkey is first used as symbol of the Democratic Party, in *Harper's Weekly*.
- Soda fountain is patented by Gustavus Dows.
- First motion picture is shown to a theater audience in Philadelphia, Pennsylvania.

- First New York subway line opens (pneumatic powered).
- First U.S. National Wildlife Preserve, Lake Meritt in Oakland, California.
- E. J. DeSemdt patents asphalt pavement.
- Congress authorizes registration of trademarks.
- Transcontinental Railway completed.

1871

- *Hints on Household Taste* is published in the United States. Published in England three years prior, it preaches "simplicity, humility and economy" in design to replace the extravagance of the popular revival styles of the time. The American edition states, "We take our architectural forms from England, our fashions from Paris, the patterns of our manufactures from all parts of the world, and make nothing really original but trotting wagons and wooden clocks."

1872

- U.S. Patent Office issues first patent list.
- George Westinghouse Jr. patents triple air brake for trains.
- First state bird refuge is authorized (Lake Merritt, California).
- Illinois becomes first state to require sexual equality in employment.
- Hydraulic electric elevator is patented by Cyrus Baldwin.
- Luther Crowell patents a machine that manufactures paper bags.
- Metropolitan Museum of Art opens, New York, New York.
- Silas Noble and J. P. Cooley patent toothpick-manufacturing machine.
- George B. Brayton patents gasoline-powered engine.
- Metropolitan Gas Company lamps are lit for the first time.
- Mahlon Loomis patents wireless telegraphy, allowing ship-to-shore communications.
- Doughnut cutter is patented by John Blondel of Thomaston, Maine.
- Fire destroys nearly 1,000 buildings in Boston.

1873

- Emperor Franz Jozef opens fifth World's Fair in Wien (Vienna).
- Dentist John Beers of San Francisco patents the gold crown.
- American Metrological Society forms weights, measures, and money.

1874

- In France, first show of the impressionist painters is displayed.

1875

- Charles Garnier's new opera opens in Paris (January).
- Georges Bizet's opera "Carmen" premieres, Paris, France.
- Electric dental drill is patented by George F. Green (March).
- Congress passes Civil Rights Act, which is invalidated by the Supreme Court, 1883.

1876

- The telephone is introduced and quickly becomes an indispensable part of daily life and business.

1877

- First news dispatch by telephone between Boston and Salem, Massachusetts.
- First cantilever bridge in United States is completed, Harrodsburg, Kentucky.
- Thomas Edison demonstrates the hand-cranked phonograph.

1878

- Full-page newspaper ads appear.

1879

- Henrik Ibsen's *Et Dukkehjem* (*A Dollhouse*) premieres in Copenhagen, Denmark.
- Joseph Swan demonstrates light bulb using carbon glow.
- First electric arc light is used (California Theater).
- George Selden files for first patent for a gasoline-driven automobile.
- Thomas Edison perfects the carbonized cotton filament light bulb.
- James and John Ritty patent first cash register to combat stealing by bartenders in their Dayton, Ohio saloon.
- First automatic telephone is switching system is patented.

1880

- Advertising copywriter becomes an occupation.

1881

- The first photographic roll film is invented.
- Women enter the business world.

1882

- Boston's Bijou Theatre, first American playhouse is lit exclusively by electricity; first performance is Gilbert and Sullivan's *Iolanthe*.
- First string of Christmas tree lights is created by Thomas Edison.
- Electric iron is patented by Henry W. Seely, New York, New York.
- The opera *Parsifal* is produced (Bayreuth).

1883

- Thomas Edison invents the incandescent lighting system, which eventually changes the concept of the workday, alters architecture, and becomes a significant aid to communication.
- The first significant impressionist exhibition in the United States is held in Boston, Massachusetts, featuring works by Manet, Monet, Pissarro, Renoir, and Sisley.
- The magazine *Ladies' Home Journal* is founded, offers readers a look into the homes of high society and the opportunity to observe the difference between good and bad taste in home furnishings.

1884

- Lewis Waterman designs a practical fountain pen that doesn't blot.
- The Stebbing Automatic Camera, first production model to use roll film.

1885

- Redfern, an English tailor, with shops in London and Paris, introduces the women's tailored suit.

- The Home Insurance Building in Chicago, Illinois is completed. It is the first building to incorporate the principles of the modern skyscraper, with a steel skeleton above the sixth floor and curtain walls. The building is designed by William le Baron Jenney, in whose offices Louis Sullivan completes his apprenticeship. Sullivan will later formulate the maxim of "form following function."

1886
- The H. Taylor House in Newport, Rhode Island, inaugurates the colonial revival building style in homes. It becomes the most popular home style in the United States and remains so for 70 years.

1887
- Edison patents the motion-picture camera.
- Cellulose photographic film is developed.
- Ads appear in magazines.

1888
- Kodak box camera makes picture taking simple. The "snapshot" is born.
- The first beauty contest is held in Spa, Belgium.

1889
- Dr. Herman Hollerith receives first U.S. patent for a tabulating machine (first computer).
- George Eastman places Kodak camera on sale for first time.
- First dishwashing machine is marketed, Chicago, Illinois.
- Universal Exposition opens in Paris, France; Eiffel Tower is completed.
- The brassiere is invented by Herminie Cadolle in France.
- Thomas Edison shows his first motion picture.
- Daniel Stover and William Hance patent a bicycle with a back pedal brake.

1890
- W. B. Purvis patents fountain pen.
- Vincent Van Gogh dies in Auvers, France.

1891
- An international agreement on copyright is established.

1892
- Elbert Hubbard publishes the monthly magazine *The Philistine*, to promote the Arts and Crafts movement in the United States.
- The magazine *Vogue* begins publication.

1893
- The Columbian Exposition in Chicago, Illinois is a triumph for Beaux-Arts style.
- Frank Lloyd Wright establishes his architectural practice.

1894
- Pneumatic hammer is patented by Charles King of Detroit, Michigan.
- First U.S. steel sailing vessel, *Dirigo*, is launched, Bath, Maine.

- First newspaper Sunday color comic section is published, *New York World*.
- Debussy's revolutionary musical composition *Prelude à l'apres-midi d'un faune* premieres. It is considered a breakthrough piece of musical modernism and a landmark in the history of music.

1895
- Siegfried Bing opens a shop in Paris and names it L'Art Nouveau ("The New Art"). Bing sells exceptional works by many of the best-known designers, and the name of his shop becomes attached to their style.
- Tchaikovsky's ballet *Swan Lake* premieres in St. Petersburg.
- National Association of Manufacturers is organized in Cincinnati, Ohio.
- Anaheim completes its new electric light system.
- First commercial movie performance occurs, 153 Broadway, New York, New York.
- British inventor Birt Acres patents film camera/projector.
- First U.S. auto race starts; six cars, 55 miles, winner averages seven miles per hour.
- First auto manufacturer opens Duryea Motor Wagon Company.
- First U.S. patent is granted for auto (George B. Selden).
- Wilhelm Rontgen discovers X-rays.

1896
- The first comic strip, *The Yellow Kid*, is published in the *New York American*.
- Architect Louis Henri Sullivan proclaims that "form follows function."
- The magazine *House Beautiful* is founded. Its first issue is designed by Frank Lloyd Wright.

1897
- The Boston subway opens, becoming the first underground metro in North America.

1898
- John Ames Sherman patents first envelope folding and gumming machine (Massachusetts).

1899
- Economist Thorsten Veblen coins the term "conspicuous consumption."

1900
- Kodak's one-dollar Brownie puts photography in almost everyone's reach.
- On Broadway, Floradora introduces what will become the chorus line.
- Henri Matisse begins the Fauvist movement in painting.
- Sigmund Freud's *The Interpretation of Dreams* is published. It describes his theory of the unconscious and introduces the id, ego, and superego. Freud's theories change the perception of the human mind and challenge traditional notions of normalcy.
- Max Planck introduces quantum theory hypothesis, prompting the birth of quantum mechanics, the underlying structure of modern physics and chemistry.

1901
- Frank Lloyd Wright gives a speech, "The Art and Craft of the Machine," in which he lays out basic principles of modern industrial design, as he sees them. He praises the Arts and Crafts Movement, but states that Morris's and Ruskin's time is over, ". . . that the machine is capable of carrying to fruition high ideals in art—higher than the world has yet seen!"

1902
- In France, magician George Méliès's *A Trip to the Moon* tells fantasy in film.
- Alfred Stieglitz publishes *Camera Work* to promote photography as art.

1903
- Wiener Werkstätte (German for "Vienna Workshop") is established in Vienna in 1903 as an association of artists and craftspeople working together to manufacture fashionable household goods. They aim to bring good design and art into every part of people's lives and establish a new art for the new century. Simplified shapes, geometric patterns, and minimal decoration is characterized Wiener Werkstätte products. They also want to break with the past and bring new style to everything they produce. Emphasis is placed on the beautiful and unique, as well as faultless craftsmanship. As well as furniture, the Wiener Werkstätte produce handpainted and printed silks, leather goods, enamel, jewelry, and ceramics. The Werkstätte exerts an enormous influence on artists and Art Deco designers throughout the first part of the 20th century.
- Edward Binney and Harold Smith coinvent crayons. Using the brand name Crayola, the crayons are sold for a nickel, and the colors are black, brown, blue, red, purple, orange, yellow, and green. The word *Crayola* was created by Alice Stead Binney (wife of Edwin Binney) who takes the French words for *chalk* (*craie*) and *oily* (*oleaginous*) and combines them.
- London's *Daily Mirror* begins illustrating with only photographs, not drawings.
- The film *The Great Train Robbery* introduces editing and creates demand for fiction movies.

1904
- New York City's subway opens.
- Anton Chekhov introduces modern realism to the theater at the premiere of *The Cherry Orchard* at the Moscow Art Theater.
- Telephone-answering machine is invented.

1905
- Albert Einstein proposes the Special Theory of Relativity to replace classical notions of space and time.
- Isadora Duncan establishes the first school of modern dance in Berlin.

1906
- Reginald Fessenden invents wireless telephony, a means for radio waves to carry signals a significant distance

1907
- Hermann Muthesius criticizes the quality of German industrial products and sets up the Deutscher Werkbund (German Work Federation) to promote high standards of design for mass production.
- Frank Lloyd Wright completes the Robie House in Chicago.
- Leo Baekeland invents the first fully synthetic plastic called Bakelite. Unveiled in 1909, Bakelite becomes so visible in so many places that it is advertised as "the material of a thousand uses." In 1924, a *Time* magazine cover story on Baekeland reports that those familiar with Bakelite's potential "claim that in a few years it will be embodied in every

mechanical facility of modern civilization." This comes to be very close to the truth. It is the material for an amazing number of products from cigarette holders and costume jewelry to radio housings, distributor caps, and telephones until well into the 1950s.

- Color photography is invented by Auguste and Louis Lumiere.
- With Les Demoiselles d'Avignon, the Spanish painter Pablo Picasso offends the Paris art scene in 1907.

1908

- Henry Ford introduces the Model T car, an automobile meant to be affordable to everyone. It sells for $850.
- Movie makers set up shop in California at a place called Hollywood.

1909

- The Ballet Russe causes a sensation in Paris, leading to a trend toward Asian-inspired dress.
- *The New York Times* publishes the first movie review.

1910

- Working as an artistic advisor for AEG in Germany, the architect and designer Peter Behrens denounces Art Nouveau for its spare abstract neoclassicism. He creates the worlds first "corporate image," designing products, lighting fixtures, advertising, graphics, and buildings for the company. Many point to him as the World's first industrial designer.
- Rayon is developed.

1911

- Pablo Picasso's cubist collages challenge traditional art.
- Fifteen years before the artist's death, the Boston Museum of Fine Arts holds the first Monet retrospective in the United States.

1912

- *Photoplay* debuts as the first magazine for movie fans.

1913

- The International Exhibition of Modern Art, better known as The Armory Show, opens on February 17, in New York City. Organized by a group of progressive artists, the show is the first large-scale exhibit of 20th-century modern art from Europe and America, including a number of ultramodern French paintings whose technique and style quickly become the focus of intense controversy. The work of two painters, Marcel Duchamp's cubist "Nude Descending a Staircase" and Henri Matisse's unconventional "Blue Nude," draw particular condemnation—both painters are attacked in the press as inept and unartistic.

  Nonetheless, the show, exhibiting more than 1,600 works, receives some praise and is heavily attended. In New York, more than 70,000 people attend during the month-long run. Even larger crowds turn out at the Art Institute of Chicago, where a smaller collection of works is displayed despite the qualms of the director and the burning of Matisse in effigy by the students of the Institute. After a final stop in Boston, where it attracts small crowds and ignites no controversy, the show returns to New York, and the works go back to the artists or to new owners.

The novel approaches to color, motion, and form displayed at The Armory Show contrast strongly with the realistic works favored by many established artists. These innovations open up a new aesthetic for American artists, museum-goers, and collectors. The Armory Show is now cited by many art historians as the most important American exhibition in the history of modern art.

- Matisse coins the term "cubism."
- On May 29, 1913, in Paris, Les Ballets Russes stages the first ballet performance of *The Rite of Spring* (*Le Sacré du Printemps*) with music by Igor Stravinsky and choreography by Vaslav Nijinsky. The intensely rhythmic score and primitive scenario—a setting of scenes from pagan Russia—shock audiences more accustomed to the demure conventions of classical ballet. The unrest in the audience escalates into a riot. *The Rite of Spring* is now regarded as a path-breaking 20th-century masterpiece.
- *Gertie the Dinosaur*, the first animated cartoon, requires 10,000 drawings.
- Gabrielle "Coco" Chanel opens a boutique in Deauville, France; she revolutionizes and democratizes women's fashion with tailored suits, chain-belted jerseys, and quilted handbags. She is the most copied fashion designer in history.

1914

- In Germany, the 35-millimeter still camera, a Leica is introduced.
- Federal Trade Commission regulates advertising.
- Henry Ford's mass production techniques of automation and moving production lines results in the price of a Model T Ford dropping to less than $300.
- World War I breaks out. Military technology progresses rapidly, and war becomes fully mechanized. Mass production is established as a prerequisite to victory in modern war. The side effects of the Great War are too numerous to count, but it extends to every type of manufactured goods. The increased capacity for production resulting from the war creates enormous potential for the manufacturing of household goods once the war is over in 1918.

1915

- D. W. Griffith's 1915 Civil War epic, *The Birth of a Nation*, with its groundbreaking camerawork—including close-ups, night photography, and tracking shots—transforms forever the way films are made and images perceived. Most white audiences in 1915 love the film, paying an unprecedented two dollars a ticket to see it. The recently formed NAACP, however, launches a crusade in the African American press against *The Birth of a Nation*, outraged by Griffith's vicious stereotyping of blacks.
- Einstein formulates the General Theory of Relativity, further displacing classical ideas of space and time. He becomes world famous. The absence of an absolute frame of reference in the universe is disturbing to some, but enters popular culture almost immediately.

1916

- The Coca-Cola bottle is introduced.

1917

- Government offices are seized, and the Romanov's Winter Palace is stormed in the Russian October Revolution.

- First U.S. combat troops arrive in France as United States declares war on Germany.
- Between 10,000 and 15,000 blacks silently walk down New York City's Fifth Avenue to protest racial discrimination and violence.

1918
- Congress authorizes time zones and approves daylight savings time. First daylight savings time in United States goes into effect ten days later.
- First regular airmail service (between New York, Philadelphia, and Washington, D.C.) is inaugurated.
- First U.S. airmail stamps are issued (24 cents).
- House of Representatives passes amendment allowing women to vote.
- First use of iron lung (Boston's Children Hospital).
- Goddard demonstrates tube-launched solid propellant rockets.

1919
- The Bauhaus School is founded in Germany.

1920
- German film expressionism is established with *The Cabinet of Dr. Caligari.*
- Stanley and Helen Resor introduce psychological ad research.

1921
- Cleveland Playhouse becomes first U.S. resident professional theater.

1922
- Paul Klee paints the *Twittering Machine.*
- T. S. Eliot's *The Waste Land* considers the sterility of modern life.
- Ludwig Wittgenstein's *Tractatus* argues that philosophy is meaningless and that its pursuit should be abandoned in favor of the natural sciences.

1923
- Neon signs begin appearing in cities.
- Paul Poiret complains that his designs are being extensively copied in the United States.

1924
- John Vassos designs a lotion bottle for the Armand company, introducing the plastic screwtop. (The bottle became popular as a hip flask.)
- For the second year running, an exhibition in New York is packed with historical styles for homes: Queen Anne, Georgian, Elizabethan, Colonial (English and Spanish), Tudor, and Louis XVI. United States style is clearly rooted firmly in the past.

1925
- *Ben-Hur* costs nearly $4 million to make, an unheard-of price to make a movie.
- John Logie Baird demonstrates the first television system, using mechanical scanning
- Warner Bros. starts experiments to make "talkies."
- Women's fashion scandalizes as skirts are knee-length.
- Exposition des Arts Décoratifs et Industriels Modernes is held in Paris and gives its

name to the style now commonly known as Art Deco. One of the strongest and most influential reactions against the Art Deco movement comes from the Swiss architect Le Corbusier. His Pavilion de l'Esprit Nouveau at the 1925 Exposition is a forceful rejection of the use of expensive, exotic materials in the extravagant, one-of-a-kind objects that typified Art Deco. He defines the house as a "machine for living in," while furniture is "domestic equipment." The pavilion itself is a prototype for standardized housing, conspicuously furnished with commonly available items such as leather club chairs. Like members of the Bauhaus, Le Corbusier advocates furniture that is rationally designed along industrial principles to reflect function and utility in its purist forms, with a strict rejection of applied ornament. Other important movements positing avant-garde theories of design and architecture are included De Stijl in Holland, which advocate a seamless unity of art and architecture, and Russian Constructivism, whose utopian projects embrace a combination of machine forms and abstract art.

1926
- Burma Shave signs dot U.S. highways.
- Rudolf Valentino dies. There is mass hysteria at his funeral and several fans commit suicide, revealing the emotional power of film.
- Don Juan, the first publicly shown "talkie," premieres in New York.

1927
- The film *Napoleon* experiments with wide-screen and multiscreen effects.

1928
- General Electric builds a television set with a 3" x 4" screen.
- Disney adds sound to cartoons; *Steamboat Willie* introduces Mickey Mouse.

1929
- The Museum of Modern Art opens in New York.
- Brokers watch stock prices soar and crash on an automated electric board.
- Les Paul, age 14, creates forerunner of the electric guitar.
- Raymond Loewy opens his industrial design office in New York. Later it becomes nearly impossible to go through a day in the United States without encountering one of his streamlined designs.
- Le Corbusier begins building The Villa Savoy. He presents the house as "a machine for living," appropriate for the new machine age.

1930
- Broadway gets professional stage lighting.

1931
- Scotch Tape arrives on the market.
- Dick Tracy joins the comic strips.
- Exposure meters go on sale to photographers.

1932
- Disney adopts a three-color Technicolor process for cartoons.
- Aldous Huxley's sci-fi classic the dystopian *Brave New World* is published.

1933

- The first *King Kong* sends the giant ape up the new Empire State Building.
- The Zippo lighter is invented.

1934

- The Volkswagen "Beetle" is proposed for design in Nazi Germany. Although ready for production in 1939, the outbreak of World War II delays its manufacture until 1945. Soon it becomes the symbol of middle-class mobility in Europe and later the hip car of the 1960s. The design is revived at the end of the 20th century to renewed popularity.
- Flash Gordon appears on the comic pages. The movie serial follows in two years.
- Surrealist René Magritte paints *The Human Condition.*

1935

- The DC-3 Dakota rolls out of its hangar for its first test flight. The aircraft's streamlined, organic design is an inspiration for designers in the late 1930s and represents the peak of the aesthetics of that period.
- New Fun Comics begins the creation of original comic book cartoons.

1936

- Penguin begins publishing paperback books with the idea of making good literature available at low prices. The first books are by Ernest Hemingway, André Maurois, and Agatha Christie. They sell 3 million copies in the first year of business.
- BBC in London starts world's first television service three hours a day.

1937

- Pablo Picasso paints the "Guernica," showing the horrors of war.
- German authorities present an exhibition of "degenerate art," condemning among other movements Cubism, Expressionism, Impressionism, and Surrealism. The Nazi's effort backfires, with more than three million visitors coming to see and mostly appreciate, not sneer at, the works.
- Theodore Geisel, "Dr. Seuss," begins writing and illustrating books for children.
- J. R. R. Tolkien opens up a fantasy world with his novel *The Hobbit.*

1938

- Two brothers named Biro invent the ballpoint pen in Argentina.
- More than 80 million movie tickets (65 percent of population) sold in the United States each week.

1939

- NBC starts first regular daily electronic TV broadcasts in the United States.
- Germany invades Poland, beginning World War II.
- Nylon is developed.

1940

- The Disney film Fantasia introduces a kind of stereo sound to U.S. movie goers.
- British develop the "Utility Line" of clothing in response to wartime shortages. The clean, spare, tailored style becomes popular and influences fashion well beyond the war years.

1941

- Orson Welles's film *Citizen Kane* experiments with flashbacks, camera movement, and new sound techniques.
- Wonder Woman follows Superman and Batman into the comic books.
- The first television commercial is aired (Bulova Watches).

1942

- Kodacolor Film for prints is the first true color negative film.
- FDR puts pressure on the synthetic fiber industry to produce materials for the war effort, by threatening to nationalize the companies. Rapid collaborative progress ensues, leading to rapid development of synthetic materials and textiles.
- Albert Camus's existentialist novel, *L'Étranger* (translated as *The Foreigner*, the *Outsider*, and *The Stranger*) is published in France.

1943

- Comic book publishers are selling 25,000,000 copies a month.

1944

- Scientists at Harvard University construct the first automatic, general-purpose digital computer.
- The first instance of network censorship occurs. The sound is cut off on the Eddie Cantor and Nora Martin duet, "We're Having a Baby, My Baby and Me."

1945

- The U.S. air force drops atomic bombs on the Japanese cities of Hiroshima and Nagasaki. The "atomic age" becomes a public perception, reinforcing the ideal of a Modern Age of new, exciting, and later frightening technologies.
- World War II ends.
- Vannevar Bush conceives idea of hyperlinks and hypermedia.
- In the Theatre de la Mode, French designers display new apparel designs on artfully created scale mannequins in elaborate sets. The theater tours Europe and the United States in the following years, reviving interest in French fashion design.

1946

- University of Pennsylvania's ENIAC heralds the modern electronic computer.
- Italian cinema counters Hollywood glitz with neorealism in Open City.
- In France, the Cannes Film Festival is debuted.
- Tupper Plastics launches its assortment of food containers: Tupperware.

1947

- Christian Dior introduces the line that becomes known as "The New Look," an opulent departure from the wartime fashions of the preceding years.
- LEGO blocks created in Denmark's first injection-molding machine.
- Bell labs develop the first transistor, opening the door to the creation of all manner of miniature electronic devices.
- Jean-Paul Sartre's play, *No Exit*, introduces the line, "Hell is other people." Existentialism begins to enter popular culture.

1948
- *The Ed Sullivan Show* premiers on television.
- The Bic ballpoint pen is invented.
- Artist Andrew Wyeth paints Christina's World.
- This is generally accepted as the starting year of the Baby Boom generation.

1949
- Network TV established in United States.
- Murphy's law is formulated at a press conference at Edwards Air Force Base.
- George Orwell's dystopian novel of a bleak, fascist future *1984* is published.
- Italian neorealism continues with the film *The Bicycle Thief,* still a staple of film-school curricula.

1950
- Fourteen million television sets are sold in the United States, increasing the number in service by ten-fold.
- Acrylic fiber developed in the United States by E. I. DuPont.

1951
- Alan "Moondog" Freed, a Cleveland disk jockey, emcees a rhythm and blues show on the radio. He begins referring to the music as rock and roll. In September of 1954, Freed is hired by WINS radio in New York. The following January he holds a landmark dance there, promoting black performers as rock and roll artists. Within a month, the music industry is advertising rock and roll records in the trade papers.
- J. D. Salinger's *The Catcher in the Rye* is published. It becomes a symbol of adolescent angst.

1952
- On television, a Univac 1 computer predicts the outcome of the presidential election, raising public awareness of computers.
- Mr. Potato Head is invented.
- Samuel Beckett presents his absurdist play *Waiting for Godot.*

1953
- Jackson Pollock paints "Blue Poles number 11." Abstract expressionism, he says, is the only possible style in the modern, electronic, nuclear age. The painting sets a price record, when it is sold at auction in 1973 for $2 million.
- Gerry Thomas invents the Swanson TV Dinner. It is made up of three sections containing turkey with cornbread dressing and gravy, sweet potatoes, and buttered peas. Priced at 98 cents, it becomes an instant hit. Thomas, a gourmet cook, who never eats TV dinners himself, immediately begins receiving hate mail from irate husbands, who miss their wives' cooking.

1954
- Coco Chanel, after a 15-year hiatus, returns to the world of apparel design. Over the next five years, she lays the foundation of the "Chanel Look," which becomes a classic staple, copied and revived the world over for the remainder of the 20th century.
- Texas Instruments introduces the silicon transistor, pointing the way to lower manufacturing costs for electronic goods.

- U.S. Senate committee holds hearings on societal effects of televised violence.
- J. R. R. Tolkien continues his fantasy world in the first of the *Lord of the Rings* trilogy with *The Fellowship of the Ring*.
- The U.S. Senate Subcommittee on Juvenile Delinquency holds hearings on whether comic books inspire juvenile delinquency and calls for self-regulation by the comics industry to keep violent titles out of young hands. Comic book publishers create *The Comics Magazine Association of America*, which publishes a strict code of guidelines to control what content the comics will permit. E.C. Comics loses every one of its titles except for *Mad*, which it republishes as *Mad Magazine* to avoid the code.

1955
- Disneyland opens in California.
- The felt-tip pen is invented.

1956
- Foreign language films get an Oscar category. *La Strada*, by Frederico Fellini, from Italy, is the first so honored.
- Elvis Presley appears on television.

1957
- Russia launches the Sputnik 1 satellite into orbit, and the "space race" begins.

1958
- Playwright Harold Pinter's *The Birthday Party* is staged in London. Pinter's threatening, absurd plays are emblematic of modern angst and alienation.
- Physicist Werner Heisenberg explains his uncertainty principle. The idea that not everything in the world can be determined by science is felt by many to be deeply disturbing.

1959
- New York sociologist C. Wright Mills refers to a postmodern period in which conformity and consumerism have begun to replace the Modern Age of liberal ideals.
- Frank Lloyd Wright's Guggenheim Museum in New York is completed.
- Barbie makes her debut at the American Toy Fair. Life-size, her measurements would be 39-18-33.
- The microchip is introduced.
- Xerox introduces the first commercial copy machine.

1960
- Ninety percent of American homes have television sets. More than 500 American television stations are broadcasting.

1961
- FCC Chairman Newton Minow calls television a "vast wasteland."
- Yuri Gagarin of the USSR is the first man in space. President Kennedy responds by accelerating the United States' space program.

1962
- Telstar relays the first live transatlantic television signal.

- The first video game, "Space Wars," is invented by MIT student Steve Russell. It is soon being played in computer labs all over the United States.
- Marshall McLuhan publishes *The Gutenberg Galaxy*, in which he argues that the communications technology of the electronic age will retribalize humankind. He coins the term "global village" to describe this situation.
- *Dr. No* begins the James Bond series.
- Andy Warhol's paintings of Campbell Soup Cans are exhibited in New York. He becomes the foremost artist of the Pop Art movement.
- *Silent Spring*, by Rachel Carson, is published. The book, a sharp critique of the use of pesticides, is credited with launching the environmental movement.
- President John F. Kennedy calls attention to the abuse of the consumer. He declares four basic consumer rights, institutionalizing and expanding consumer expectations in the United States to include the right to safety, the right to be informed, the right to choose, and the right to be heard.
- Yves St. Laurent opens his couture house in Paris. Beatnik street style meets couture.

1963
- Fans go wild after a Beatles concert in London. *The Daily Mirror* coins the term "Beatlemania."
- President John F. Kennedy is assassinated in Dallas, Texas.

1964
- IBM develops a computer aided design (CAD) system.
- Doug Engelbart invents the computer mouse.
- *McLuhan's Understanding Media: The Extensions of Man* proposes that "the medium is the message:" that the effect of a mode of communication far outweighs the effect of the content being communicated. Television would, for example, have the same effect on society, no matter what kind of programming took place.

1965
- André Courrèges introduces the miniskirt.
- Ralph Nader's book, *Unsafe at Any Speed*, attacks Detroit's auto industry, raising awareness about safety issues in automotive design and sparking a disillusionment with manufacturing in general.
- The Beatles perform their first concert at Shea Stadium. This concert set new world records for attendance (55,600).
- San Francisco writer Michael Fallon applies the term "hippie" to the San Francisco counterculture.
- Bergdorf Goodman, a New York upscale department store, hitches its wagon to youth culture and opens a store within a store, BiGi's, at its Fifth Avenue location. BiGi's caters to young fashions and is designed in a pop style. Many older customers protest this invasion to no avail.

1966
- *Star Trek* lands on TV.
- Neorealistic style gives the film *The Battle of Algiers* a documentary look. Its influence is felt in films for decades.
- Yves St. Laurent opens his groundbreaking Rive-Gauche boutiques in Paris, the first ready-to-wear collections associated with a couture house.

1967

- The Beatles release *Sergeant Pepper's Lonely Hearts Club Band.* Pop music metamorphoses toward an art form.
- Jacques Derrida's and Francois Leotard's philosophies "deconstruct" Western rationalist thinking. Deconstructionist thinking points to a world in which there are no absolute viewpoints and no narratives that are universally applicable. This begins immediately to cause rifts in academic circles and later begins to influence architecture.
- From IBM comes the floppy disk.
- Adult, underground comics arrive with R. Crumb's *Zap Comix.*
- A computer hypertext system is developed at Brown University.

1968

- The rock musical *Hair* hits Broadway.
- *2001: A Space Odyssey* hits movie theaters.
- Intelsat completes global communications satellite loop.
- Noam Chomsky influences linguistics with *Language and Mind* .
- Andy Warhol predicts that "in that future everyone will be famous for 15 minutes".

1969

- Pop art movement's Claes Oldenburg makes large sculptures of mundane objects.
- The Woodstock music festival is held in upstate New York, later seen as the high-water mark of hippie culture.
- The Who release the album *Tommy*, the first musical work billed as a rock opera. It is later filmed.

1970

- The Beatles break up, to fans' great dismay. "It's only a band," says John Lennon.

1971

- *Jesus Christ Superstar*, a rock opera, released as an album the year before, opens on Broadway. Its London production becomes the longest running musical. Authors Andrew Lloyd Webber and Timothy Rice change the world of theater and musical performance.
- The New York Dolls create a new form of rock that presages punk rock and inspires the New York underground music scene.
- ARPANET, Internet forerunner, has 22 university and government connections.
- *A Clockwork Orange* is released in Britain. "Being the adventures of a young man whose principal interests are rape, ultra-violence and Beethoven." The tagline for American director Stanley Kubrick's 1971 film *A Clockwork Orange* makes headlines in Britain, where controversy erupts at its release. Based on Anthony Burgess's 1962 futuristic novel of juvenile delinquency in London, the film depicts extreme brutality in a highly stylized, and heretofore unseen, manner. Kubrick's unpredictable camera techniques coupled with protagonist Alex's language (an English-Russian-slang hybrid invented in the novel) disrupt the narrative flow and disorient the viewer. Kubrick's opposition of ultraviolent acts with a mostly classical score also unsettles viewers.

1972

- The Pruitt-Igoe housing development, in St. Louis, Missouri, is demolished. Charles Jencks asserted that its destruction signaled the end of the modern style of architecture.

- The video game *Pong* is developed for Atari.
- Sony sells a videotape system for the home, the Betamax.
- HBO starts pay-TV service for cable.
- David Bowie releases the album *Ziggy Stardust*. Concerts meld music with abstract theater. The Ziggy persona becomes an instant icon; glam-rock emerges.

1973
- Reggae music spreads out from Jamaica.
- The Jamaican film *The Harder They Come*, starring Jimmy Cliff, launches the popularity of reggae music in the United States.
- An American family, the Louds, comes apart in a documentary on national television, presaging "reality TV."
- Skylab, the first American space station, is launched.
- A ceasefire is signed, ending involvement of American ground troops in the Vietnam War.

1974
- *People* magazine debuts, with Mia Farrow gracing the cover.

1975
- Steven Spielberg's *Jaws* will be the first film to earn more than $100 million. It sets the precedent for the summer blockbuster.

1976
- The Sex Pistols release their first single. They play their gigs in outfits designed by Vivienne Westwood. They become the face of punk rock.
- IBM develops an ink-jet printer.

1977
- Steve Jobs and Steve Wozniak incorporate Apple Computer.
- Bill Gates and Paul Allen found Microsoft.
- Disco music becomes the rage.

1978
- Will Eisner's *A Contract with God* is the first graphic novel.

1979
- The annual volume of plastic manufactured overtakes that of steel, the symbol of the Industrial Revolution.
- George Lucas forms Lucasfilm.
- Sony introduces the Walkman, a portable, personal cassette tape player, changing people's relationship to their music and surroundings.

1980
- Ettore Sottsass founds the Memphis Group of designers, which then goes on to create a sensation at the Milan Furniture Fair in 1981. The goal of the Memphis Group is to direct design away from the European functionalism of the late 1970s, by transferring "into the world of the Western home the culture of rock music, travel and a certain excess." The group, always intending to be temporary, disbands in 1988.

- *Donkey Kong* is introduced by Nintendo.

1981
- MTV begins broadcasting, with 120 videos to choose from.
- IBM introduces first IBM PC.
- The Center for Disease Control's first report on AIDS points to a growing epidemic.

1982
- The Vietnam Veterans' Memorial in Washington, D.C. is dedicated on Veterans' Day. Maya Lin, a 21-year-old undergraduate at Yale's school of architecture, had won the commission to design it. Her vision, a dark cut in the earth, with its emphasis on the chronological listing of the names of the fallen, has changed the way memorials are viewed and designed. She described it as follows:

  > I went to see the site. I had a general idea that I wanted to describe a journey . . . a journey that would make you experience death and where you'd have to be an observer, where you could never really fully be with the dead. It wasn't going to be something that was going to say, "It's all right, it's all over," because it's not.

- *Bladerunner*, a film by Ridley Scott, presents a vision of future cities that is much darker and fragmented than ever seen before. It becomes the design standard of future-vision for almost two decades.
- Autodesk is founded and ships its first version of AutoCAD.
- *Time* magazine names the computer as its "Man of the Year."

1983
- Sally K. Ride, 32, becomes the first U.S. woman astronaut in space as a crew member aboard space shuttle *Challenger*.
- With the introduction of compact discs, the vinyl record begins a steep decline.
- Nicolas Hayek markets the first collection of Swatch watches.

1984
- William Gibson's *Neuromancer*, the first "cyberpunk" novel, introduces the term "Cyberspace," and underscores the trend toward depicting the future in dark, chaotic terms, in a new type of science fiction.
- The Macintosh computer is unveiled with an unprecedented ad campaign, featuring Orwellian imagery.
- Sony and Philips introduce the CD-ROM.
- The film *The Last Starfighter* uses extensive super-computer generated graphics.

1985
- Pagemaker allows easy creation of professional-looking layouts on home and office computers.
- The debut of Max Headroom, a computer-mediated live action figure.

1986
- Comic books turn grim and violent with *The Dark Knight Returns*.

1987

- From Japan, the anime cartoon film emerges.

1988

- *Who Framed Roger Rabbit* mixes live action and animation.
- Ninety-eight percent of U.S. homes have at least one television set.
- Sally Fox, an entomologist, improves an ancient agricultural art and successfully breeds and markets varieties of naturally colored cotton she calls *FoxFiber*. Fox's cotton is naturally resistant to pests and naturally colorfast so the fabrics don't fade. Manufacturers and designers respond enthusiastically and pale colored cottons abound. Dye manufacturers and other cotton growers are less happy.

1989

- *Cinema Paradiso*, from Italy, wins the Academy Award for Best Foreign Language Film.
- The Berlin Wall is dismantled, hastening the disintegration of the Soviet bloc in Eastern Europe. To some this is understood to mean that Capitalism has won and is vindicated. Chaos follows in some areas, as Eastern Europe realigns.

1990

- World Wide Web originates at CERN in Europe. Tim Berners-Lee writes the program.
- Adobe ships PhotoShop 1.0. Photos can now be digitally manipulated on a home computer.
- DuPont produces polyester microfiber.

1991

- Operation Desert Storm begins. The United States leads a coalition to reclaim Kuwait from Iraq. "Stealth" aircraft and "smart bombs" become openly part of modern warfare. The B1 "Stealth" bomber's faceted look becomes a design inspiration over a wide spectrum of products.
- In Europe, Internet sites more than triple in one year and pass 100,000.
- Nirvana-mania sweeps the United States. MTV plays *Smells Like Teen Spirit* incessantly. Grunge, an outsider's style, is vaulted to the center of popular culture and fashion, negating itself overnight.

1992

- Disneyland comes to Paris.

1993

- Mosaic, a graphical interface for Internet navigation is created and allows the World Wide Web to be accessed by common users. The creators eventually form the company Netscape Communications.
- *Myst* is released (Cyan)—in 1998, it becomes the top-selling game of all time. The look and feel of the game's environments are of a kind never seen before and have influenced game design since.
- HTML is introduced as the code for Web design.

1994

- Netscape's first Web browser becomes available. The number of Web surfers increases exponentially.

1995

- *Toy Story* is the first completely computer-generated feature length movie.
- Sony Playstation is introduced.
- The Vatican develops a Web site.
- John Galliano, an Englishman, is appointed designer of Givenchy in Paris.

1996

- Computer makers begin selling flat-panel displays.

1997

- The Guggenheim Museum Bilbao completed. The architect, Frank Gehry, brings his style of curved, clashing, free-form surfaces to fruition.
- DVD technology is unveiled.
- The first weblogs, or "blogs," appear on the Internet.
- From Kodak, the first point-and-shoot digital camera is presented.
- John Galliano goes to Dior. Alexander McQueen takes over as designer at Givenchy. Two English graduates of St. Martins School of Design are now heading two of the greatest French couture houses. ("Sad, very sad," says YSL's Pierre Bergé.)

1998

- Google Inc. opens for business. Its search engine will change how information is accessed, and thought of.
- Megapixel digital cameras become available at the consumer level.
- Apple unveils the colorful iMac computer.

1999

- The number of Internet users worldwide reaches 150 million by the beginning of 1999. More than 50 percent are from the United States.
- *Star Wars Episode One: The Phantom Menace* uses 66 digital characters composited with live action.
- *The Matrix* presents moviegoers with a dark, postmodern vision. The movie's use of new visual effects and stylistic blend of influences sets a new tone for action films. The look of the film is extensively copied.
- The $35,000 *Blair Witch Project* shows the potential of low cost video production.

2000

- The world celebrates the new millennium (a year early.) Apocalyptic prophecies and computer virus scares prove to be groundless.

2001

- Terrorists hijack four airplanes, fly two into the World Trade Center in New York City, fly one into the Pentagon in Washington, D.C., and crash one into a field in Pennsylvania. A wave of patriotism arises in the United States, and war in Afghanistan and Iraq begins. President Bush urges Americans to go shopping to mitigate any economic effects the attacks may have.
- From *Shrek* to *Harry Potter* to *Crouching Tiger*, films are defined by their special effects.

2002

- Euro banknotes and coins are put into circulation in Europe.

- The MTV show *The Osbournes* debuts. It follows the daily events of aging heavy metallist Ozzy Osbourne and his family. The offbeat and often bizarre show becomes an instant hit, fuelling the trend for reality TV.
- Black actors win top Oscars: Denzel Washington and Halle Berry win acting awards for *Training Day* and *Monster's Ball*, respectively.

2003
- Hollywood releases this year are heavy on special effects, violence, and sequels, typified by the third *Matrix* film, *The Matrix Reloaded*, which, due to extensive stylistic copying of the first release, looks like a parody of itself.

2004
- The iPod becomes the "must have" gadget. It holds 10,000 tunes, but fits into a shirt pocket.

2005
- Kyoto protocol goes into effect. The international environmental treaty requires 35 industrialized nations to reduce heat-trapping gases, such as carbon dioxide. Developing nations have promised to try to limit their emissions of such gases. The United States, which emits the largest amount of heat-trapping gases in the world, refused to sign the treaty.
- Christo and Jeanne-Claude's *The Gates in Central Park*—the husband-and-wife artist team's first temporary outdoor work of art in New York, their home of more than 40 years—consists of 7,500 saffron-colored vinyl gates (each 16 feet in height and hung with saffron fabric panels) placed at 12-foot intervals over 23 miles of pedestrian walkways that lace the park.

1. The Muses, daughters of Memory were born in this order: Calliope, epic poetry and eloquence; Clio, history; Melpomene, tragedy; Euterpe, music; Erato, the poetry of love; Terpsichore, choral song and dance; Urania, astronomy; Thalia, comedy; Polymnia, oratory or sacred poetry.
2. Plato. *Phaedrus* 245a, Harold North Fowler, translator.
3. Ibid., 244a–244b.
4. This is the basis for the myth of Pandora's Box.
5. Pablo Picasso: "A Palm Tree can become a Horse," *Sunday Observer* (London), July 10, 1950.
6. Archimedes, on having a sudden realization while taking a bath, ran naked through the streets of Athens shouting "Eureka!"
7. Dr. Stickgold, et al.: "Visual Discrimination Task Improvement: A Multi-Step Process Occurring during Sleep", *The Journal of Cognitive Neuroscience*, March 2000.
8. D. Shand-Tucci, *The Art of Scandal: The Life and Times of Isabella Stewart Gardner* (New York, NY: Harper Collins Publishers, 1998).
9. "Searching for a Sound to Bridge the Decades." *The New York Times*, 9 February 1997, Arts and Leisure section, p. 10. Franz Kafka, Max Brod ed.: The Blue Octavo Notebooks, translation: 1991.
10. Franz Kafka, Max Brod eds: *The Blue Octavo Notebooks*, trans. 1991.
11. "Exploring The Unmaterial World;" *Wired Magazine* (June 2000): 316.

CHAPTER 2
1. Louis H. Sullivan, "The Tall Office Building Artistically Considered," *Lippincott's Magazine* (March 1896).
2. Captain Murphy was actually only giving voice to a law that had been long known in Britain as "Sod's Law" and in France as "La Loi de I' Emmerdement Maximum"
3. Edward Tenner, *Why Things Bite Back: Technology and the Revenge of Unintended Consequences* (New York: Knopf, 1996), 19.
4. London Telegraph: January 8, 2004 "Public have fouled Diana memorial fountain, says minister."
5. Robert K. Merton, "The Unanticipated Consequences of Purposive Social Action American," *Sociological Review*, vol. 1, no. 6 (1936): 894-904.
6. Robert Matthews, "The Science of Murphy's Law," *Scientific American* (April 1997): 88.
7. Robert K. Merton, "The Unanticipated Consequences of Purposive Social Action American," *Sociological Review*, vol. 1, no. 6 (1936): 901.
8. Ibid., p. 903.
9. Ibid.
10. Ibid., p.904.
11. World Commission on Environment and Development (WCED): Document A/42/427: "Our Common Future," *The Brundtland Report*, 1987, p. 24.
12. United Nations Development Programme (UNDP): *Human Development Report*, 1998, p. 56.
13. Ibid., p. 71.
14. Dr. Anthony D. Cortese, *Education for Sustainability: The Need for a New Human Perspective* (Boston: Second Nature, Inc., 1999), 4.
15. United Nations Development Programme (UNDP): *Human Development Report*, 1998, p. 81.

16. Dr. Anthony D. Cortese, *Education for Sustainability: The Need for a New Human Perspective* (Boston: Second Nature, Inc., 1999), 2.

17. Rio de Janeiro: United Nations Department of Economic and Social Affairs (DESA): Annex I, A/CONF.151/26: *Report of the United Nations Conference on Environment and Development*, vol. 1, 1992.

18. Ibid.

19. Graham Prophet: "Green Design: a Delicate Balancing Act," EDNEurope, www.edn-mag.com (1999).

20. Dr. Anthony D. Cortese, *Education for Sustainability: The Need for a New Human Perspective* (Boston: Second Nature, Inc., 1999), 4.

21. "Ecological Footprint Accounts: Moving Sustainability from Concept to Measurable Goal," *Redefining Progress*, Oakland CA, www.redefiningprogress.org (2004).

22. Dr. Anthony D. Cortese, *Education for Sustainability: The Need for a New Human Perspective* (Boston: Second Nature, Inc., 1999), 5.

23. DESA, 1992: Principle 3.

24. www.cdc.gov/nceh.

25. www.checnet.org.

26. "Mobile industry to set up phone recycling system," *The Guardian* (UK, 2002).

27. Edward Tenner, *Why Things Bite Back: Technology and the Revenge of Unintended Consequences* (New York: Knopf, 1996), 275.

28. World Commission on Environment and Development (WCED): Document A/42/427: "Our Common Future," *The Brundtland Report*, 1987, p. 24.

CHAPTER 3

1. Linda Tain, *Portfolio Presentations for Fashion Designers*, 2nd ed., (New York: Fairchild Publications, Inc., 2004). (For more information, also see: Mark Oldach. *Creativity for Graphic Designers: A Real-World Guide to Idea Generation—from Defining Your Message to Selecting the Best Idea for Your Printed Piece* (F&W Publications, Inc., 2000).

2. Billy Collins, "Budapest," *Sailing Alone Around the Room* (New York: Random House, 2001).

3. Robert Kunzig, "Curing Congestion—Traffic Congestion," *Discover Magazine* (1999).

4. Joseph D. Novak, *The Theory Underlying Concept Maps and How to Construct Them*, Cornell University, http://cmap.coginst.uwf.edu/info.

5. http://cmap.ihmc.us/ (accessed: October 2004).

CHAPTER 4

1. Noam Chomsky, *Language and Mind* (Harcourt Brace, 1968).

2. www.1.ibm.com/solutions/plm/doc/content/casestudy/762804113.html (accessed: August 2004).

3. www.rtqe.net/ObliqueStrategies. Oblique Strategies by Brian Eno and Peter Schmidt. Copyright © 1975, 1978, and 1979.

CHAPTER 5

1. "At Modern, Architect Is Content (Mostly)," *New York Times*, 16 November 2004, section E, p. 1.

2. Concept adapted from Will Lidwell, Jill Butler, and Kritina Holden, *Universal Principles of Design* (Massachusetts: Rockport Publishers, Inc., 2003), 106.
3. Jesse James Garret, *The Elements of User Experience*, (New York: AIGA New Riders Publishing, 2003), 46.
4. Ralph Caplan, *By Design*, 2nd ed., (New York: Fairchild Publications, Inc., 2005), 4.

CHAPTER 6

1. John Corner, "Textuality, Communication, and Media Power." In Howard Davis & Paul Walton (Eds.), *Language, Image, Media* (England: Basil Blackwell Publisher Ltd. 1983), p. 266.
2. See Edward Tufte's essay: "The Cognitive Style of PowerPoint" (Connecticut: Graphics Press LLC, 2003).

CHAPTER 7

1. "Building a Bad Reputation." *New York Times*, 8 August 2004, Art/Architecture section.
2. Will Lidwell, Jill Butler, and Kritina Holden, *Universal Principles of Design* (Massachusetts: Rockport Publishers, Inc., 2003), 158.

APPENDIX 1

1. www.colormarketing.org.
2. Le Corbusier (Charles Edouard Jeanneret), *The Modulor: A Harmonious Measure to the Human Scale Universally Applicable to Architecture and Mechanics and Modulor 2* (Let the User Speak Next), vol. 2, (Birkhauser Verlag AG Birkhäuser, 2000), 130.
3. James P. Kohn, *The Ergonomic Casebook: Real World Solutions* (CRC Press, 1997).
4. MIL-STD 1472D: *Human Engineering Design Criteria for Military Systems, Equipment and Facilities.*
5. Will Lidwell, Jill Butler, and Kritina Holden, *Universal Principles of Design* (Massachusetts: Rockport Publishers, Inc., 2003), 188.

APPENDIX 4

1. McLuhan, Marshall. *Understanding Media,* (Ginko Press, 2003), 143.
2. For a discussion on this topic, see Jean Baudrillard, *Simulacra and Simulation* (Ann Arbor: The University of Michigan Press, 1994).
3. Jean Baudrillard, *Simulacra and Simulation* (Ann Arbor: The University of Michigan Press, 1994), 43.
4. Ibid., 79
5. For a closer look at postmodern decentralization, try looking at an introduction to the thinking of Jaques Derrida and Francois Lyotard: Jeff Collins and Bill Mayblin, *Introducing Derrida* (Totem Books, 2001).
6. Sherry Turkle, "Sex, Lies and Avatars," *Wired Magazine* (April 1996).

PHOTO CREDITS

11	Photograph © Scala/Art Resource, NY. Reprinted with permission.
30	Photograph © Neal Preston/Corbis.
31	Photograph © Lawrence Manning/Corbis.
31	Photograph © Richard Melloul/Sygma/Corbis.
34	Courtesy of The Seattle Public Library.
39	Photograph © Marvin Koner/Corbis.
39	Digital Image © The Museum of Modern Art/Licensed by SCALA/Art Resource, NY. Reprinted with permission.
43	Photograph © AP Photo/PA, John Stillwell.
45	Photograph © AP Photo/Francois Mori.
45	Photograph © Corbis/Sygma/Thierry Orban.
50	Courtesy, the History Office, Edwards AFB.
51	Courtesy, NASA.
75	Photograph © Royalty-Free/Corbis.
79	Photograph © Bettman/Corbis.
80	Digital Image © The Museum of Modern Art/Licensed by SCALA/Art Resource, NY. Reprinted with permission.
84	Courtesy, Maria Nasso.
104	Photograph © Royalty-Free/Corbis.
115	Photograph © AP Photo/Zack Seckler.
118	Photograph of the Rheo Knee, courtesy of Ossur.
119	Photograph of Áron Losonczi, copyright © LiTraCon Bt, 2001–2005.
146	Original image © The National Gallery, London. Reprinted with permission.
148	Photograph © Hulton-Deutsch Collection/Corbis.
156	Courtesy, National Theater, Iceland.
166	Original image © David Pu'u/Corbis.
168	Photograph © The Milwaukee Art Museum. Reprinted with permission.
170	Photograph © Reuters/Corbis.
180	Photo of the Rheo Knee, courtesy of Ossur.

evolutionary prototype, 173

evolution of ideas, 121

experiment, 20, 101, 213

expert opinions, 52, 103

exploration/refinement, xiv, 3–4, 7, 12,
    91–104
    alchemy and, 92
    CAD, 101–2
    exercises, 110–11
    observing and testing in, 92–93
    perspective, 105–9
    reflection and, 103–4
    sketching and, 93–100

F

fabric, 22–23, 49, 193, 236
    See also apparel design
    modeling and, 126, 128, 172

fabricators, 44–45, 103
    See also manufacturing

facilitator, in brainstorms, 75

fashion designers, 22–25, 30–31, 200
    See also apparel design; specific designers
    in timeline, 216, 225, 229, 230, 232, 237

feedback, 85, 103, 168–71, 175
    as *dead fish,* 169–70

feelings. See emotion/feelings

Fibonacci series, 191

"fifteen-minute" rule, 47, 146

figurative style, 105

film (motion pictures) in timeline, 218,
    221, 222, 223, 225, 227–29, 233,
    235, 237–38

fixative, for pastels, 151

focus, 26–27, 144, 190

"follow the money," 55–56

form, 11, 48
    function and, 41–42, 221, 222

forte-piano, 147–48

fossil fuel dependence, 57

Foster, Norman, 203

Fox, Sally, 236

Freed, Alan "Moondog," 230

freewheeling, 76

function and functionality, 5, 12, 117,
    133, 227, 234
    in apparel design, 24, 44, 45
    constraints and, 39, 44
    in detailing, 121, 122
    form and, 41–42, 221, 222
    materials and, 44, 48–49
    in models, 123, 128, 135

"Funeral Blues" (Auden), 78

G

Gabbana, Stefano, 30–31

The Gates in Central Park, 238

Gehry, Frank, 101, 203, 237

generation gap, 210

gestalt perception, 69–73, 75, 79, 93, 189
    Law of Pragnanz and, 70, 72
    open vs. closed, 72–73

"The Gift" (Man Ray), 39

Glaser, Milton, 203

global consumption, 55

globalization, xiii, 42

global village, 209, 211

Goethe, Johann, 185

Golden Section (*Phi*), 191, 192

grand entrance, in presentation, 147–48

graphic design, 127, 148, 156, 164

Graves, Michael, 203

color, 187–88

events and, 211

future challenges, 212–13

media and, 208, 209, 210

technology and, 208–9, 211

Zeitgeist and, 32, 207–10, 211

Tschumi, Bernard, 204

Tupper, Earl S., 202

U

Ukraine, orange in, 187

unintended consequences, 50–54

United Kingdom, recycling in, 58

U.S. military design guidelines, 192

universal design, 25

usability, 118. See also function

V

value (color), 186

values and beliefs, 53

Van Gogh, Vincent, 29, 195, 216, 221

venue, for presentation, 143–44

Vietnam Veterans' Memorial, 205, 235

virtual models, 125, 127, 155

visualization, 26, 83, 93, 100–101

See also modeling

visual language, 7, 93–96, 122

W

watercolor paints, 151

webbing, 81, 82, 89

Web pages/sites, 58, 154–55, 161, 193, 236

Wegner, Hans, 202

Wertheimer, Max, 69

Western culture, 42, 187

Westwood, Vivienne, 45, 234

Wiener Werkstätte (Vienna), 223

Wirkkala, Tapio, 80

world of imagination vs. world of objects, 2, 3, 6

Wright, Frank Lloyd, 200, 221, 222, 231

Z

Zeff, Mark, 160–63

Zeitgeist, 32, 207–10, 215

See also trendspotting

events and, 211

media and, 209–10

observation of, 207–8

technology and, 208–9

Zen koan, 20, 33, 103–4

Zen Mind, Beginner's Mind (Suzuki), 33